JAR

PPL-CPL

Helicopter Manual

Principles of Flight
Technical 'H'
Flight Performance & Planning
Turbine Engine 'H'
Question & Answers

H R Quantick

Nothing in this manual supersedes any legislation, rules, regulations or procedures contained in any operational document issued by Her Majesty's Stationery Office, the Civil Aviation Authority, the Joint Aviation Authority, ICAO, the manufacturers of aircraft, engines and systems, or by the operators of aircraft throughout the world.

JAR PPL-CPL Helicopter Manual

Principles of Flight, Technical 'H'
Flight Performance & Planning
Turbine Engine 'H'
Question & Answers

H.R. Quantick

Second Edition 2005.

Copyright 2005 © H. R. Quantick & Pooleys Flight Equipment Ltd

ISBN 1-84336-109-4

Pooleys Flight Equipment Ltd
Elstree Aerodrome
Hertfordshire
WD6 3AW
England

Tel: 0208 953 4870
Fax: 0208 953 2512

www.pooleys.com

Roy Quantick

Roy Quantick FRAeS, FRmetS was a former RAF pilot and Airline Captain and operated the World air routes. He holds the British Airline Transport Pilots Licence and the Flight Navigators Licence. For 15 years he specialised in crop protection and insect control, working as Operations Manager and Aviation Manager in large programmes for the chemical industry and the UN World Health Organisation. He became director of the International Agricultural Aviation Centre at the Cranfield Institute of Technology. He has published a number of papers on the safety aspects of this industry, both in aircraft design and the use of toxic chemical formulations. He is author of two books in this field: The Handbook for Agricultural Pilots, and Aviation in Crop Protection and Insect Control (1985). Since translated into 4 languages. Also the author of Climatology for Airline Pilots: Blackwells 2001. Author of the Cranfield Aviation Studies Home Study Courses for JAR PPL(A) & (H). Roy Quantick has taught for over 20 years at the Cranfield Institute of Technology and since 1985 has been an approved CAA instructor at training schools on the campus of Cranfield University teaching ATPL students. He is now Head of Training for Cranfield Aviation Studies/Pooleys Distance learning.

Editors

Dorothy Pooley

Dorothy holds an ATPL (A) and is both an instructor and examiner on fixed wing, running Flight Instructor courses at Shoreham. She is also a CAA Flight Instructor Examiner. She holds a CPL 'H' with R22 and R44 type ratings. Dorothy is the author and editor of a number of flying training books and has published articles in legal and insurance journals. Dorothy is a Honourary Solicitor for the Guild of Air Pilots and Air Navigators (GAPAN) and is Chairman of the Education and Training Committee.

Daljeet Gill

Daljeet is Head of Design & Development for Pooleys Flight Equipment and editor of the Pooleys Private Pilots Guides, Pre-flight Briefing, R/T Communications, Pooleys ATPL Manuals and Air Presentations, Ground School Training Transparencies. Daljeet has been involved with editing, typesetting, illustrations and design for all these publications including this manual.

Acknowledgments

The Civil Aviation Authority, David Patterson, Ron Jenkins, Ian MacGregor, Ken Bannister, David Evans and many other instructors whose comments and help have been invaluable.

Pooleys JAR Helicopter Manual

This book is intended to provide study material to cover the JAR syllabus for the following examinations, PPL 'Aircraft General & Principles of Flight', 'Flight Performance & Planning' and the alternative engines paper in 'Aircraft General' covering turbine engines. However, this book would be a useful reference for all helicopter JAR examinations. There are some excellent books available about Helicopter flight principles, but this book is concerned mainly in preparing students for the above JAR examinations. The JAR syllabus expands the knowledge required since it replaced the former CAA syllabus. Aircraft weight and balance is now incorporated in the new subject – ' Flight Performance & Planning'. The student must understand basic principles of Helicopter aerodynamics, and control. This is covered in the Aircraft General section Part 1. Also, gyroscopic and air pressure instruments, theory of gyros – also applicable to Helicopter rotors. Certain flying characteristics are described, like the vortex-ring state.

Aircraft Flight Performance and planning is mainly concerned with the loading of the Helicopter for safe flight, it is concerned with the Centre of Gravity when loaded with fuel and payload, both in the longitudinal and lateral axis. Section 2 covers weight and balance, and includes certain aspects of aerodynamics affecting flight efficiency. This includes a section on airframe and rotor icing. The Turbine section, Part 3, is a section dealing with the basic theory of the gas turbine engine. This leads to the general principles of the Turbo-shaft engine as used in the light single engine Helicopter. An understanding of this section will enable students to sit the JAR Turbine engine section of the Aircraft General & Principles of Flight paper. Practice sample questions and answers are included to complete these studies.

Index

For the Private Pilot, the JAR Examination is based
on a single piston engine, single rotor helicopter.

Part 1 Aircraft (GENERAL) and Principles of Flight

Part 2 Flight Performance and Planning

Part 3 PPL (H) Turbine Engine Section

PART 1 Aircraft (GENERAL) and Principles of Flight
Single Engine Helicopter

Introduction:

The helicopter is defined as "an aircraft deriving its lift in flight chiefly from power-driven horizontally-rotating rotors".

There are many configurations of helicopters, but these notes are concerned with a single engined, single rotor helicopter, although the number of blades in the rotor may be two, three or four. The general configuration is shown below.

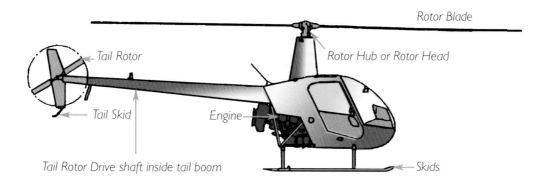

Fig. A1.   Robinson R 22 Light helicopter. Rotor is free to Teeter and Cone, and has a rigid inplane. Power plant, Lycoming 0-320, 150 BHP on standard R22.

The rotors of helicopters can be further sub-divided into types. An articulated rotor, is one where the individual blades are free to flap, drag and change pitch. This is made possible by mounting the individual blades on dragging and flapping hinges and pitch-change bearings (or torsion bars). Fig A2.

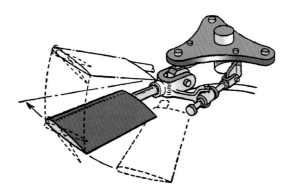

Fig. A2.   An Articulated Rotor

The term semi-rigid is generally used to denote a rotor in which the blades are without individual flapping and dragging hinges. The blades can, however, flap like a see-saw about a central gimbal. A rigid rotor is one in which the blades are not mounted on flapping or dragging hinges.

Rotors normally have any number of blades from two upwards, and some helicopters have five. Rotor blades are aerofoils and can be of metal, wood or composite construction.

Helicopters can be powered by piston engines or gas turbine engines. Undercarriages can consist of wheels, skids or floats. The aircraft may have a flying boat hull. Some land helicopters are fitted with inflatable flotation gear for emergency landings on water. The most popular helicopter used by the Private Pilot is the Robinson R22, see fig. A1. It is a single piston engine, single rotor, light utility helicopter.

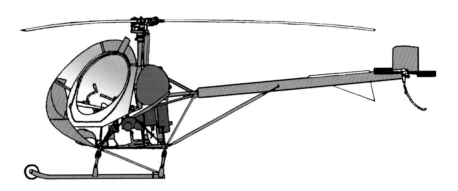

Fig. A3.   Schweizer 269/300C Light Helicopter.   Power Plant Lycoming H10 360-DIA. 190 BHP (De-rated).

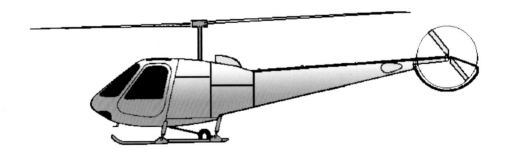

Fig A4.   Enstrom F-28. Another example of a light helicopter currently used in training. Power plant, one Lycoming TI0-360 Turbocharged piston engine.

Note: *A number of different helicopters are shown schematically in these notes, which are used to illustrate the points raised.*

1   PRINCIPLES OF FLIGHT

1.1   General Introduction

1.1.1   Helicopters justify their existence by their ability to hover and take-off and land vertically. That is not enough however. They must also be able to fly from Point A to Point B. In the early days of the development of the Sikorsky VS-300, the machine could hover, climb vertically (barely), and fly backwards and sideways. It couldn't however, fly forwards without going out of control. When asked about it, Igor Sikorsky explained, "This is just a minor engineering problem that we have not yet solved." Fortunately, by relocating the horizontal tail rotors he was then using for control, he soon solved this particular "minor" problem.

1.1.2   The basic laws that govern the flight of fixed wing aircraft also apply to rotary wing aircraft. Equally, both types face the same basic problem in that the aircraft concerned is heavier than air and must therefore produce an aerodynamic force (lift) to overcome the weight of the aircraft before it can leave the ground.

1.1.3   In the case of both types of aircraft, the force "lift" is obtained from an aerodynamic reaction resulting from a flow of air around an aerofoil section. The primary difference between the helicopter and the fixed wing aircraft is the relationship between the aerofoil and the fuselage. In the case of the fixed wing aircraft the aerofoil is attached to the fuselage in the form of a wing or mainplane, whilst in the case of the helicopter the aerofoils are attached to a centre drive shaft and hub assembly which is in turn given a rotational velocity. The rotation of the hub assembly causes air to flow over the aerofoil sections of the blades and thereby generate lift.

1.1.4   Both autogyros and helicopters have rotating wings or blades, but those of the autogyro rotate freely in flight under the influence of the airflow which passes through them, sometimes termed a windmill effect, but those of the helicopter *are engine driven in normal flight*. A pure autogyro must be provided with a source of horizontal thrust by, for example, a propeller, the rotor of a pure helicopter however provides both lift and thrust.

1.1.5   Autogyros have some advantages over the helicopter in forward flight, but cannot take off vertically in still air, consequently the autogyro, although comparatively simple in design, has now been replaced (by and large) by the more complex, but much more versatile, helicopter.

1.2 General Helicopter Aerodynamics

1.2.1   Before launching into a detailed discussion of the various forces acting on a helicopter in flight, it is first necessary that you understand the meaning of a few basic aerodynamic terms; how the force of lift is created; and the effect that certain factors have on lift.

1.2.2   **Aerofoil**. An aerofoil is any surface designed to produce lift or thrust when air passes over it. The wings of aeroplanes are aerofoils, also the propellers. Aerofoils on a helicopter are the rotor blades. The wing of an aeroplane is normally a non-symmetrical aerofoil, that is, the top surface has more curvature than the lower surface. The rotor blade of a helicopter is normally a symmetrical aerofoil having the same curvature on both upper and lower surfaces. See fig 1.1. In a symmetrical aerofoil, the Chord Line bisects the aerofoil into equal halves.

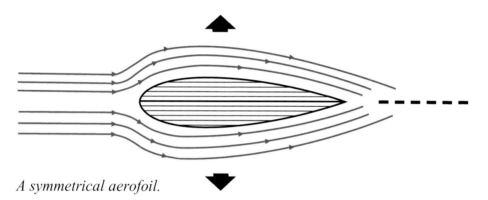

Fig. 1.1   A symmetrical aerofoil.

1.2.3   On a non-symmetrical aerofoil, the centre of pressure is less variable. As the angle of attack is altered, the distribution of pressure over the aerofoil changes (not so much as with a non-symmetrical aerofoil) and there is a movement of the centre of pressure. The position of the centre of pressure is usually defined as a certain proportion of the chord from the leading edge. The centre of pressure is NOT the centre of gravity, it is that point on the CHORD LINE through which the total reaction **(TR)** of the aerodynamic forces is considered to act. TR can be drawn as a vector and is 90° to the chord line. See fig 1.2

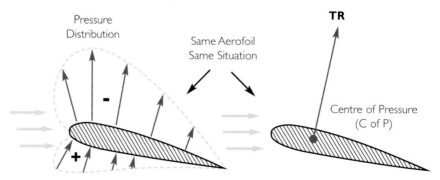

Fig. 1.2   Centre of pressure through which the Total Reaction (TR) vector is drawn 90° to the Chord Line.

1.2.4 As the angle of attack increases, the centre of pressure moves forward along the chord line; as the angle of attack decreases, the centre of pressure moves rearwards. See fig 1.3. A to B shows the distance from the leading edge to the centre of pressure at two angles of attack. Point C is the trailing edge. On a symmetrical aerofoil, the centre of pressure movement is limited. A symmetrical aerofoil is required for rotor blades so that a relatively stable centre of pressure is maintained; otherwise, dangerous forces would be introduced.

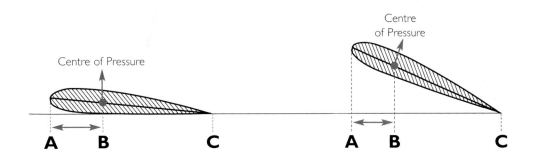

Fig. 1.3   In the first diagram the angle of attack is about 4°, in the second diagram the angle of attack is about 12°. The minimum pressure point moves forward with increasing angle of attack, (Distance A to B), leaving a greater distance to the trailing edge for air to overcome an adverse pressure gradient. ie., the pressure is showing an increase B to C as the C of P moves forward.

1.2.5   **Chord line.** The chord line of an aerofoil is an imaginary straight line from the leading edge to the trailing edge of the aerofoil. See fig 1.4.

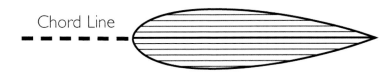

Fig. 1.4   The Chord Line of an aerofoil section.

1.2.6   **Relative Airflow. (RAF).** If a rotor blade is moved horizontally through a column of air, the effect will be to displace some of the air downwards. If a number of rotor blades are travelling along the same path in rapid succession (with a three-bladed rotor system at 240 rotor rpm (Rrpm), a blade will be passing a given point every twelfth of a second. Then the column of still air will eventually become a column of descending air, **INDUCED AIRFLOW**. See fig 1.5.

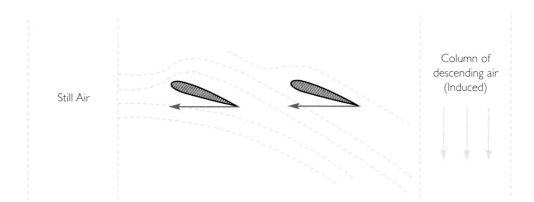

Still Air

Column of descending air (Induced)

Fig. 1.5   Induced airflow.

1.2.7   Forwards and backwards as used here are relative to the fore and aft axis of the helicopter - forwards means in the direction that the nose of the helicopter points, and backwards meaning the direction the tail is pointing. Relative airflow may be affected by several factors including the rotation of the rotor blades, horizontal movement of the helicopter, flapping of the rotor blades, (more later) and wind speed and direction.

1.2.8   Relative airflow is created by the motion of an aerofoil through the air, by the motion of air over an aerofoil or by a combination of the two. For a helicopter, the relative airflow is the flow of air with respect to the rotor blades. When the rotor is stopped, wind blowing over the blades creates a relative flow; when the helicopter is hovering in a no-wind condition, relative airflow is created by the motion of the rotor blades through the air; when the helicopter is hovering in a wind, the relative airflow is a combination of the wind and the motion of the rotor blades through the air.

1.2.9   When the helicopter is in horizontal flight, the relative airflow is a combination of the rotation of the rotor blades and the movement of the helicopter.

1.2.10   **Pitch Angle**. The rotor blade pitch angle is the acute angle between the blade chord line and a reference plane determined by the main rotor hub. Since the rotor plane of rotation is parallel to the plane containing the main rotor hub, the rotor blade pitch angle could also be described as the acute angle between the blade chord line and the rotor plane of rotation. (POR). See fig 1.6. The pitch angle can be varied by the pilot through the use of cockpit controls (collective and cyclic pitch controls) provided for this purpose.

1.2.11   **Angle of attack**. The angle of attack is the angle between the chord line of the aerofoil and the direction of the relative airflow. See fig. 1.7.

7

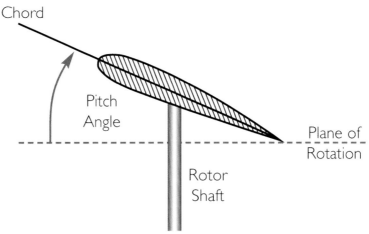

Fig. 1.6 *The pitch angle of a rotor blade is the angle between the chord line and a reference plane determined by the rotor hub, or plane of rotation.*

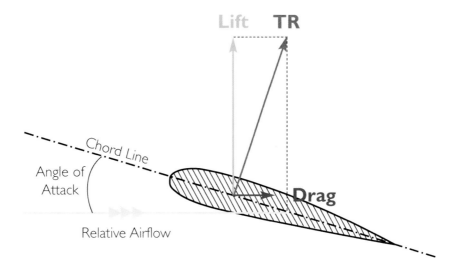

Fig. 1.7 *The Angle of Attack is the angle between the relative airflow and the Chord line. The aerofoil is inclined to the direction of the airflow producing a resultant force (Total Reaction – TR) at 90° to the chord line.*

1.2.12   The angle of attack should not be confused with the pitch angle of the rotor blades. The pitch angle is determined by the position of the appropriate cockpit controls, (collective and cyclic pitch, more later), whereas the angle of attack is determined by the direction of the relative airflow. The angle of attack may be less than, equal to, or greater than the pitch angle. During forward flight, the angle of attack is less than the pitch angle for the forward going blade, (as it is going through the air faster being the sum of the forward speed of the helicopter and the rotation speed). The angle of attack is greater than the pitch angle for the retreating blade, (as the blade is going more slowly through the air being the rotation speed minus the helicopter speed), and equal at the fore and aft positions. How this is achieved will be dealt with later.

1.2.13   The pilot can increase or decrease the angle of attack by changing the pitch angle of the rotor blades. If the pitch angle is increased, the angle of attack is increased; if the pitch angle is decreased, the angle of attack is decreased. Since the angle of attack is dependent on the relative airflow, the same factors that affect the relative airflow also affect the angle of attack.

1.2.14   **Lift.** The force, lift, is derived from an aerofoil through a principle often referred to as Bernoulli's Principle, or the "venturi effect." As air velocity increases through the constricted portion of a venturi tube, the pressure decreases. Compare the upper surface of an aerofoil with the constriction in the venturi tube (fig. 1.8). They are very similar.

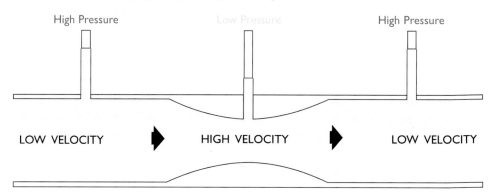

High Pressure   Low Pressure   High Pressure

LOW VELOCITY   ▶   HIGH VELOCITY   ▶   LOW VELOCITY

Fig. 1.8   Bernoulli's principle: increased air velocity produces decreased pressure. Lift is produced by an aerofoil through a combination of decreased pressure above the aerofoil (as per Bernoulli's principle) and increased pressure beneath.

1.2.15   The upper half of the venturi tube is replaced by layers of undisturbed air. Thus, as air flows over the upper surface of an aerofoil, the curvature causes an increase in the speed of the airflow. The increased speed of airflow results in a decrease in pressure on the upper surface of the aerofoil. At the same time, airflow travels relatively more slowly over the lower surface of the aerofoil thus the pressure underneath is increased. The combination of decreased pressure on the upper surface and increased pressure on the lower surface results in an upward force. This force is LIFT.

1.2.16   **Drag (aerofoil).** At the same time as the aerofoil is producing lift, it is also subject to a drag force. Drag is the term used for the force that tends to resist movement of the aerofoil through the air, the retarding force of inertia and air resistance. It acts parallel and in the opposite direction to the movement of the aerofoil or, if you prefer, in the same direction as the relative airflow. It is this force that causes a reduction in rotor RPM (revolutions per minute) when the angle of attack is increased. An increase in angle of attack then not only produces an increase in lift, but it also produces an increase in drag (fig. 1.9).

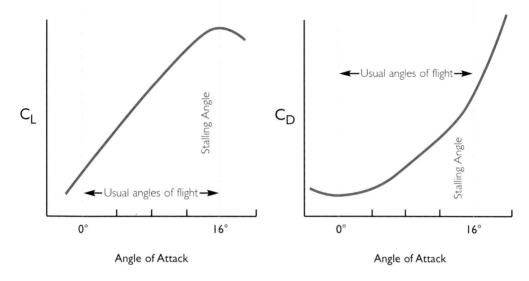

Fig. 1.9   *The relationship between Angle of Attack (AoA) and Lift and Drag forces (C_L and C_D). As the angle of attack increases, Lift and Drag increase.*

1.2.17   **Stall.** When the angle of attack increases up to a certain point, the air can no longer flow smoothly over the top surface because of the excessive change of direction required. This loss of streamlined flow results in a swirling, turbulent airflow and a large increase in drag. The turbulent airflow also causes a sudden increase in pressure on the top surface resulting in a large loss of lift. At this point, the aerofoil is said to be in a stalled condition. See fig 1.10.   Although the lift has dropped considerably, it is not zero.

Note: *The aerofoil stalls at a certain angle, not a certain speed.*

Direction
of Airflow

Fig. 1.10   *An aerofoil in a stalled condition.*

1.2.18   **Lift and angle of attack**. As the angle of attack of an aerofoil increases, the lift increases (up to the stall angle) provided that the velocity of the relative airflow remains the same. Since the pilot can increase or decrease the angle of attack by increasing or decreasing the pitch angle of the rotor blades through the use of the collective pitch cockpit control, then he can increase or decrease the lift produced by the rotor blades. He must remember, however, that any increase in angle of attack will also increase drag on the rotor blades tending to slow down the rotor rotation. Additional power will be required to prevent this slowing down.

1.2.19   **Lift and velocity of airflow**. As the velocity of the relative airflow increases, the lift increases for any given angle of attack. Since the pilot can increase or decrease the rotor RPM which, in turn, increases or decreases the velocity of the airflow, he can change the amount of lift. As a general rule, however, the pilot attempts to maintain a constant rotor RPM and changes the lift force by varying the angle of attack.

1.2.20   **Lift and air density**. Lift varies directly with the density of the air; as the air density increases, lift and drag increase; as air density decreases, lift and drag decrease.

1.2.21   **What affects air density?** Altitude and atmospheric changes affect air density. The higher the altitude the less dense is the air. At 10,000 feet the air is only two thirds as dense as the air at sea level. Therefore, if a helicopter is to maintain its lift, the angle of attack of the rotor blades must be increased. In order to increase the angle of attack, the pilot must increase the pitch angle of the blades. We have already seen that, as the pitch angle increases, drag on the rotor system increases and the rotor RPM tends to decrease. Therefore, more power must be applied to prevent a decrease in rotor RPM. This is why a helicopter requires more power to hover at higher altitudes than under the same conditions at lower altitudes.

1.2.22   Due to the atmospheric changes in temperature, pressure, or humidity, the density of the air may be different, even at the same altitude, from one day to the next or from one location in the country to another. Because air expands when heated, hot air is less dense than cold air. In order for the helicopter to produce the same amount of lift on a hot day as on a cold day, the rotor blades must be operated at a higher angle of attack. This requires that the blades be operated at a greater pitch angle which increases the drag and tends to reduce rotor RPM. To maintain a constant rotor RPM, more power is required. For this reason, a helicopter requires more power to hover on a hot day than on a cold day.

1.2.23   Because air expands as pressure is decreased, there will be fluctuations in the air density due to changes in atmospheric pressure. The lower the pressure, the less dense the air, and, for the same reason stated previously, the greater the power required to hover.

1.2.24   Because water vapour weighs less than an equal amount of dry air, moist air (high relative humidity) is less dense than dry air (low relative

11

humidity). Because of this, a helicopter will require more power on a humid day than on a dry day. This is especially true on hot, humid days because the hotter the day, the greater the amount of water vapour the air can hold. The more moisture (water vapour) in the air, the less dense the air. From the above discussion, it is obvious that a pilot should beware of high, hot, and humid conditions, high altitudes, hot temperatures, and high moisture content.

1.2.25   The pilot should be especially aware of these conditions at his destination, since sufficient power may not be available to complete a landing safely, particularly when the helicopter is operating at a high gross mass.

1.2.26   **Lift and mass**. The total mass (gross) of a helicopter is the first force that must be overcome before flight is possible. Lift, the force which overcomes or balances the force of mass, is obtained from the rotation of the main rotor blades. *Note: The term MASS in these notes is used generally to conform with JAR definition, however the term WEIGHT is used in some areas relating to helicopters not working to the JAR definition.*

1.2.27   **Thrust and drag**. Thrust moves the aircraft in the desired direction; drag, the retarding force of inertia and air resistance, tends to hold it back. In vertical flight drag acts downward; in horizontal flight, drag acts horizontally and opposite in direction to the thrust component. Thrust, like lift, is obtained from the main rotor. Drag, as discussed here, is the drag of the entire helicopter, not just the drag of the rotor blades, which was discussed earlier. The use of the term "drag" in subsequent sections of these notes should be considered as having this same connotation. In future references, the drag of the rotor blades, or rotor system will be used.

1.3   Gyroscopic Precession

1.3.1   The principle of the gyroscope is a principle that should be understood as the main rotor of a helicopter acts like a gyroscope, and the forces of precession are considerable. This chapter draws on the description of the gyroscope from aircraft instrumentation, and will help in the understanding of how precessional forces affect the plane of rotation of the rotor blades, and how these forces are controlled.

1.3.2   The spinning main rotor of the helicopter acts like a gyroscope. As such, it has the properties of gyroscopic action, one of which is precession. Gyroscopic precession is the resultant action or deflection of a spinning object when a force is applied to this object. This action occurs approximately 90° in the direction of rotation from the point where the force is applied. See figs 1.11A & B. Through the use of this principle, the tip-path plane of the main rotor may be tilted from the horizontal, although in Helicopter terminology, different expressions will be used (more later).

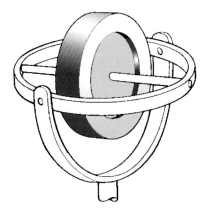

1. The Gyroscope

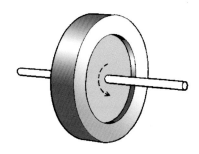

2. The Wheel is rotating rapidly, in an upright position

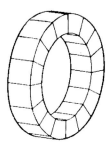

3. Suppose the rim is spilt into segments

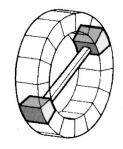

4. Attend to two of these segments

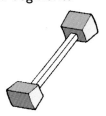

5. Forget all the rest

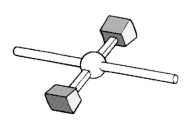

6. These segments are rigidly connected to the axle

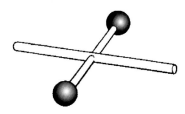

7. Their shape does not matter

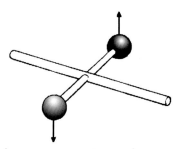

8. As the segments turn about the axle, one moves up and the other moves down

Fig. 1.11A. Gyroscopic precession principle. *(Courtesy of Sperry Gyroscope Company)*

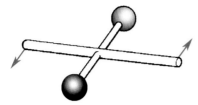

9. Now suppose we apply a torque to the axle in the horizontal plane.

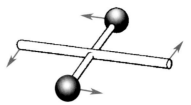

10. This imparts a motion in the horizontal direction to the segments, one to the right and the other to the left.

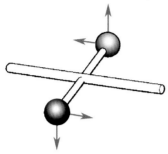

11. Thus the segments now have both a horizontal and a vertical motion.

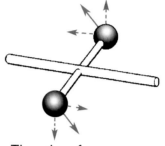

12. They therefore move diagonally.

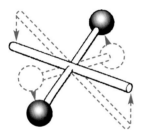

13. This is the key diagram. Study it carefully. The axle is rigidly connected to the segments and must therefore tilt when the segments move diagonally.

14. All the other segments must tilt in the same way.

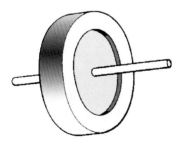

15. Therefore, the whole wheel tilts.

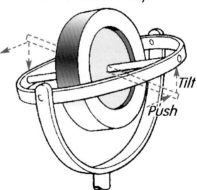

16. Thus when a gyroscope is given a push, it tilts at right angles to the direction of the push.

Fig. 1.11B. Gyroscopic precession principle. *(Courtesy of Sperry Gyroscope Company)*

1.3.3   The movement of the cyclic pitch control in a two bladed rotor system increases the angle of attack of one rotor blade with the result that a greater lifting force is applied at this point in the plane of rotation. This same control movement simultaneously decreases the angle of attack of the other blade a like amount thus decreasing the lifting force applied at this point in the plane of rotation. The blade with the increased angle of attack tends to rise; the blade with the decreased angle of attack tends to lower. However, because of the gyroscopic precession property, the blades do not rise or lower to maximum deflection until a point approximately 90° later in the plane of rotation.

1.3.4   In the illustration (See fig 1.12), the retreating blade angle of attack is increased and the advancing blade angle of attack is decreased resulting in a tipping forward of the tip-path plane, since maximum deflection takes place 90° later when the blades are at the rear and front respectively.

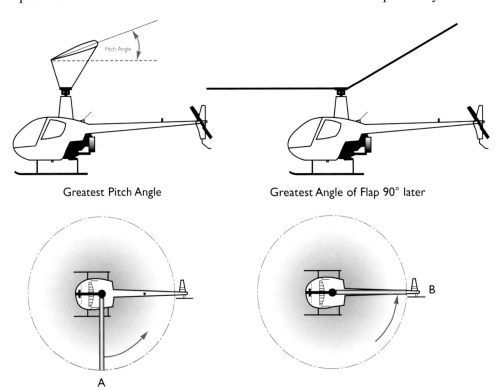

Greatest Pitch Angle   Greatest Angle of Flap 90° later

Fig. 1.12.   Rotor disc acts like a gyroscope. When a rotor blade pitch change is made, maximum reaction occurs approximately 90° later in the direction of rotation.

1.3.5   In a three-bladed rotor, the movement of the cyclic pitch control changes the angle of attack of each blade an appropriate amount so that the end result is the same, a tipping forward of the tip-path plane when the maximum change in angle of attack is made as each blade passes the same points at which the maximum increase and decrease are made. In the illustration (fig 1.12) for the two bladed rotor, as each blade passes the 90° position on the left, the maximum **increase** in angle of attack occurs. As each blade passes the 90° position to the right, the maximum **decrease** in angle of attack occurs.

1.3.6   Maximum deflection takes place 90° later, maximum upward deflection at the rear and maximum downward deflection at the front, and the tip-path plane tips forward.

1.3.7   It can be seen that the Rotor Disc acts like a gyroscope, however, there is a further significant aspect to understand. A gyroscope tends to maintain its position in space and, and so would the Rotor Disc if there were no aerodynamics involved. ie., if the Rotor Disc were to spin in a vacuum, it would certainly exhibit all the gyroscopic aspects of stability. The effect of very large aerodynamic forces cause a degree of instability. In air, the aerodynamic forces will cause any rotor to align itself perpendicular to the shaft. Flapping and other movements of individual blades as a result of unbalanced external inputs, ie., gusts near the ground, or cyclic pitch changes, may last up to one revolution while alignment takes place.

1.3.8   The rotor disc then does NOT HAVE the gyroscope's inherent stability. If required, this last drawback can be compensated for. Early Bell Helicopters used a stabilizer bar that acted like a gyroscope, and controlled cyclic pitch in a way that transferred some of the gyroscopic stability to the rotor. The Lockheed rotor and gyro system did the same thing. Nowadays, the designer can use a hidden "black box" containing a rapidly turning gyroscope with appropriate electronic connections to the control system to make the helicopter achieve as much stability as desired.

2   AERODYNAMICS OF THE ROTOR

2.1   The same force - LIFT, keeps an aeroplane and a helicopter airborne by placing an aerofoil in the airflow which deflects air downwards.

2.1.1   The wings of a fixed wing aircraft are fitted to the fuselage at some specified angle. The datums are the Chord and a line longitudinally down the fuselage. The angle between to two is known as the **ANGLE OF INCIDENCE.**   See fig 2.1.

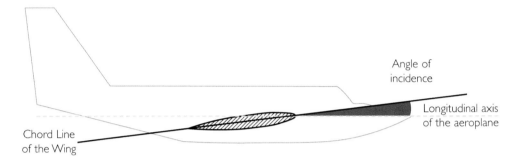

Fig. 2.1   *The angle of incidence on a fixed wing aeroplane. Exaggerated for illustration. It is fixed during the design and construction.*

2.1.2   The aerofoils of a helicopter are ROTOR BLADES attached to a ROTOR SHAFT which extends vertically from the fuselage. They form the ROTOR which turns independently through the ROTOR SHAFT. The SHAFT AXIS is the axis through the Rotor Shaft about which the Rotor Blades are permitted to rotate. See fig 2.2.

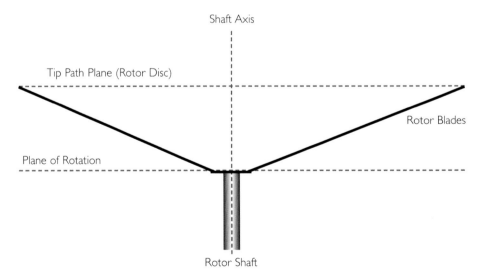

Fig. 2.2   *The Rotor Head arrangement.*

2.1.3   The Rotor Blades are connected to the Rotor Head. The angle of the blades relative to the PLANE OF ROTATION is called the PITCH ANGLE. See fig 2.3

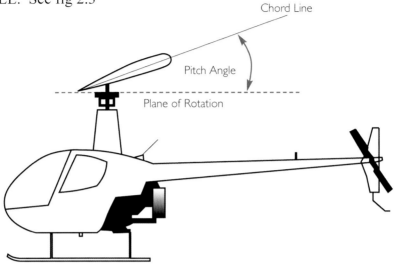

Fig. 2.3   The Pitch Angle on a helicopter.

2.1.4   The AXIS OF ROTATION (which is perpendicular to the PLANE OF ROTATION) is a line through the Rotor Head about which the blades actually rotate. Under ideal conditions of steady flight in equilibrium, the AXIS OF ROTATION will coincide with the SHAFT AXIS. This, however, will not always be so since the rotor is permitted to tilt under certain flight conditions. See fig 2.4.

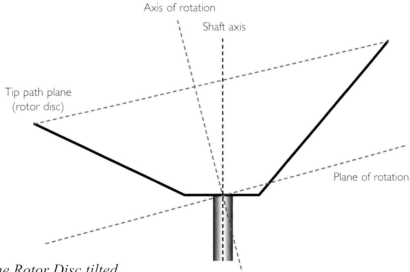

Fig. 2.4   The Rotor Disc tilted.

2.1.5   The TIP PATH PLANE is the imaginary circular plane outlined by the rotor blade tips in making a cycle of rotation. It is at right angles to the Axis of Rotation and parallel to the Plane of Rotation. The area encompassed within this path is known as the ROTOR DISC.

2.2 Basic Forces on the Aerofoil

2.2.1 The airflow around an aerofoil gives rise to a pressure distribution. The pressure differences produce a force distribution which can be represented by TOTAL REACTION. See fig 2.5.

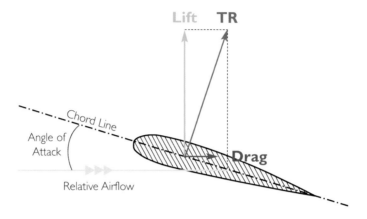

Fig 2.5   *Total reaction.*

2.2.2 The Total Reaction is resolved into a force perpendicular to the Relative Airflow (RAF) called LIFT, and a force parallel to the RAF called DRAG. The angle which the chord line makes to the RAF is the ANGLE OF ATTACK. The magnitude of lift is given by the formula:

LIFT   = $C_L \frac{1}{2} \rho V^2 S$

Where ρ =   Air Density
         V   =   Velocity of RAF
         S   =   Plan Area of Aerofoil
         C_L =   Coefficient of Lift

The magnitude of DRAG is given by the formula:

DRAG   = $C_D \frac{1}{2} \rho V^2 S$

2.3 Blade Design

2.3.1 The design requirements for a rotor blade are complicated:

1   The combined area of the blades is small compared to the wings of an aeroplane of similar weight. A high maximum C_L is needed.

2   The Power to Weight Ratio of a helicopter is important, and good lift to drag characteristics are needed.

3 The Pitch Angle of a blade is held by a control arm and a large pitching moment would cause excessive stress in this component. A symmetrical aerofoil has a very small pitching moment and is also suitable for high blade tip speeds.

4 Torsional stiffness is required so that the pitch angle is not changed by the airflow twisting the blade. The blade is symmetrical, with a thickness to chord ratio of about 1:7. (Also referred to as Fineness Ratio) See fig 2.6.

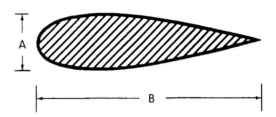

Fig. 2.6 *Determining the "Thickness to Chord Ratio", If "A" is 4 cm and "B" is 26 cm then the ratio is approximately 1:7. The "Fineness Ratio is the thickness of the aerofoil expressed as a percentage of chord length, approximately 15%. The maximum value of "A" should be about a quarter to one-third of the way back from the leading edge. This ratio offers the least resistance to airflow.*

2.4 Determining the Direction of Airflow Relative to the Rotor Blade

2.4.1 A rotor produces vertical thrust by accelerating air downwards.

2.4.2 Consider a column of air through which a rotor blade is moving horizontally. The effect will be to displace some of the air downwards. If a number of rotor blades are traveling along the same path in rapid succession, then the column of air will eventually become a column of descending air. This downward motion of air is known as INDUCED FLOW. See fig 2.7.

2.4.3 The Plane of Rotation, Axis of Rotation and Chord line have been described. There is rotational airflow due to the horizontal movement of the rotor blade through the air in the plane of rotation. In producing thrust, there is the induced flow. The resultant of the two vectors is the Relative Airflow (RAF).

Fig.2.7   Induced flow caused by the rotors displacing air downwards.

To recap on the definitions:

*   The angle between the RAF and the Chord line is the **Angle of Attack (∝)**
*   The angle between the Chord line and the Plane of Rotation is the **Pitch Angle, or Blade Angle.**
*   Lift is produced perpendicular to the RAF, and Drag is produced parallel to the RAF. The resultant is the Total Reaction. See fig 2.8.

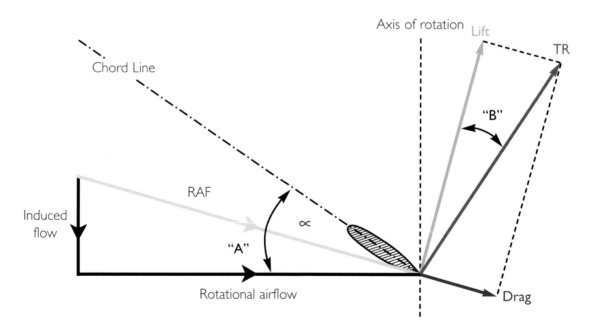

Fig. 2.8   The Total Reaction. **Note:** *Angle "A" is the Pitch Angle. Angle "B" is determined by the L/D ratio. RAF is Relative Airflow. If no other airflows are present, then blade angle "A" would be the same as angle of attack.*

21

2.4.4   Lift is not producing a force in direct opposition to the mass, as in the case of fixed wing aircraft. The lift component of Total Reaction (the useful force) must therefore be that part which is acting along the Axis of Rotation. This component is known as Rotor Thrust. The other component of Total Reaction will act in the Rotor Blade's Plane of Rotation and is known as Rotor Drag. See fig 2.9.

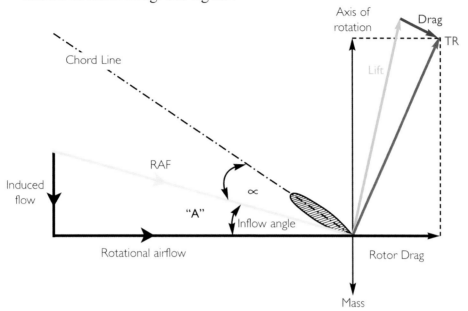

Fig. 2.9   *Forces acting on a rotor blade.*
Note: ∝ *(angle of attack) + inflow Angle = Pitch Angle.*

2.4.5   In further consideration of Induced flow: the rotor experiences two airflows, one from straight ahead (Rotational Airflow V_R) caused by rotation, and one from above (the Induced flow). These two airflows create a resultant, the Relative Airflow (RAF). The RAF is no longer parallel to the plane of rotation. See fig. 2.9.

2.4.6   **The angle between the RAF and the rotational airflow is called the INFLOW ANGLE.**

2.4.7   The angle between the chord line and the plane of rotation is controlled by the pilot by raising or lowering the collective lever. Pulling upwards, the blade angle increases, and pushing downwards, the blade angle decreases. If no other airflows are present, this angle is also the angle of attack. **Note:** The blade angle does NOT affect the direction from which the plane of rotation is orientated. ie., it does not matter whether the plane of rotation is parallel with the ground or tilted, the plane of rotation will always be parallel to the rotational airflow (V_R).

        Remember, V_R is the velocity as a result of rotation, sensed on the leading edge of the rotor. This varies along the length of the rotor.

2.4.8   The angle of attack decreases when the induced flow becomes established. See fig. 2.9. For a given blade section and rotor RPM; when the induced flow decreases, the angle of attack increases. **The angle of attack and induced flow are inversely proportional for a given rotor section and RPM.**

2.4.9   The inflow angle is the angle between the plane of rotation and the RAF. For a given rotor RPM, the inflow angle increases as the induced flow increases, and decreases as the inflow angle decreases. **The inflow angle and the induced flow are directly proportional for a given rotor RPM (Nr).**

2.4.10   If the induced flow remains constant, and the N_R increases, the angle of attack increases, and the inflow angle will decrease. A reduction of (N_R) will decrease the angle of attack and the inflow angle will increase. **The induced flow remaining constant, the inflow angle and the N_r are inversely proportional.**

2.4.11   Referring to fig. 2.8, notice that the lift is at right angles to the relative airflow, and the drag is in line with the relative airflow, these vectors resolve into Total Reaction (TR). Notice that the **TR** vector "leans backwards" from the lift vector. This vector does not act in line with the weight (except in the hover in nil wind), so, in forward flight the vector that is in line with and opposite to the weight vector must be Rotor Thrust **(RT)**. However, to achieve forward flight, a forward component of rotor thrust must be present. See fig. 2.10.

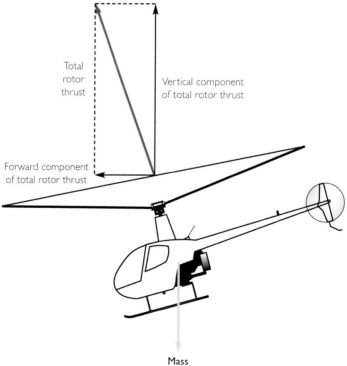

Fig. 2.10   In forward flight, the total rotor thrust (TRT) is resolved into two components: Vertical and Horizontal. The vertical component is equal and opposite to the gross mass, and the forward component provides the forward motion.

2.4.12   The Rotor Thrusts of each blade are added together and make up the Total Rotor Thrust. **(TRT).** Total Rotor Thrust is defined as the sum of all blade Rotor Thrusts and acts along the Axis of Rotation through the Rotor Head.

2.4.13   **Rotor Drag.** This is the component of total reaction at right angles to rotor thrust. See fig. 2.9. Rotor drag is in the plane of rotation, but in the opposite direction to the blade rotation. Do not confuse Rotor Drag (which acts in the plane of rotation) with Aerodynamic Drag (which acts in line with the relative airflow).

2.4.14   **Angle of attack and rotor thrust.** Total Rotor Thrust **(TRT)** is the force that overcomes the weight, however, rotor drag must also be considered in terms of power available (which is limited). For efficiency, the TRT must be as high as possible with the rotor drag as low as possible, ie., TRT/rotor drag ratio as high as possible. The total reaction determines the amount of rotor thrust and rotor drag. In fig. 2.8 it is noticed that the TR vector "leans" backwards from the lift vector. If the degree of "leaning" increases, possibly due to a high angle of attack, the amount of rotor thrust decreases, and the rotor drag will increase. **Therefore, the TRT/rotor drag ratio is determined by the size and orientation of the Total Reaction (TR).** For the best TRT/rotor drag ratio, the TR should be as close as possible to the axis of rotation, where the blades are operating at the best lift/drag ratio, maximum lift and minimum drag.

2.4.15   For a constant rotor RPM and a decrease in induced flow, the angle of attack increases (and the inflow angle decreases) for a constant blade angle. To avoid an increase in the angle of attack, the pilot would lower the collective control, which reduces the blade angle. Now, the inflow angle will reduce causing the total reaction vector to re-orient closer to the axis of rotation. Rotor thrust then increases, and rotor drag decreases. **The best efficiency (Best TRT/drag ratio) is obtained when the angle of attack produces the least amount of drag and when the collective control is at the lowest position.**

Note: *Generally speaking, the higher the collective control is set, the higher will be the inflow angle, the greater amount of rotor drag requires a greater amount of power.*

2.5   Washout

2.5.1   The rotational velocity of each part of the Rotor Blade varies along its length or radius from the Rotor Head. The blade tip will always experience a greater velocity of airflow than the root. Lift, and hence Rotor Thrust is proportional to V^2 and will be much greater at the blade tip than at the root.

2.5.2   This unequal distribution of lift would cause large bending stresses in the Rotor Blade and is also aerodynamically inefficient.

2.5.3   The Rotor Thrust at the blade tip is reduced by WASHOUT, that is, making the Rotor Blade with a built-in twist such that the Pitch Angle decreases from the root to the tip. Angle of Attack, and hence Rotor Thrust is decreased with the Pitch Angle at the tip. However, in practice, lift from the Rotor Blade will still have its greatest value at the tip but its distribution is more uniform. See 2.11

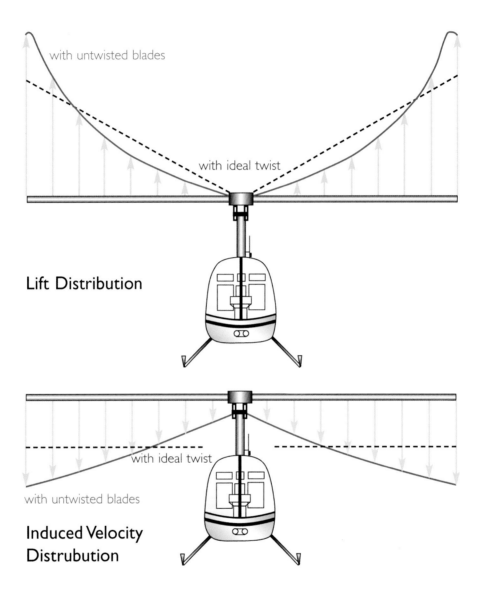

Fig. 2.11   Washout (twisting) of rotor blades improves the lift distribution along the blades. The induced velocity distribution is also improved.

2.5.4   Another way of reducing the lift towards the tips is by tapering, and the optimum blade would be both twisted and tapered. Most helicopters use twisted blades but no taper, but tapering may become more common because of the improving technology with composite materials, which can be made into odd shapes compared with metal.

2.5.5   There are limits however, to the amount of both twist and taper that can realistically be used. Theoretically, a twist distribution that reduces the pitch 20° to 30° between the tip and the root is desired for the best hover. Unfortunately, experience has proved that vibration and oscillatory loads in forward flight are increased by twist, and a compromise has been reached in the order of about 10°.

2.5.6   The desire to taper the blade also runs up against practical constraints. Almost every rotor blade has a concentrated tip weight made up of heavy metal. It's there for two reasons: to modify the blades' dynamic characteristics to reduce vibration and oscillatory loads; and to increase rotor inertia to help keep the rotor speed up during those critical seconds following a power failure. If the designer decides tapering to a very small chord at the tip is a good idea from the aerodynamic standpoint, he may find there is not enough volume to install the required tip weight. See fig 2.12.

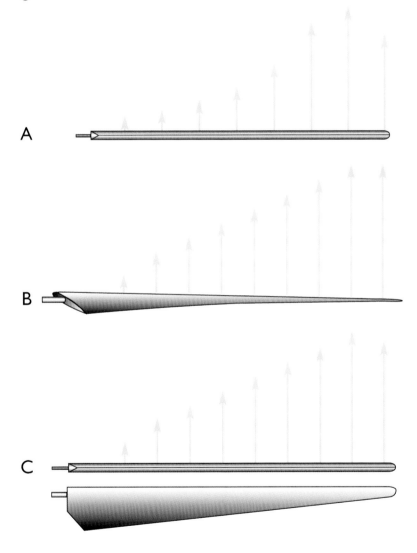

Fig. 2.12   "A" is the lift distribution along the span of a parallel section non twisted rotor blade. "B" is the lift distribution along the span of a twisted blade. C" is the lift distribution along the span of a tapered blade.

2.5.7   For small helicopters, the designer may also find that if the tip chord goes below about 13 cm, the rotor starts losing its good aerodynamic characteristics even at normal helicopter tip speeds. Tapering also assists in helicopters with high tip speeds in reducing compressibility losses.

2.6   Collective Pitch

2.6.1   At various stages of flight, the Total Rotor Thrust requirements will change. Although Rotor RPM (Nr) and hence Rotational Velocity can be changed, the reaction time is slow and the range of values is small. The other controllable variable is PITCH ANGLE.

2.7   Collective Pitch Changes

2.7.1   The Pitch Angle of a Rotor Blade is altered by turning it about a Sleeve and Spindle bearing on its FEATHERING HINGE by means of a Pitch Operating Arm. Each blade is given the same Pitch Angle by connecting the lower ends of the Pitch Operating Arms to a ROTATING SWASH PLATE (more later). **(Feathering describes the movement of the blade about its feathering axis, which is the straight line axis from root to the tip of the blade).** Feathering takes place as a result of changes in collective or cyclic pitch. See fig 2.13.

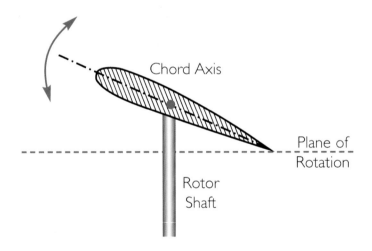

Fig. 2.13   *Feathering or cyclic-pitch change.*

2.7.2   The rotating Swash Plate is raised or lowered by a Non-Rotating Swash Plate below it. It is connected to the COLLECTIVE PITCH LEVER in the cockpit by rods which are often hydraulically assisted, or by electronic inputs to computer regulated servo jacks. The Pitch Angle of the blades is thus increased or decreased COLLECTIVELY by the pilot raising or lowering the Collective Pitch Lever. See Fig 2.14.

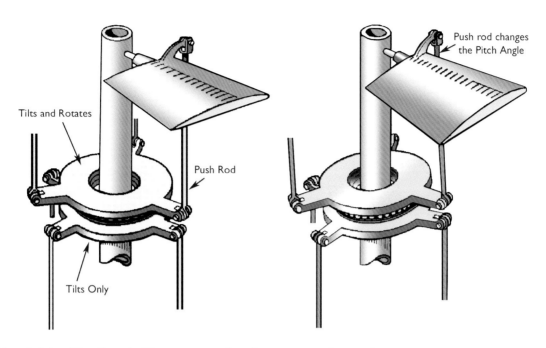

Fig. 2.14   The Swash-Plate system for changing cyclic pitch.

2.7.3   The Swash-Plate is divided into upper and lower sections with a bearing between the two. The upper section can tilt in any direction and it also rotates at the same speed as the rotor, as do all the rods and appendages above it. The lower section can only tilt, and it is from this lower plate (or fixed star) that control rods lead off through a control transmission to the pilot's cockpit, to the cyclic-pitch stick. See fig. 2.15. In order to tilt the rotor disc in any required direction for any manoeuvre, the swash plate must be tilted. The resulting up and down movement of the push-pull rods attached to the upper section (or rotating star) of the swash plate is transferred to the blades in the form of cyclic-pitch changes as the blades move round. The rods which alter the cyclic pitch of the blades also control the mean collective pitch. This is done by making the whole of the swash plate move up and down bodily, or by arranging for part of the rotor hub or control linkage system to move up or down as required.

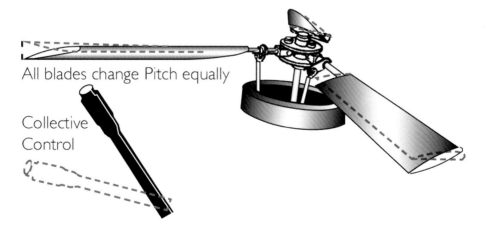

Fig. 2.15   Raising the collective control (pitch lever) up, will increase the Blade pitch angle equally on all the blades.

2.8   Control of Rotor RPM (Nr)

2.8.1   An increase in Total Rotor Thrust will produce an increase in Rotor Drag. Engine power must therefore be increased to maintain Nr when increasing Total Rotor Thrust, and vice versa. In older types of helicopters, this was achieved by a cam operated linkage between the collective lever and the engine. A twist-grip manual throttle was also provided for fine adjustments. Modern helicopters have automatic devices to sense the slightest variation of rotor speed and to compensate by altering the fuel supplied to the engine, hence maintaining constant Nr.

2.9   Dissymmetry of Lift

2.9.1   The area within the tip-path plane of the main rotor is known as the disc area or rotor disc. When hovering in still air, lift created by the rotor blades at all corresponding positions around the rotor disc is equal. Dissymmetry of lift is created by horizontal flight or by wind during hovering flight, and is the difference in lift that exists between the advancing blade half of the disc area and the retreating blade half.

2.9.2   At normal rotor operating RPM and zero airspeed, the rotating blade-tip speed of most helicopter main rotors is approximately 350 kt. When hovering in a no-wind condition, the speed of the relative airflow at the blade tips is the same throughout the tip-path plane. The speed of the relative airflow at any specific point along the rotor blade will be the same throughout the tip-path plane, however, the speed is reduced as this point moves closer to the rotor hub.

2.9.3   As the helicopter moves into forward flight, the relative airflow moving over each rotor blade becomes a combination of the rotational speed of the rotor and the forward movement of the helicopter. At the 90° position on the advancing side, the advancing blade has the combined speed of the blade velocity plus the speed of the helicopter. At the 90° position on the retreating side, the retreating blade speed is the blade velocity less the speed of the helicopter. In other words, the relative airflow is at a maximum at the 90° position on the advancing side and at a minimum at the 90° position on the retreating side.

2.9.4   Earlier in these notes, the statement was made that for any given angle of attack, lift increases as the velocity of the airflow over the aerofoil increases. It is apparent that the lift over the advancing blade half of the rotor disc will be greater than the lift over the retreating blade half during horizontal flight or when hovering in a wind unless some compensation is made. It is equally apparent that the helicopter will roll to the retreating side unless some compensation is made. How is this done, to equalize the lift over the two halves of the rotor disc ?

2.9.5   **Juan de la Cierva**, in the 1920's solved this problem after he had two rollovers when attempting a take-off in his Cierva Autogyro. Both attempts reduced the autogyro to splinters. Yet, his model autogyro always flew with no tendency to roll. In a sudden flash of inspiration, the difference between his full-scale autogyro and the model was apparent, it was the difference between rigidity and flexibility. On the aircraft, he had obtained structural integrity by rigidly bracing the blades with struts and wires, just as aeroplane wings were braced in those days. On the other hand, the model had been built with flexible rattan spars, since in model size this type of construction was adequate. As the rigidly braced autogyro taxied forward, the airspeed seen by one blade changed during each revolution. On the advancing side, the air speed was higher than on the retreating side. Since each blade had the same pitch setting and, therefore, angle of attack, the difference in velocity produced more lift on the advancing side than on the other, thus generating an unbalanced rolling moment. But on the model, the flexible rattan spars could bend up and down. Thus the advancing blade, which had high lift, began to flap upwards. As it did, it was also being rotated toward the nose, where the local velocity was reduced to its mean value. The retreating blade was undergoing a similar experience, except that it was flapping downwards as it rotated to a position over the tail. This flapping produced a climbing condition on the advancing side, decreasing its angle of attack and the opposite effect on the retreating side. Flapping equilibrium came when the model's rotor had an angle of attack just sufficient to compensate for the airspeed at each point in the revolution. In this equilibrium condition, the model rotor was tilted fore and aft and the lift distribution was balanced. Cierva knew what he had to do, add flexibility to his full-scale rotor. The simplest solution, he decided, would be mechanical hinges allowing the blades to flap, just as they had on the model. In flight, the blades were kept extended by centrifugal forces and coned slightly upward by the lift. With this technological breakthrough, Cierva was able to fly his autogyro and begin a long line of development that resulted in most present-day helicopters having mechanical flapping hinges. *(from: Prouty R W: Helicopter Aerodynamics. PJS Publications Inc 1985 pp17-18).*

2.10   The Cyclic Pitch

2.10.1   First of all, let us be clear about the differences between COLLECTIVE and CYCLIC pitch. In a collective-pitch change, all rotor blades change their pitch (collectively) together, by the same amount, and in the same direction. In a cyclic-pitch change (sometimes called cyclic feathering) the pitch of each blade is altered consecutively from the minimum to a maximum, as determined by the position of the pilot's control (Cyclic Pitch Control). The cyclic pitch control will alter the angle of tilt of the rotor disk.

2.10.2   The degree of alteration of the pitch angle of each blade is determined by the position of the pilot's control. In a two bladed rotor, the blades reach minimum and maximum pitch positions respectively at one particular instant, see fig 2.16.

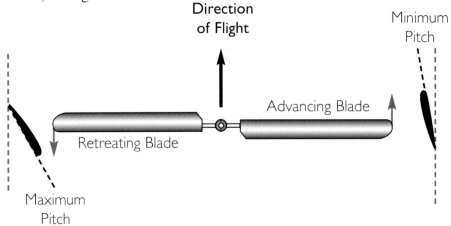

Fig. 2.16   Cyclic pitch changes in a two bladed rotor.

2.10.3   In a three bladed rotor, if one blade were passing through the minimum pitch position, the other two would be in the process of increasing and decreasing their pitch respectively, see fig 2.17.

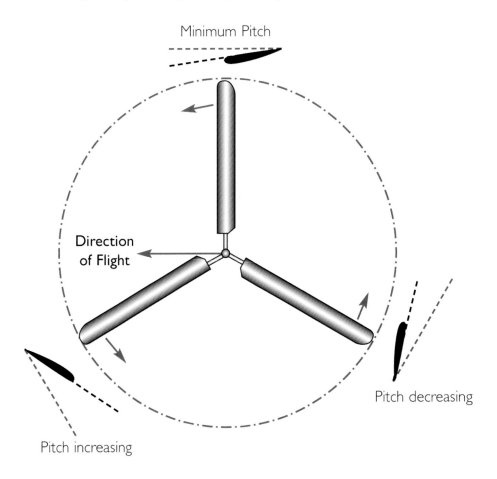

Fig. 2.17   Cyclic pitch changes in a three bladed rotor.

2.11 Blade Flapping

2.11.1 In a three-bladed rotor system, the rotor blades are attached to the rotor hub by a horizontal hinge which permits the blades to move in a vertical plane, i.e., flap up or down, as they rotate in forward flight. See fig 2.18. Flapping by definition is, *"the angular oscillation of the rotor blade about a substantially horizontal axis"*. Where individual hinges are fitted they are referred to as flapping hinges. Fig. 2.18. The axis of the hinge is usually set at 90° to the span of the blade, but some are set at an angle – The Delta Three Hinge for example. See paragraph 9.12.15.

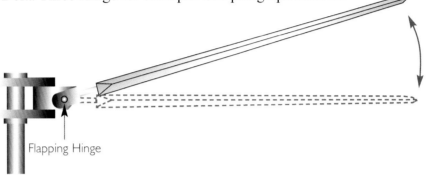

Flapping Hinge

Fig. 2.18   Blade flapping.

In the case of a gimbal mounted rotor, the blades move like a see-saw about the gimbal. See fig. 2.19.

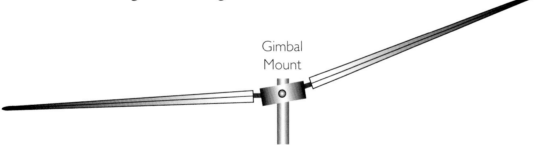

Gimbal
Mount

Fig. 2.19   Blade flapping of a gimbal mounted rotor. There is a built-in Coning angle. (Upward bending of the rotor blades: See paragraph 2.12.1).

Assuming that the blade-pitch angle remains constant, the increased lift on the advancing blade will cause the blade to flap up decreasing the angle of attack because the relative airflow will change from a horizontal direction to more of a downwards direction. The decreased lift on the retreating blade will cause the blade to flap down increasing the angle of attack because the relative airflow changes from a horizontal direction to more of an upwards direction. The combination of decreased angle of attack on the advancing blade and increased angle of attack on the retreating blade through blade flapping action tends to equalize the lift over the two halves of the rotor disc. (The blade moving forward into the relative airflow is called the advancing blade, on moving into the opposite sector it becomes the retreating blade. See fig 2.16.

2.11.2   In a two-bladed system, the blades flap as a unit. As the advancing blade flaps up due to the increased lift, the retreating blade flaps down due to the decreased lift. The change in angle of attack on each blade brought about by this flapping action tends to equalize the lift over the two halves of the rotor disc.

2.11.3   The position of the cyclic pitch control in forward flight also causes a decrease in angle of attack on the advancing blade and an increase in angle of attack on the retreating blade. This together with blade flapping equalizes lift over the two halves of the rotor disc. The reaction to dissymmetry of lift is often referred to as Blow-back, or flap-back and has an undesirable effect on airspeed by slowing the helicopter down.

Note: The flapping motion is the result of the cyclical change of balance between the lift, centrifugal and inertia forces, and while the rotor is maintaining any substantially fixed plane, the resultant of these forces acting on each blade root will be equal. It is only when the resultants are momentarily unequal, due to say, a cyclic stick movement that the plane of the disk will alter.

2.11.4   To give an individual blade more or less lift is merely a matter of giving it more or less pitch as it rotates, giving it in fact, a cyclic-pitch change. Naturally, any changes of cyclic pitch are superimposed on the mean collective pitch, and the total lift force will therefore remain substantially the same.

2.12   Coning

2.12.1   *Coning is the upward bending of the blades caused by the combined forces of lift and centrifugal force.* Before takeoff, the blades rotate in a plane nearly perpendicular to the rotor mast, since centrifugal force is the major force acting on them. As a vertical takeoff is made, two major forces are acting at the same time, centrifugal force acting outward perpendicular to the rotor mast, and lift acting upward and parallel to the mast. The result of these two forces is that the blades assume a conical path instead of remaining in the plane perpendicular to the mast. See fig 2.20.

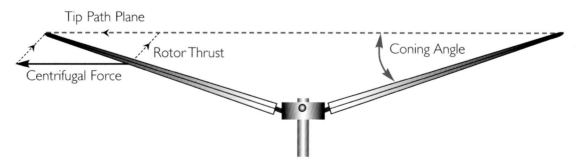

Fig. 2.20   The coning angle.

33

2.12.2   In normal operation, the blades are said to be coned upwards, the coning angle being measured between the spanwise length of the blade and the blades tip path plane. The coning angle will vary with combinations of rotor thrust and Nr.

2.12.3   If rotor thrust is increased and Nr remains constant, the blades cone up. If Nr is reduced, centrifugal force decreases, and if rotor thrust remains constant, the blades again cone up. The weight of the blade will also have some effect but for any given helicopter this will be a constant.

2.12.4   It can be seen that it is important that the pilot maintains a certain minimum rotor speed. If the RPM becomes too low, centrifugal force becomes less and the blades will ride higher. With loss of effective disc area the helicopter will sink, (loss of lift) and the upward flow of air through the rotor will assist in lifting the blades up to a point where it may be no longer be possible to bring them down again.

2.12.5   **Over-pitching.** Further to the previous para: 2.12.4, the pilot error of *"over-pitching"* should be considered. When the rotor blades are over-pitched, it means that their angle of attack is so great, and the drag so large, that the engine is no longer able to keep driving them round and the rotor quickly slows down and loses lift. The correction is to reduce pitch to increase Nr, but this must be done quickly or the helicopter will sink rather rapidly

2.13   Dragging

2.13.1   *Dragging is the freedom given to each blade to allow it to move in the plane of rotation independently of the other blades.* To avoid bending stresses at the root, the blade is allowed to drag about a dragging hinge, see fig 2.21, but movement about the hinge is retarded by some form of drag damper to avoid undesirable oscillations, see fig 2.22A & B.

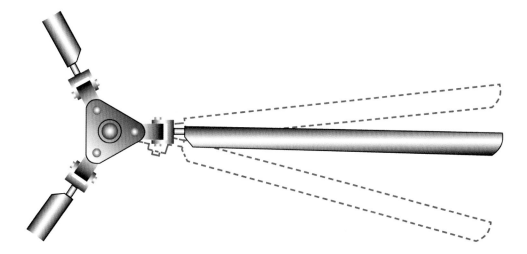

Fig. 2.21   Dragging hinge.

34

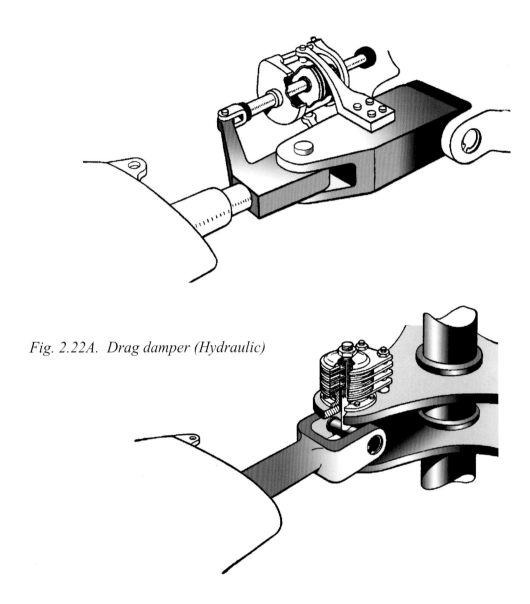

Fig. 2.22A. Drag damper (Hydraulic)

Fig. 2.22B. Drag damper, friction-pad stack.

Dragging occurs because of:

(1)   **Periodic Drag Changes**. When the helicopter moves horizontally, the blades's angle of attack is continually changing during each complete revolution to provide asymmetry of rotor thrust. **This variation in angle of attack results in variation in rotor drag** and consequently the blade will lead or lag about the dragging hinge.

(2)   **Changing Position of the Blade C of G relative to the Hub.** Consider the Helicopter stationary on the ground in still air conditions, rotor turning. The radius of the blade's C of G relative to the axis of rotation will be constant. See fig 2.23.

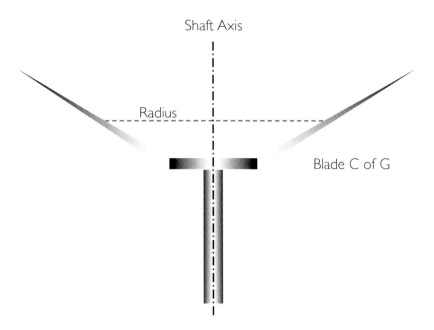

Fig. 2.23   *C of G radius constant distance from the shaft axis.*
(Helicopter stationary).

If the cyclic stick is moved the blade will flap up on one side of the disc
and flap down on the other to produce a change in the disc attitude. With
the helicopter stationary on the ground, the axis about which the blades
are turning will not have altered, so the radius of the blade's C of G
relative to the axis will be changing continuously through each 360° of
travel. See fig 2.24.

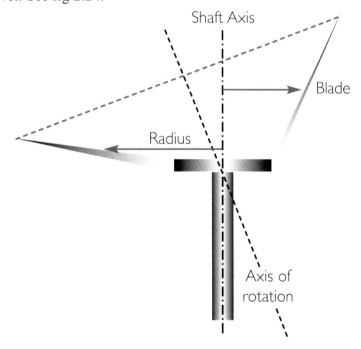

Fig. 2.24   *Blades flap up and down during the cycle because the cyclic stick has*
been moved changing the disc attitude. The flapped-up blade C of G has
moved closer to the shaft axis.

This variation in the radius will cause the blade to speed up or slow down about the dragging hinge, depending upon whether the radius is reducing or increasing (This is called **CORIOLIS EFFECT**). The same effect will occur when the helicopter first moves into horizontal flight.

(3)   **HOOKE'S JOINT EFFECT**. *Applied to Helicopter rotor blades is the movement of the blade to reposition itself relative to the other blades after application of cyclic stick.*

A Hooks Joint is a universal joint, but NOT a constant velocity joint. This can be described by assuming two shafts (which may not be in-line) are connected with a joint, one shaft is rotating at a constant speed, but the other shaft is rotating in a series of speeding up and slowing down. It is similar to the movement of the blade's C of G in relation to the rotor hub. See fig. 2.24.   Referring to fig. 2.25(A), which shows a rotor ground running or hovering. The position of the blades A,B,C and D are symmetrical about the rotor hub, and the plan view, fig. 2.25(B), shows a symmetrical tip path plane. ie, a perfect circle. Now when cyclic tilt is applied, fig. 2.25C, the cone axis would have tilted like fig. 2.24, and viewed down onto the shaft axis WHICH HAS NOT TILTED, Blade A will appear to have increased its radial path and Blade C decrease its radial path, fig. 2.24(D). The other blades B and D maintain position as in fig. 2.25(C). B and D maintain this position in order to achieve their correct positions in the cone. Furthermore, this means that the blades move relative to the shaft axis to take up positions as in fig. 2.25(D). *In fig. 2.25(D) point "E" now becomes the centre of rotation, instead of the shaft axis. The tip path plane has been displaced towards the lowest blade.*

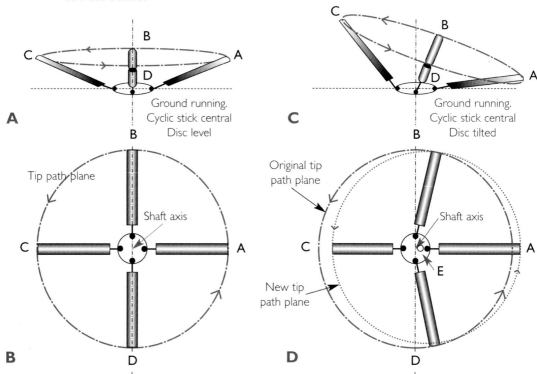

Fig. 2.25   *The Hooke's Joint Effect.*

2.14 Flapping to Equality

2.14.1 Moving the cyclic stick does not alter the magnitude of total rotor thrust but simply changes the disc attitude. This is achieved by the blades flapping to equality when the cyclic pitch change is made. Consider a blade of a helicopter in the hover where the angle of attack is 6° (Fig. 2.26(A)).

2.14.2 A cyclic stick movement decreases the blade pitch and assuming that initially the direction of the RAF remains unchanged, the reduction in pitch will reduce both the blade's angle of attack and rotor thrust (Fig. 2.26(B)). The blade will now begin to flap down causing an automatic increase in the blade's angle of attack. When the angle of attack is back to 6° again, rotor thrust will return to its original value and the blade will continue to follow a path to keep the angle of attack constant (Fig. 2.26(C)).

2.14.3 Thus cyclic pitch will alter the plane in which the blade is rotating but the angle of attack remains unchanged. The reverse takes place when a blade experiences an increase in cyclic pitch. Therefore any change in angle of attack through control action or in-flight conditions causes the blades to flap, and they will do so until they restore the rotor thrust. **They have "FLAPPED TO EQUALITY".**

2.14.4 Remember that when a Cyclic Pitch change is made, the blades continuously flap to equality as they travel through 360° of movement.

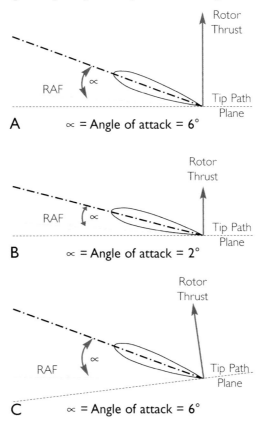

Fig. 2.26   *Flapping to equality.*

3   PHASE LAG AND ADVANCE ANGLE

3.1   Control Orbit

3.1.1   In its simplest form of operation, movement of the collective lever causes a flat plate mounted centrally on the rotor shaft to rise and descend. (Swash plate mechanism: See para: 2.7.2 & fig. 2.14). Movement of the cyclic stick causes it to tilt, the direction of the tilt being controlled by the direction in which the cyclic stick is moved. Rods of equal length, known as Pitch Operating Arms, connect the flat plate to the rotor blades.

3.1.2   As the Pitch Operating Arms (POA) are connected to the flat plate, then movement of the flat plate will move the POA's. This will increase or decrease the pitch angle of the blades. Fig. 3.1(A) and 3.1 (B). The amount of movement is dependent on the amount and direction the flat plate is moved.

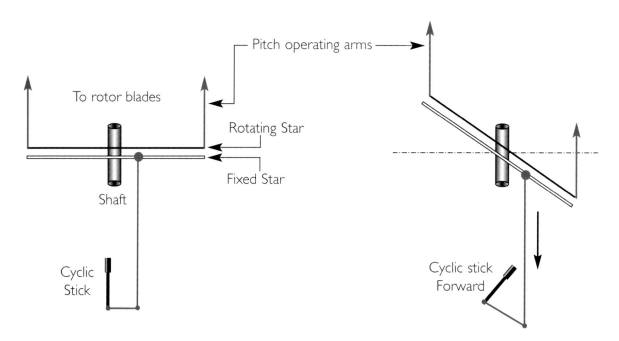

Fig. 3.1   Control orbit.

3.1.3   The flat plate can be more accurately described as a CONTROL ORBIT because it represents the plane in which the pitch operating arms are rotating. To enable reference to be made to a CONTROL ORBIT for mechanical systems which do not incorporate a flat plate, the CONTROL ORBIT can be defined as **THE PLANE OF ROTATION OF ANY COMMON POINT ON THE PITCH OPERATING ARMS.**

39

3.2   Pitch Operating Arm Movement

3.2.1   Assuming the control orbit tilts in the same direction as the cyclic stick is moved, (see fig. 3.2A), then when the control orbit has tilted, say 2° by the pitch operating arms, the plan view in fig. 3.2A shows how the control orbit has altered at four positions. A is at 0°, B is -2°, C is 0° and D is at + 2°.

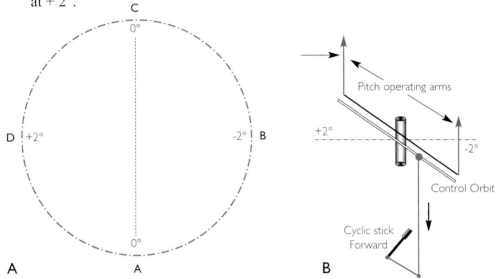

Fig. 3.2   Pitch operating arm movement.

3.2.2   The pitch operating arms move up and down throughout the 360° of rotation. In fig. 3.3 it can be seen the plane of the control orbit and the position of the pitch operating arms in one complete rotation.

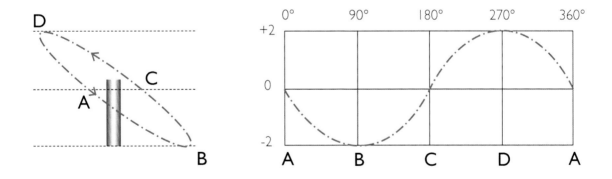

Fig. 3.3   Movement of Pitch Operating Arms through 360°.

3.2.3   The RATE at which the POA's move up and down in the orbit is not linear. See fig. 3.4, which shows the varying blade movement for 90° angular movement of the control orbit. The plan view shows three segments of 30°. The side elevation shows how the varying movement takes place for each 30° segment in a total of 90° of the control orbit.

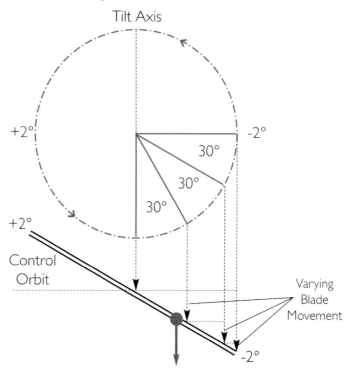

Fig. 3.4   Rate of movement of the Pitch Operating Arms.

3.3   Resultant Change in Disc Attitude

3.3.1   The rotor blades will respond to the cyclic pitch change by flapping, and the resultant change in disc attitude can be determined by following the movement of each blade, of a two-bladed rotor fitted with flapping hinges, through 180° of travel. Consider the rotor blades to be positioned at A and C when the control orbit is tilted and the pitch operating arms are attached to the control orbit directly beneath the blades. See fig. 3.5.

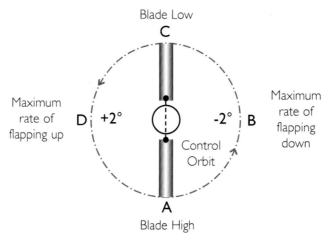

Fig 3.5   Relationship of Blade Position to Control Orbit Position.

41

3.3.2   As the blade moves anti-clockwise from position A, it will experience a reduction in pitch and the blade will begin to flap down. RATE of flapping varies with the amount of pitch change so the blade will be experiencing its greatest RATE of flapping down as it passes position B (maximum pitch change). In the next 90° of travel the pitch is returning from -2° back to 0° so the RATE at which the blade is still flapping down will slowly die out and disappear entirely when the blade has reached position C. So the blade which started at A is flapping down for 180° of travel and will therefore reach a low position at C.

3.3.3   The reverse will take place with the other blade. As it rotates anti-clockwise from C to A the increase in pitch will cause the blade to flap up, the maximum RATE of flapping occurring as the blade passes position D. Beyond this point the RATE OF FLAPPING UP begins to slow down but will not disappear entirely until the blade has reached position A. So the blade which started at C is flapping up for 180° of travel and will reach a high position at A and the disc will now be tilted along an axis (BD) 90° removed from the tilt axis of the control orbit (AC). If the movement of the blade through 360° of travel is plotted on a graph similar to the one showing movement of the pitch operating arm in fig 3.3, the result would be as in fig. 3.6. This is called PHASE LAG.

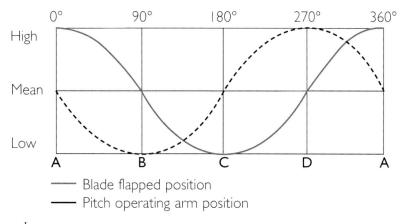

Fig 3.6   Phase lag.

3.3.4   For the same reason as explained in section 3.2, the RATE of flapping is not uniform. By superimposing the movement of the pitch operating arm from fig 3.3 into fig 3.6, it will be seen that blade flapped position will always be 90° out of phase with the control orbit.

3.4   Phase Lag

3.4.1   When cyclic pitch is applied, the blades will automatically flap to equality, and in so doing, the disc attitude will change, the blade reaching its highest and lowest positions 90° later than the point where it experiences the maximum increase and decrease of cyclic pitch.

3.4.2   The variation between the tilt of the control orbit in producing this cyclic pitch change and subsequent tilt of the rotor is known as PHASE LAG.

3.4.3   Phase lag will also occur when the blades experience a cyclic variation resulting from a change in speed or direction of the RAF, as occurs in horizontal flight.

3.5   Advance Angle

3.5.1   If the control orbit tilts in the same direction as the cyclic stick is being moved, and as a result of the changes in cyclic pitch, the rotor disc tilts 90° out of phase with the control orbit, then the disc will also be tilting 90° out of phase with the cyclic stick.

3.5.2   **There is need of compensation, because putting the cyclic stick forward will cause the helicopter to MOVE SIDEWAYS.**   To overcome this effect would be to arrange the MAXIMUM pitch change 90° before the blade has reached the highest and lowest points in its orbit. See fig. 3.7.

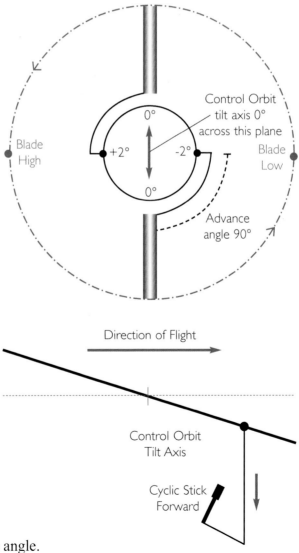

Fig 3.7   90° Advance angle.

43

3.5.3   The angular distance that the pitch-operating arm is positioned on the control orbit in advance of the blade to which it relates is known as the **ADVANCE ANGLE.**

3.5.4   It has been shown that when the control orbit tilts to follow the cyclic stick input, advance angle must be set at 90°. However, if the control orbit tilt is 45° out of phase with the cyclic stick input, then phase lag can be fully compensated with an advance angle of 45°. See fig. 3.8.

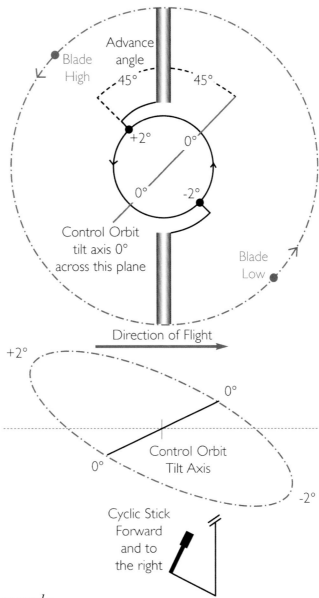

Fig. 3.8   *45° Advance angle.*

3.5.5   When discussing collective pitch changes, it was noted that rods attached to the blades can change the pitch of the blade by an up and down motion. If the movement of the rod in fig 3.9 were traced in a complete revolution, it would move up and down once, thereby giving a cyclic pitch change to the blade. This system is called a SWASH-PLATE (Some texts call this an azimuth star).

3.5.6   The Swash-Plate is divided into upper and lower sections with a bearing between the two. The upper, or rotating plate of the swash plate can go up and down and tilt in any direction whilst rotating. The lower or stationary plate of the swash plate can go up and down and tilt in any direction but cannot rotate. The lower plate is mounted on the main drive shaft via a universal or ball joint, which permits it to be tilted in any direction, and it is from this lower plate (or fixed star) that control rods lead off through the usual type of control transmission to the pilot's cockpit and the cyclic-pitch control.

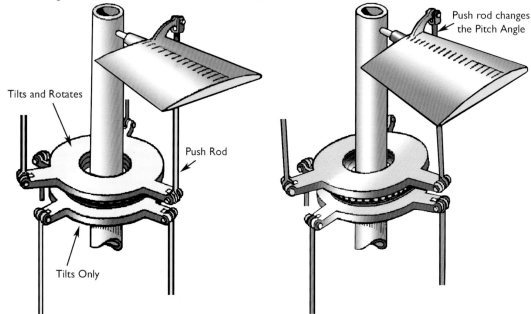

Fig. 3.9   The Swash-Plate system for changing Cyclic Pitch.

3.5.7   In order to tilt the rotor disc in any required direction for translational flight or other manoeuvre, the swash plate must be tilted. The resulting up and down movement of the push pull rods attached to the upper section (or rotating star) of the swash plate is transferred to the blades in the form of cyclic-pitch changes as the blades move round.

3.5.8   The rods which alter the cyclic pitch of the blades also control the mean collective pitch. This is done by making the whole of the swash plate move up and down bodily, or to arrange for part of the rotor hub or control linkage system to move up and down as required.

3.5.9   There is another system used on light types of helicopter and that is the spider system. In the spider system of pitch control (see fig 3.10) the arms are connected to the leading edge of the blades by control rods. The spider spindle being contained inside the rotor shaft. A ball joint mounting allows the spider to tilt when cyclic pitch changes are made. Collective pitch changes are made by raising or lowering the whole spider.

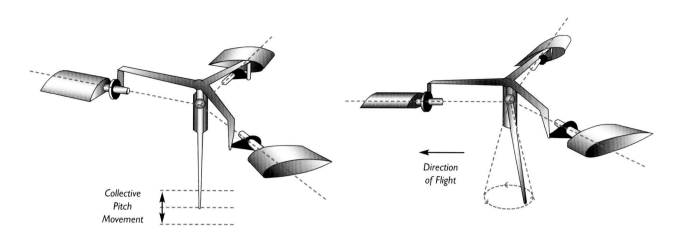

Fig. 3.10   Spider type control for changing cyclic pitch.

3.5.10   Load Factors: A point to consider when comparing the load factor of a fixed-wing aeroplane and a helicopter. A wing on an aeroplane increases its load factor capability in forward flight, but a rotor does not. This is because a retreating rotor blade is actually going slower through the air than in the hover. Its maximum lifting capability decreases and, to avoid unbalancing the rotor, the lift on the advancing side must be decreased using cyclic pitch.

3.5.11   This means that since only the blades over the nose and tail retain the same potential in forward flight as in the hover, the maximum lifting capability of the entire rotor decreases as speed increases.

3.5.12   Referring back to a fixed-wing aeroplane, it cannot develop a load factor above 1.0 until it reaches its minimum flying speed. From then on, its load factor capability increases as the square of the airspeed. Conversely, a helicopter rotor develops its maximum load factor at zero airspeed.

4   THE TAIL ROTOR

4.1   **Torque.** Newton's third law of motion states, "To every action there is an equal and opposite reaction." As the main rotor of a helicopter turns in one direction, the fuselage tends to rotate in the opposite direction. See fig 4.1.

4.1.1   This tendency for the fuselage to rotate is called torque. Since torque effect on the fuselage is a direct result of engine power applied to the main rotor, any change in engine power brings about a corresponding change in torque effect. The greater the engine power, the greater the torque effect. Since there is no engine power being applied to the main rotor during autorotation, there is no torque reaction during autorotation. (More later).

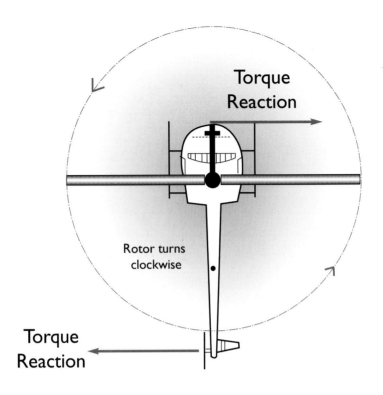

Fig. 4.1   Torque reaction. (Anticlockwise rotor).

4.1.2   **Anti-torque rotor.** The force that compensates for torque and keeps the fuselage from turning in the direction opposite to the main rotor is produced by means of an auxiliary rotor located on the end of the tail boom. This anti-torque rotor, generally referred to as a tail rotor, produces thrust in the direction opposite to the torque reaction developed by the main rotor. See fig 4.2. Thrust is increased by increasing the tail rotor pitch. Since the value of thrust required is a product of force × distance, the greater the distance that the tail rotor acts from the main rotor axis of rotation, the smaller the force required. In practice, tail rotors are normally positioned just clear of the main rotor.

Fig. 4.2   Location of tail rotor on a Robinson R 22.

4.1.3   Foot pedals in the cockpit (yaw pedals or anti torque pedals) permit the pilot to increase or decrease tail-rotor thrust, as needed, to neutralize torque effect. See fig 4.3.

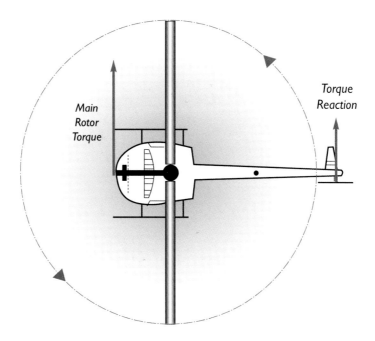

Fig. 4.3   Tail rotor torque compensates for the torque effect of the main rotor. (Anti-clockwise rotor).

4.1.4   Heading control in the hover is achieved by increasing or decreasing the tail rotor thrust so that torque reaction is not balanced and the helicopter turns about the rotor shaft.

4.1.5   Aerodynamic balance in forward flight is adjusted by tail rotor thrust in a similar fashion to the rudder control of a fixed-wing aeroplane.

4.1.6   **In power-off flight (Autorotation) there is NO Torque Reaction**. The rotor is turning and there is friction in the transmission system which tends to turn the helicopter in the SAME DIRECTION AS THE ROTOR. The turn is prevented by negative pitch on the tail rotor producing thrust opposite to that in powered flight. Tail rotor blades are also symmetrical, and must be capable of being adjusted to produce plus or minus values of pitch. See fig. 4.4.

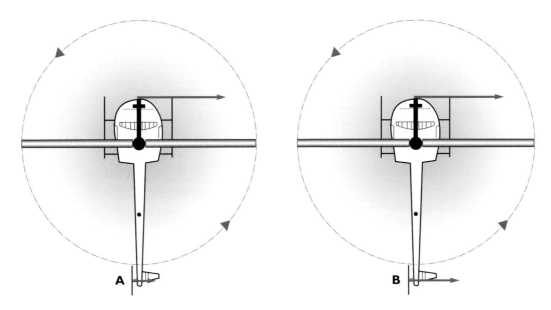

Fig. 4.4   "A" turning RIGHT - "B" turning LEFT (Anti-clockwise rotor).

4.2   Tail Rotor Drift

4.2.1   The tail rotor of a helicopter produces a moment to overcome the COUPLE arising from torque reaction of the main rotor, which in turn causes a side pull on the pivot point or axis of rotation of the main rotor. This side force produces a movement known as **TAIL ROTOR DRIFT and unless corrected would result in the helicopter moving sideways over the ground.**

4.2.2   To describe the forces that cause Tail Rotor Drift**, assume an anti-clockwise turning rotor,** consider the helicopter fuselage (in plan view) being turned under the influence of the fuselage torque reaction couple (XX) about the hub, see fig 4.5.

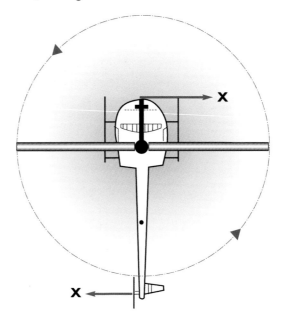

Fig 4.5   Fuselage torque reaction couple about (XX).

49

4.2.3   The *rotation* will stop if forces of equal value (YY) acts in the opposite direction to the couple XX. (Tail rotor thrust), see fig 4.6.

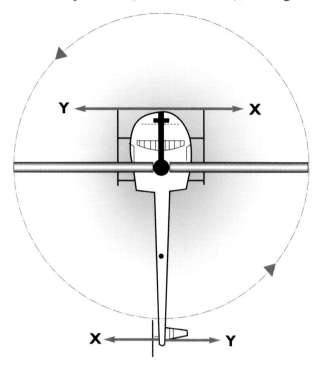

Fig 4.6   Fuselage torque reaction cancelled by the equal force (YY) produced by the tail rotor thrust.

4.2.4   The *rotation* would also stop if a force generated by the tail rotor thrust (YY) acts in the opposite direction to the couple XX. See fig. 4.7.

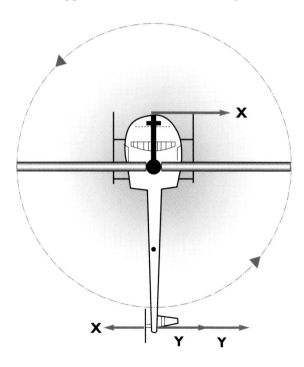

Fig 4.7   Tail rotor thrust (Y) has cancelled the 'turning' of the fuselage.

4.2.5   At first sight, this seems to solve the problem, however, using equations, we can cancel X and Y which now leaves a sideways force as shown in fig 4.8 (X and Y) acting on the pivot point, or axis of rotation of the main rotor. This is what causes drift and is known as **TAIL ROTOR DRIFT.**

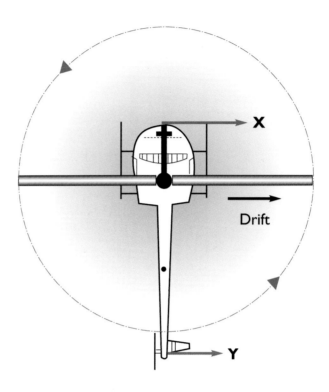

Fig 4.8   *Cancelling the rotational forces leaves a "residual" force acting on the pivot point of the main rotor causing DRIFT. X = Torque reaction – main motor. Y = Tail rotor torque, both forces acting in the same direction.*

4.2.6   Correction for tail rotor drift. Tail rotor drift can be corrected by tilting the rotor disc away from the direction of drift, see fig 4.9. This can be achieved by:

1   The pilot making a movement of the cyclic pitch stick.

2   Rigging the controls so that when the stick is in the centre the disc is actually tilted by the right amount.

3   By mounting the engine so that the drive shaft to the rotor is offset. See fig 4.10.

4   By causing the disc to tilt when the collective pitch lever is raised.

4.2.7   *From the foregoing, items 2 and 3 are the usual methods (normally combined) of overcoming tail rotor drift. This is noticed in the hover where one side of the aircraft hangs lower than the other and combines with the effect of tail rotor roll (see para: 4.3).*

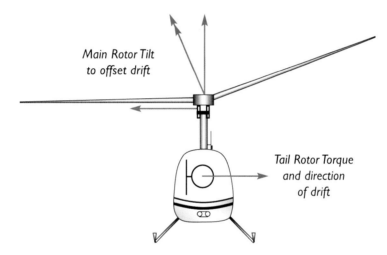

Fig. 4.9   *Drift is prevented by tilting the main rotor in the opposite direction.*

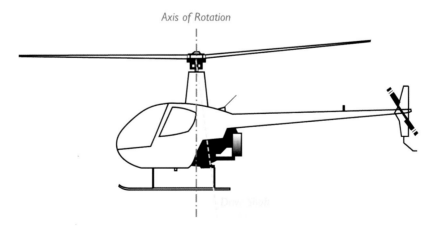

Fig. 4.10   *Drift can also be reduced by mounting the engine drive-shaft axis offset to the rotor axis. Tail rotors are usually positioned just clear of the main rotor.*

4.3   Tail Rotor Roll

4.3.1   If the tail rotor is mounted on the fuselage below the level of the main rotor, the tail rotor drift corrective force being produced by the main rotor will create a rolling couple with the tail rotor thrust, causing the helicopter to hover one skid low. See fig 4.11. This can be overcome if the tail rotor is raised to the level of the main rotor by slanting the tail boom upwards, or fitting the tail rotor to a pylon or fin, but this condition will only be achieved if the fuselage is loaded with the Centre of Gravity in the ideal position. On some helicopters the tail rotor assembly has been mounted at an angle off the vertical to compensate for tail rotor roll. (Not normally seen on small helicopters, but is on multi engine military types).

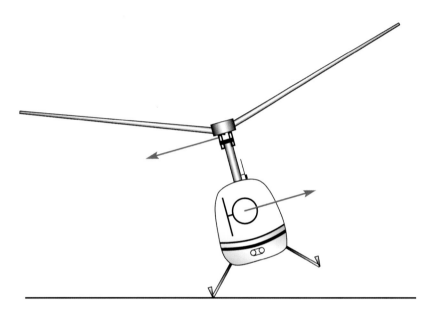

Fig. 4.11   The tail rotor can cause a rolling couple (Tail Rotor Roll).

4.3.2   The amount of roll depends on the size of the tail rotor and vertical separation between the main and tail rotor hubs. In the hover, the helicopter will roll about the horizontal couple until the movement is balanced by the couple of the vertical component of Total Rotor Thrust and the helicopter All Up Mass (AUM). A helicopter is usually designed so that the tail rotor is in line with the main rotor head at forward speed. In the hover, tail rotor roll has to be lived with.

5 VERTICAL CLIMB AND DESCENT

5.1   A helicopter is capable of climbing and descending vertically, moving horizontally in any direction, and while hovering over a spot on the ground, turn on to any selected heading. To achieve this degree of performance the helicopter is fitted with special controls and the manner in which these are used to produce various in-flight conditions is described in the following paragraphs.

5.2   Vertical Movement

5.2.1   To achieve a vertical climb the total rotor thrust must be increased. This can be done by increasing the pitch of the blades, which in turn produces an increase in angle of attack. It is important to note that each blade must produce an equal amount of increase in total rotor thrust. Therefore the increase in pitch must be exactly the same on each of the rotor blades and must be operated at exactly the same time. This change in pitch is known as a collective pitch change and is achieved by the pilot raising the collective pitch lever.

5.2.2   When the blades are rotating at take-off RPM (flight idle), and the collective pitch lever is fully down, very little rotor thrust is being produced. As the collective pitch lever is raised the blades will begin to cone up and eventually the rotor thrust will equal the weight of the helicopter. In this state, the undercarriage will be in light contact with the ground. If the collective pitch lever is raised further, the rotor thrust will exceed the weight, and the helicopter will accelerate (in still air conditions) vertically upwards. In practice, this phase of the take-off is passed through quickly to avoid setting up a condition known as ground resonance, which is described later.

5.2.3   As the rate of climb increases, by virtue of upward motion there is a relative airflow down through the rotor. This adds to and increases the Induced flow. The Angle of Attack and Total Rotor Thrust are automatically reduced and the acceleration decreases until a steady rate of climb is achieved with Total Rotor Thrust = AUM.

5.2.4   When the acceleration settles to become a steady rate of climb, the helicopter continues in this state, assuming that constant power is available, until the pilot lowers the collective pitch lever. At a height well clear of the ground, say 150 feet or so, if the pilot lowers the collective pitch lever by just the right amount to stop the helicopter from climbing, the helicopter will now be in the hover, and being well clear of the ground it is referred to as a Hover Outside Ground Effect **(Hover OGE).**

5.3 Control of Rotor (RPM)

5.3.1 An increase in total rotor thrust can only be obtained from a bigger total reaction. If the total reaction is increased then the component acting in the plane of rotation will also increase. See fig 5.1.

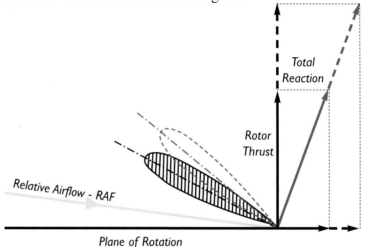

Fig. 5.1 Control of rotor RPM. Increase in total reaction sees an increase in angle of attack (more lift) and an increase in rotor drag.

5.3.2 Normally a change in power must be made if rotor RPM is to be kept constant when the collective pitch lever is moved. This is achieved by incorporating a throttle control or correlator in the collective pitch lever mechanism so that power will either increase or decrease automatically when the lever is respectively raised or lowered, or a fuel control unit which will alter the power corresponding to engine load.

5.3.3 In the climb, the total reaction vector is tilted to the right (because the direction of the RAF has been changed and also the Pitch Angle has been increased). ROTOR DRAG is increased. More power is required to maintain rotor RPM (Nr). See fig 5.2.

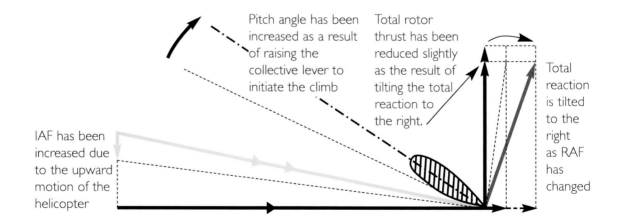

Fig. 5.2 Rotor drag increases – more power is required.

55

5.4   Vertical Descent

5.4.1   If the collective pitch is reduced in the free air hover, the angle of attack will reduce and the helicopter will start to accelerate downwards. However, the airflow resulting from this descent will oppose the induced flow through the disc and the resulting change in direction of the RAF to the blade will cause the angle of attack to increase. When the angle of attack reaches the 4° position again (this was the angle of attack to maintain the hover in para: 5.2.5), rotor thrust will equal the All-up mass (AUM) and downward acceleration will become a steady rate of descent.

5.4.2   Less collective pitch and power is required in vertical descent than in free air hover to produce a rotor thrust equal to the AUM, but the required angle of attack can, of course, only be maintained provided that the helicopter continues its steady rate of descent. See fig 5.3A and B. At higher rates of descent, the airflow is more complex and is discussed under "Vortex Ring".

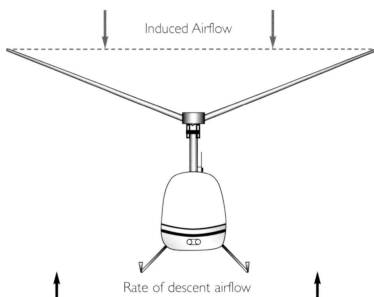

Fig. 5.3A   Steady rate of descent.

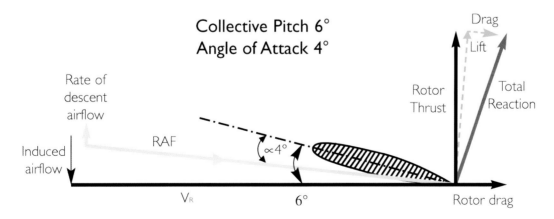

Fig. 5.3B   Vertical descent.

5.5 Horizontal Movement

5.5.1　The thrust required to move the helicopter horizontally must be obtained from the total rotor thrust. This can be achieved by tilting the disc so that the rotor thrust is tilted in the direction of the required movement. If rotor RPM (Nr) is maintained constant, raising the collective lever will increase the coning angle and all the blades will rise together. The reverse occurs when the lever is lowered.

5.5.2　If a two-bladed rotor is considered and the pitch on one blade is increased while at the same time the pitch on the other blade is decreased by an equal amount, then one blade will rise and the other blade will fall which will result in a tilt of the rotor disc. To keep the rotor disc in the tilted position the pitch must vary throughout the blades' 360° cycle of travel. This change in pitch is therefore known as a cyclic pitch change and is achieved by the pilot moving the cyclic pitch stick.

5.5.3　Consider a helicopter in a perfect hover with the C of G in the ideal position. Assume the helicopter moves into forward flight, but no change takes place in the fuselage attitude. The rotor disc will be tilted forward and the disposition of forces is shown in fig 5.4A.

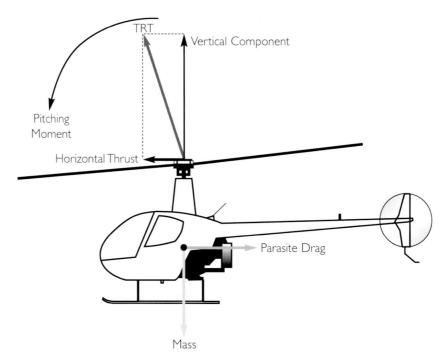

Fig.5.4A　Disposition of forces at the moment the pilot selects forward (horizontal) movement (cyclic stick forward).

5.5.4　Total Rotor Thrust (TRT) is now inclined forward, and produces a nose down turning movement about the C of G. The vertical component of TRT and the AUM (All Up Mass) remain in line, but a couple now exists between the horizontal component of TRT and the fuselage Parasitic Drag as the helicopter increases speed

5.5.5   The fuselage will pitch forward, but the moment will now be opposed by the vertical component of TRT and AUM. The forces will resolve themselves as in fig 5.4B.

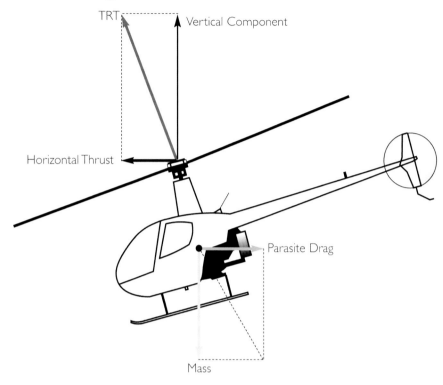

Fig. 5.4B   Disposition of forces when balance is obtained between the TRT and the C of G.

5.5.6   Therefore, the fuselage will only pitch forward until the couples are in balance, and this will occur when the TRT is in line with the C of G. The C of G controls the position of the fuselage in relation to the disc.

5.5.7   This relationship however will be affected in forward flight by the negative lift effect of a tail stabiliser (if fitted) and the moment exerted by it will tend to keep the fuselage attitude slightly more nose up.

5.6   Limits of Rotor RPM (Nr)

5.6.1   When the coning angle increases, the rotor disc area decreases. It is therefore critical to maintain RPM(Nr) above a certain limit, as published in the relevant operating manual. The centrifugal force of the rotor gives a degree of control of the coning angle. Therefore, the RPM (Nr) must ALWAYS by maintained above the published lower limit. There is also a published upper limit. This limitation is set be the manufacturers as a function of rotor gear-box limitations and blade root stresses. Compressibility at the blade tips is a further limitation.

5.7 Overtorquing

5.7.1 If RPM (Nr) reduces and the power required to maintain Total Rotor Thrust is the same, the torque from the engine applied to the rotor shaft via the transmission increases and may exceed the design limitations of the transmission system. Overtorquing can be avoided by monitoring the torque gauge fitted to most helicopters.

5.8 Overpitching

5.8.1 It may sometimes be possible for the pilot to apply pitch to the rotor blades without sufficient engine power to compensate for the extra rotor drag. This may be due to either:

1   A limited engine power condition
2   A fixed throttle setting due to an engine malfunction.

A stage will be reached where, as pitch (and hence rotor thrust) increases, no further power will be available to maintain rotor speed with the result that RPM(Nr) will decay rapidly. The coning angle will become greater and greater. This dangerous situation is termed **OVERPITCHING. Recovery must be made by lowering the collective lever.**

5.9 Ground Effect

5.9.1 In a free air hover (hover OGE) the resistance to the induced flow is only the resistance of the surrounding air. In a hover close to the ground (hover IGE), the ground will also resist the induced flow, this additional resistance being at a maximum when hovering just above the ground surface. A dome of air, at a slightly increased pressure, is formed beneath the helicopter. **The dome of air formed in the ground effect is normally a height equivalent to three quarters the diameter of the rotor.**

5.9.2 The formation of this dome is illustrated in fig. 5.5. The downwash from the rotor is deflected by the ground into a flow radiating outwards from the helicopter and is dissipated against the surrounding air. At the same time, some downwash is deflected inwards underneath the aircraft and is brought to rest, forming a dome of stagnant or slow moving air. This dome of "dead air" or ground cushion slightly increases pressure and causes a reduction in induced flow.

Note: *The induced flow, which passes over or close to the fuselage, and is then deflected outwards, is similar to airflow in a divergent duct, thus adding to the pressure under the fuselage.*

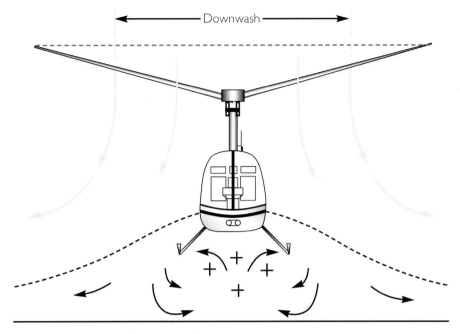

Pressure build-up opposing induced flow

Fig. 5.5   Helicopter hovering in Ground Effect.

5.9.3   The direction of the flow relative to the blade changes, thus increasing angle of attack, or, the same angle of attack can be maintained in ground effect **(IGE)** with less collective pitch and power than that required out of ground effect **(OGE).** The reduction in power being possible because of reduced rotor drag. See Fig. 5.6A. and 5.6B.

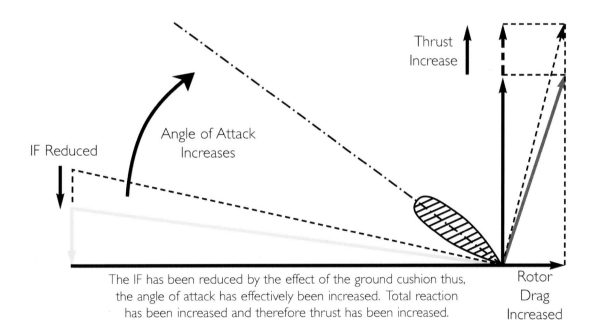

The IF has been reduced by the effect of the ground cushion thus, the angle of attack has effectively been increased. Total reaction has been increased and therefore thrust has been increased.

Fig. 5.6A   Hovering in ground effect.

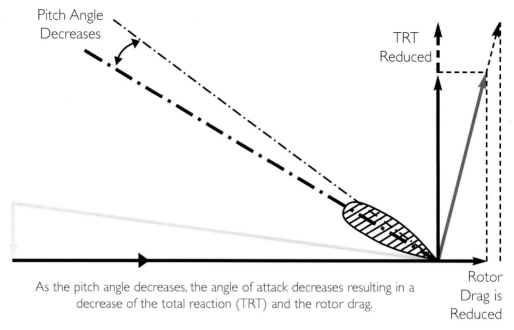

Pitch Angle Decreases

TRT Reduced

As the pitch angle decreases, the angle of attack decreases resulting in a decrease of the total reaction (TRT) and the rotor drag.

Rotor Drag is Reduced

Fig. 5.6B   Hovering out of ground effect.

5.10   Factors Affecting the Ground Cushion

5.10.1   The factors affecting the Ground Cushion are:

1   The height the helicopter is hovering above the ground. Its effect disappears at a height equal to approximately three quarters of the diameter of the rotor disc.

2   Nature of the ground. (Rough ground dissipates the cushion.)

3   Slope of the ground which will produce an uneven ground cushion.

4   Wind. (The cushion is displaced downwind.)

5.11   Recirculation

5.11.1   In considering a helicopter hovering over a flat even surface, some of the air is recirculated. It is observed that the recirculated air going through the rotor disc a second time increases speed. The increase in induced flow, particularly at the rotor tips causes a loss of rotor thrust. However, this is more than compensated by the ground cushion. Note: recirculation is always present to a degree. It is exacerbated by nearby obstructions. See fig: 5.8.

5.11.2   However, if the helicopter is hovering over a grassy surface, then the escape of air at the surface is impeded, ie., it does not flow evenly away and results in a loss of lift due to recirculation. Under these conditions, the pilot will need to increase power and collective pitch. The ground cushion is NOT available to help the helicopter to lift off. So, **more power and collective pitch** is required to hover near the ground than in the free air.

5.11.3   The top of the rotor disc is a region of low pressure and below one of high pressure. Since on most helicopters, the blades do not extend all the way to the rotor shaft, air will leak upwards through this hole in its desire to equalise the pressure. (Fountain Effect). This is especially evident when hovering near the ground. See fig 5.7. This assists taking off heavily loaded, since the up-flow reduces the normal download on the fuselage caused by rotor wake. There is also a combined root vortex.

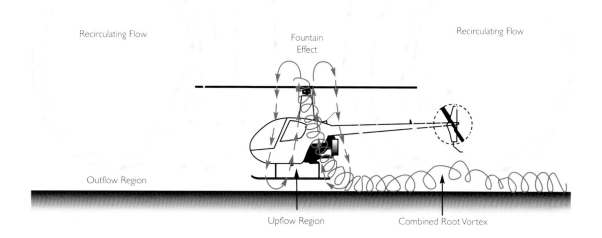

Fig. 5.7   *Flow pattern around a helicopter hovering near the ground, showing recirculation, fountain effect and root vortex. (After Prouty R.W. More Helicopters Aerodynamics: Rotor & Wing International; PJS Publications Inc. 1988 pp 2)*

5.11.4   However, a disadvantage when hovering over dusty or sandy surfaces is that dust or sand laden air is being fed by the Fountain Effect into the engine intakes. A lesser, but real problem can exist when similar debris is stirred up by the outflow along the ground, and then rises to be eventually recirculated back down through the rotor. This is the primary cause of blade erosion damage.

5.11.5   Fig 5.8 shows one of the most noticeable effects that can occur when taking off near an obstacle. The recirculating wake produces an increasingly non-uniform inflow pattern at the rotor disc as thrust is increased to lift-off. This will require a non-standard hover cyclic stick position that might come as a surprise to the unsuspecting pilot.

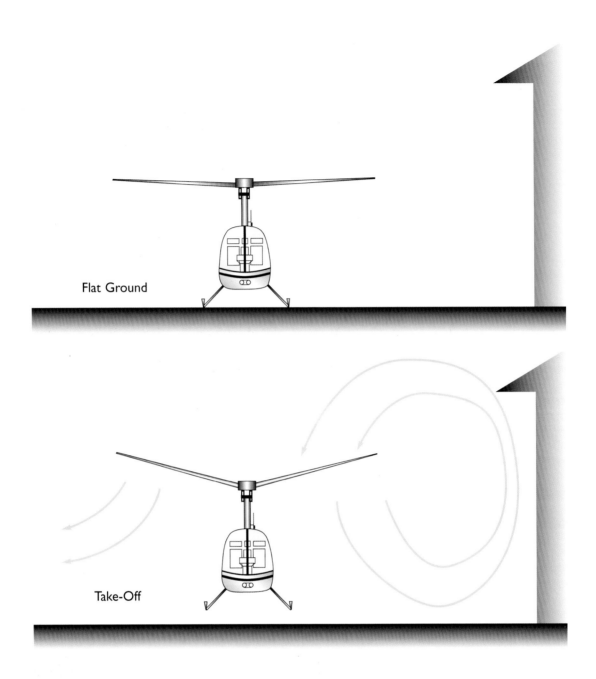

Flat Ground

Take-Off

Fig. 5.8   Non uniform inflow pattern.

5.11.6   For example, if because of recirculation, the downflow is stronger on the left side, the helicopter will tend to move backwards because of the 90° lag in flapping. Not only is the cyclic pitch affected but the increased downflow looks like a climb condition, which requires more power to the main rotor and therefore to the tail rotor also. This represents a decrease in ground effect and might keep a heavily loaded helicopter on the ground.

6   TRANSITION

6.1   When the helicopter is hovering in still air conditions the total Rotor Thrust produced by the rotor is equal to the mass. There will, in fact, be some fuselage parasite drag to be overcome but for simplicity this drag will be considered to be included in the mass. To achieve forward flight the rotor disc has to be tilted forward and the total Rotor Thrust must now provide not only a vertical force to balance the mass but a horizontal force in the direction in which the helicopter is moving. This change in state from a hover to movement in a horizontal direction is known as a TRANSITION, the same term being used to describe a change from horizontal flight back to the hover.
(See paragraph 6.2)

6.1.1   When the helicopter is travelling forward at uniform speed, the horizontal component, Thrust, will be balanced by the parasite drag of the fuselage and since the parasite drag increases as the square of the speed, the faster the helicopter is moving forward the greater must become the tilt of the disc, to provide the thrust. (See again section 5.5 - Horizontal Movement and the disposition of forces when changing to horizontal flight).

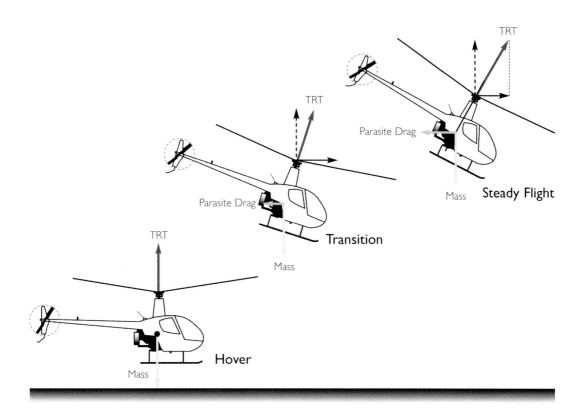

Fig. 6.1   The balance of forces in transition.

6.1.2   For level flight the vertical component of total Rotor Thrust must remain equal to weight. To meet this requirement it follows therefore that when the helicopter moves forward from a hover state, the total Rotor Thrust must increase, and that the faster the forward speed the greater must become the total Rotor Thrust being provided by the rotor. See fig. 6.1.

6.1.3   As total Rotor Thrust is a function of collective pitch, it would appear from the foregoing that the collective pitch lever must be progressively raised for any given increase in forward speed, with power being increased to overcome the rising rotor drag. However, it is found in practice that for speeds up to 45-55 kt depending upon the type of helicopter, both the collective pitch and power can be progressively reduced and it is only for speeds beyond this figure that the pitch and power have to be increased.

6.1.4   This gain in rotor efficiency when moving forward is known as TRANSLATIONAL LIFT and the same effect will occur if the helicopter is hovering stationary over the ground in wind conditions. *As the rotor becomes more efficient, then by definition, more lift is obtained for no increase in power, this also means a gain in height takes place without increasing power.*

6.2   Translational lift

6.2.1   Assuming a helicopter is in the hover, in still-air conditions. Assume too that the collective pitch is say 8° for the rotor RPM to maintain a perfect hover. The induced airflow will be continuously moving downwards towards the rotor disc. It is important to consider the direction of airflow relative to the rotor blade. In fig.6.2, it is shown that the angle of attack is 5°. This is LESS than the pitch angle. This reduction is due to the induced airflow. If there were no induced airflow, then the angle of attack and pitch angle would be the same.

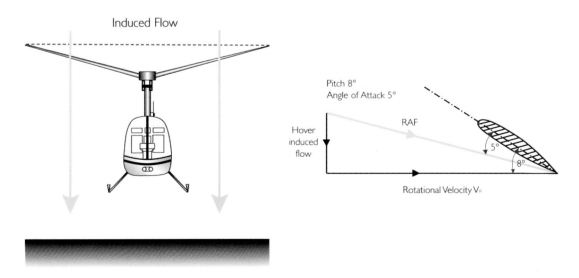

Fig. 6.2   *Translational lift.*

65

6.2.2 Consider the effect now if the helicopter is facing into a 20 kt wind, and assume that it is possible to maintain the hover without tilting the disc (for the purposes of this explanation). The horizontal flow of air (the wind) will blow across the vertically induced column of air and deflect it "downwind" BEFORE it reaches the disc.

6.2.3 The column of air which was flowing down towards the disc will therefore be modified and gradually be replaced by a mass of air which is moving horizontally across the disc. The rotor will act on this air mass to produce an induced flow but the velocity of the induced flow will be greatly reduced. See fig. 6.3. **Therefore, an airflow parallel to the disc must reduce the induced flow and increase the angle of attack and therefore the rotor thrust.**

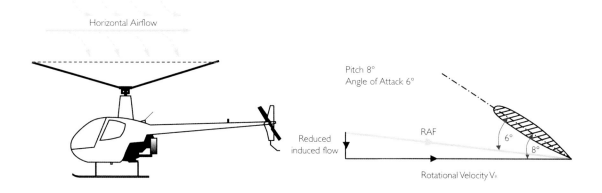

Fig. 6.3 *The wind modifies the induced air flow towards the horizontal, reducing the induced velocity.*

6.2.4 However, to maintain the hover condition when facing into wind the disc must be tilted forward. The horizontal flow of air will not now be parallel to the disc, and a COMPONENT of it can now be considered to be actually passing through the disc at right angles to the plane of rotation, effectively increasing the induced flow, see fig 6.4. To consider an extreme case, if the rotor disc was tilted 90° to this horizontal flow of air then all of it would be passing through the disc at right angles to the plane of rotation.

6.2.5 The effect of this horizontal airflow across the disc when hovering facing into wind is therefore to reduce the induced flow, but because the disc has had to be tilted forward, a component of this horizontal airflow will now be passing through the disc, effectively increasing the induced flow, and both of these effects must now be taken into consideration when determining the direction of the airflow relative to the blades.

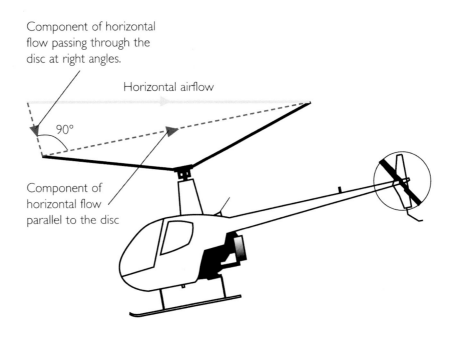

Component of horizontal
flow passing through the
disc at right angles.

Horizontal airflow

90°

Component of
horizontal flow
parallel to the disc

Fig. 6.4   Effect of tilting the disc towards the horizontal airflow.

6.2.6   Provided that the reduction in induced flow is greater than the component of horizontal airflow passing through the disc then the relative airflow will be nearer the plane of rotation than when the helicopter is in the hover, and the angle of attack will increase and the helicopter will climb. Therefore the collective pitch can be decreased to, say, 7° while still maintaining the SAME ANGLE OF ATTACK of 5°. See fig 6.5. The lift/drag ratio for this angle of attack remains unchanged so the total reaction must move FORWARD when the collective pitch is reduced. There will therefore be less rotor drag and rotor RPM can be maintained with less power.

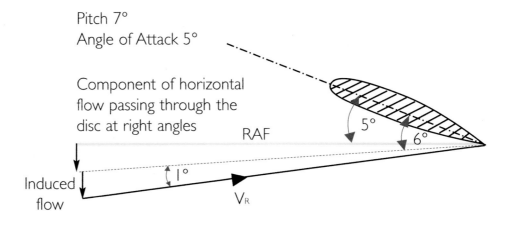

Pitch 7°
Angle of Attack 5°

Component of horizontal
flow passing through the
disc at right angles

RAF

5°

6°

Induced
flow

1°

V_R

Fig. 6.5   Total flow through the disc.

6.2.7   TRANSLATIONAL LIFT: occurs because of the reduction in induced airflow which is first observed when the air is moving towards the disc at approximately 12 kt. The induced flow continues to decrease as the helicopter increases its forward speed. This is not a linear relationship, as can be seen in fig: 6.6A.

6.2.8   As the helicopter increases its forward speed, a further consideration is the increase in parasite drag. Parasite drag is directly related to speed. As the parasite drag increases then the tilt of the rotor disc must increase to provide an increase in thrust to compensate the increasing parasite drag. Increasing the tilt of the rotor will see an increase in the horizontal airflow passing through the rotor disc. See fig. 6.6B

6.2.9   To summarise: As the helicopter increases its forward speed, the disc must be tilted forward to provide the necessary increase in thrust. The tilting must be increased as speed increases, however, parasite drag increases as the square of the speed, moreover, the horizontal airflow approaching the disc also increases and the greater will be the component of air passing through the disc at right angles to the disc plane. See fig. 6.6B.

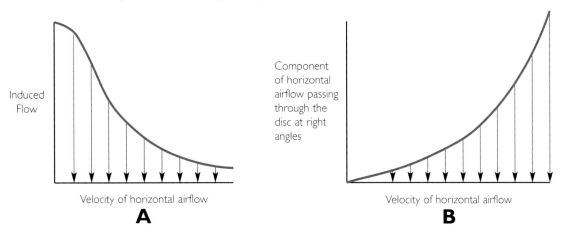

Fig. 6.6   *Variation of induced flow and component of horizontal airflow passing through the disk with forward speed.*

6.2.10   If the graphs in fig. 6.6 are superimposed onto one graph (fig. 6.7) it will be seen that the flow of air at right angles to the plane of rotation decreases at first then increases again being a minimum when the two airflows have the same value.

6.2.11   As the flow of air through the disc decreases less collective pitch and power will be required to maintain the required angle of attack. When the flow of air through the disc begins to increase again, collective pitch and power must be increased if the required angle of attack is to be maintained.

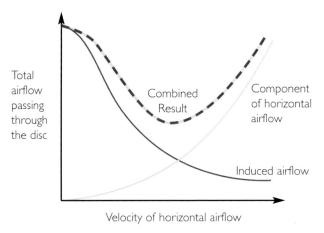

Total airflow passing through the disc

Combined Result

Component of horizontal airflow

Induced airflow

Velocity of horizontal airflow

Fig. 6.7   Variation of total airflow through the disc with forward flight.

6.3   Flapback

6.3.1   As forward speed increases (during transition) the disc experiences an increasing airflow from ahead. The effect of this is to INCREASE the rotational airflow on the advancing blade (V_R+V_W), and to DECREASE the rotational airflow on the retreating blade. (V_R-V_W).

6.3.2   Due to increased velocity on the advancing blade, rotor thrust will increase and the blade will flap up. The reverse will take place on the retreating blade. The blades are in fact flapping to equality. As with cyclic pitch change, there is a phase lag of 90° and it will be seen in fig 6.8 that the disc will tilt about the axis BD (athwartships) and will FLAPBACK.

6.3.3   Total Rotor Thrust has not changed, but the disc has risen at the front and lowered at the rear without any control movement. **FLAPBACK is the tilting back of the rotor when the rotor is in horizontal airflow, if no corrective action is taken, the fuselage will pitch up.**

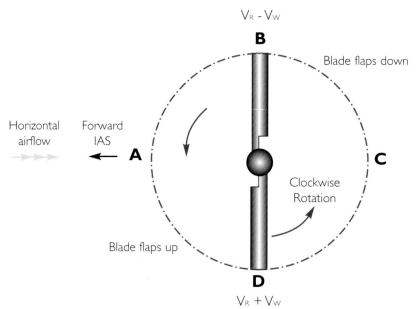

$V_R - V_W$

B

Blade flaps down

Horizontal airflow

Forward IAS

A

Clockwise Rotation

C

Blade flaps up

D

$V_R + V_W$

Fig. 6.8   Rotor tilting during transition with no cyclic input from the pilot, FLAPBACK.

69

6.3.4   The corrective action is to move the cyclic stick forward. The amount of flapback increases with increased airspeed and is most noticeable at about 10 - 15 kt. The Rotor Disc attitude is maintained as airspeed increases by progressive forward movement of the cyclic stick.

6.4   Inflow Roll

6.4.1   As the helicopter moves forward, the disc will be tilted and the blades will be coned. As a result of this the relative airflow meets the disc at different angles during the rotation. Fig 6.9.

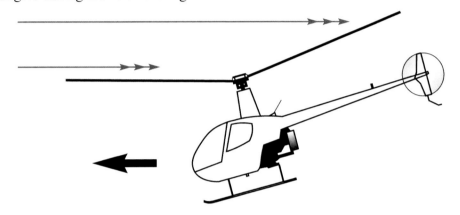

Fig. 6.9   The relative airflow meets the forward and rearwards blades at different angles.

6.4.2   At the front of the disc, the angle is shallow and has the effect of reducing the induced airflow, thus INCREASING Rotor Thrust in this area. At the rear of the disc the angle is steeper to the blade and induced airflow is increased thus REDUCING Rotor Thrust in this area. (See again section 6.2 Para: 6.2.3).

6.4.3   The overall effect is to tilt the disc, but because of phase lag, the Rotor Disc tilts sideways and to the advancing side. *This is known as inflow roll.* See fig 6.10. **Note:** *Some texts describe this as Transverse Flow Effect.*

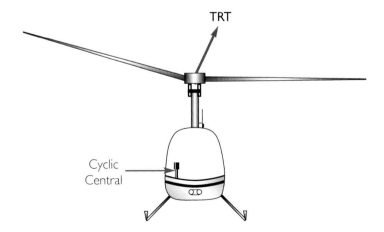

Fig. 6.10   Phase lag makes the disc tilt sideways.

6.4.4   Rotor Disc attitude is maintained by cyclic stick control to the retreating side, but less than is required for flapback. See fig 6.11.

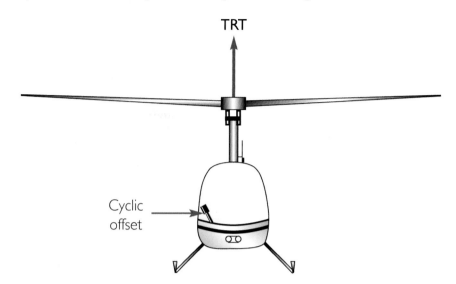

Fig. 6.11   Inflow roll corrected by offsetting the cyclic stick towards the retreating blade side.

6.4.5   Flapback and Inflow Roll normally occur together and are most noticeable at about 12 - 15 kt. However, as airspeed increases, Inflow Roll reduces as the flow through the disc becomes more uniform.

6.5   Flare and its Effects

6.5.1   **Transition.** If the transition from forward flight to the hover is made by reducing the forward speed in many stages allowing the helicopter to settle at each speed reduction, then the collective pitch and power changes would be the same but in the reverse sense as making a transition from the hover to forward flight. However, the general method of coming to a hover from forward flight is by the pilot executing a FLARE, and this is done by tilting the disc in the opposite direction to that in which the helicopter is moving. When this method of reducing speed is employed collective pitch and power changes to control the manoeuvre will differ considerably from those required to produce a more gentle transition.

6.5.2   **Flare effects.** To execute a flare the cyclic stick is moved back in the opposite direction to which the helicopter is moving, the harshness of the flare depending upon how much and how fast the stick is moved. The flare will bring about a number of effects, which will now be considered.

6.5.3   **Thrust Reversal.** By tilting the disc away from the direction in which the helicopter is travelling the horizontal thrust component of the Total Rotor Thrust will now act in the same direction as the fuselage Parasite Drag causing the helicopter to slow down very rapidly. See fig 6.12.

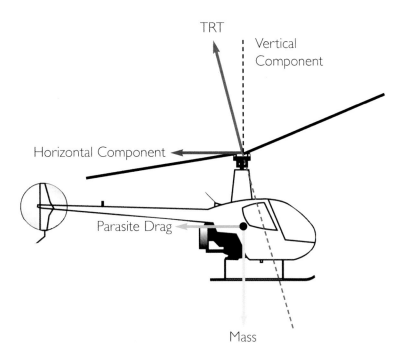

Fig. 6.12   With the disc tilted backwards, the TRT horizontal component is acting in the same direction as the parasite drag, decelerating the helicopter very rapidly.

6.5.4   The fuselage will respond to this rapid deceleration by pitching nose up because reverse thrust is being maintained while Parasite Drag decreases. If the pilot takes no corrective action, the disc will be tilted further still adding to the deceleration effect. See fig 6.13.

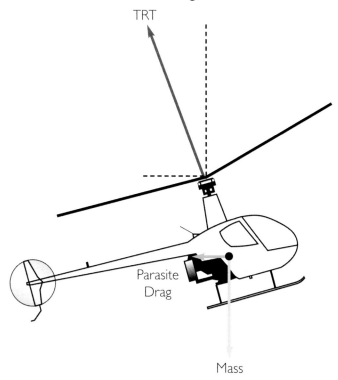

Fig. 6.13   Fuselage response with steeper pitch-up as reverse component of thrust is maintained. (Parasite drag reduces as speed reduces).

6.5.5   **Increase in Rotor Thrust**. Another effect of tilting the disc back while the helicopter is moving forward is to change the airflow relative to the disc. See Fig 6.14.

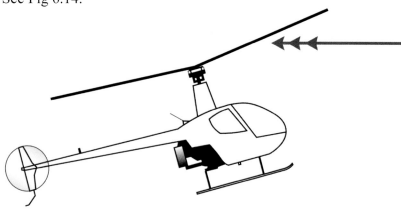

Fig. 6.14   Flare changes the flow relative to the disc.

6.5.6   As explained in Translational Lift, a component of the horizontal airflow (due to the helicopter moving forward) is passing through the disc at right angles to the Plane of Rotation in the SAME direction as the Induced flow. When the helicopter is flared, a component of the horizontal flow will now be opposing the Induced flow and the changed direction of the flow relative to the blades **will cause an increase in the Angle of Attack** and therefore an increase in Total Rotor Thrust. See fig 6.15.

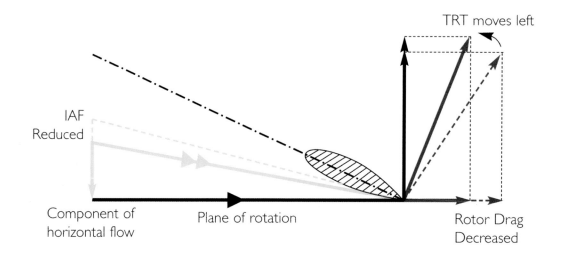

Fig. 6.15   The horizontal airflow opposes the induced flow and increases the angle of attack, (and the TRT).

6.5.7   If the pilot took no corrective action, the helicopter would climb. The collective pitch lever must therefore be lowered if constant height is to be maintained.

6.5.8   **Increase in rotor RPM (Nr).** The changes in the airflow and forces on the Rotor Disc cause the rotor RPM (Nr) to increase rapidly in the flare for the following reasons:

1   **Reduction in Rotor Drag:**
Rotor Drag is reduced in the flare because the total reaction moves towards the axis of rotation. This results from the changed direction of the relative airflow. The forward movement of the total reaction vector causes the rotor drag component to be reduced as shown in fig 6.15.

2   **Conservation of Angular Momentum:**
The increase in Total Rotor Thrust will cause the blades to cone up. The radius of the blades C of G from the axis decreases and the rotor RPM (Nr) will automatically rise.

6.5.9   As a result of the flare, the speed reduces rapidly and the flare effects disappear. Collective pitch and power which had been reduced during the flare must be replaced and in addition, MORE collective pitch and power must be used to replace the loss of translational lift caused by the speed reduction, otherwise the aircraft would sink.

6.5.10   The cyclic stick must also be moved forward to level the helicopter and to prevent the helicopter moving backwards. The power changes necessary during the flare affect the aircraft in the yawing plane, therefore yaw pedals must be used to maintain heading throughout.

6.6   Landing

6.6.1   If collective pitch is reduced slightly in a hover (IGE), the helicopter will descend but settle at a height where ground effect has increased Total Rotor Thrust to equal AUM again. Therefore, a progressive lowering of the lever is required to achieve a steady descent until the aircraft is on the ground and the mass supported by the undercarriage.

6.6.2   When the helicopter is close to the ground, the tip vortices (more later) are larger and unstable which causes variation in the thrust around the Rotor Disc and turbulence around the tail which can make control difficult.

7   AUTOROTATION

7.1   Introduction

7.1.1   To maintain the rotor RPM in normal flight, the drag is overcome by engine power. Should the engine fail, or the rotor is deliberately disengaged from the rotor drive chain, then the rotor RPM must be maintained by some alternative means.

7.1.2

Should engine failure happen, then the pilot has as his primary objective to control the helicopter down to the ground (or sea) in a controlled and predicable manner. The following procedures are to be followed.

7.1.3   As soon as engine failure occurs, the first action by the pilot is to allow the helicopter to descend, and lower the collective pitch lever fully. Now, the resulting airflow will drive the rotor. This is the alternative means in maintaining rotor RPM. It can be described as the rate of descent replaces the engine power. This decent without engine power is described as AUTO ROTATION.

7.2   Autorotation in Still Air

7.2.1   Normally, autorotation is carried out with forward speed, but to clarify the explanation of the forces involved, it is assumed the helicopter is autorotating in still air and descending vertically.

7.2.2   Under such conditions, if the various forces are calculated on one blade, the calculations will be valid for all the other blades irrespective of the position of the blade in its 360° of travel. See fig. 7.1 for flows and angles referred to in the following text.

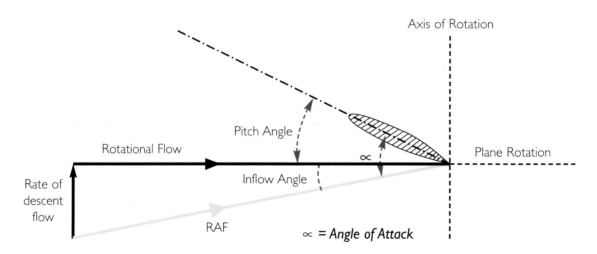

Fig. 7.1   Autorotation in still air (terms used).

7.2.3   The blade's rotational velocity and the airflow resulting from the rate of descent determines the inflow. However, this is not strictly true because the action of the blade slows down the rate of descent airflow. This can be likened to induced flow. This in turn will REDUCE the inflow angle to something a bit smaller than indicated.

7.2.4   For the purpose of this explanation, the inflow angle shown in fig. 7.1 is deemed correct. The fact that it is a bit smaller will be considered at a later stage including how this effects the blade.

7.3   Autorotative Force / Rotor Drag

7.3.1   In fig. 7.2 a rotor blade has been divided into three sections, A, B and C. At each section the relative airflow can be determined from the local rotational velocity and the helicopter's rate of descent. The rotational velocity decreases from the tip to the root, but of course the rate of descent will be the same for each section.

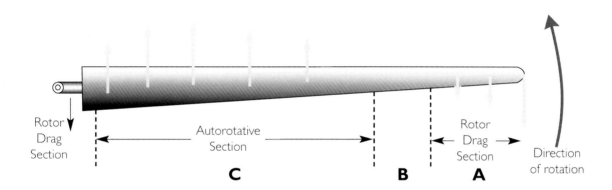

Fig. 7.2   Autorotation – Blade section.

7.3.2   In comparing the sections from A to C, the INFLOW ANGLE must be increasing. See also fig. 7.3. The blade pitch angle is also increasing as washout is incorporated in the blade. Therefore, the angle of attack is increasing, as too is the inflow angle. Maximum angle of attack being at the root.

7.3.3   The lift/drag ratio at each of the above sections can be determined from the angle of attack and the aerofoil data tabulations. When the vectors of lift and drag are added in the correct ratio, total reaction can be obtained. See fig. 7.3.

76

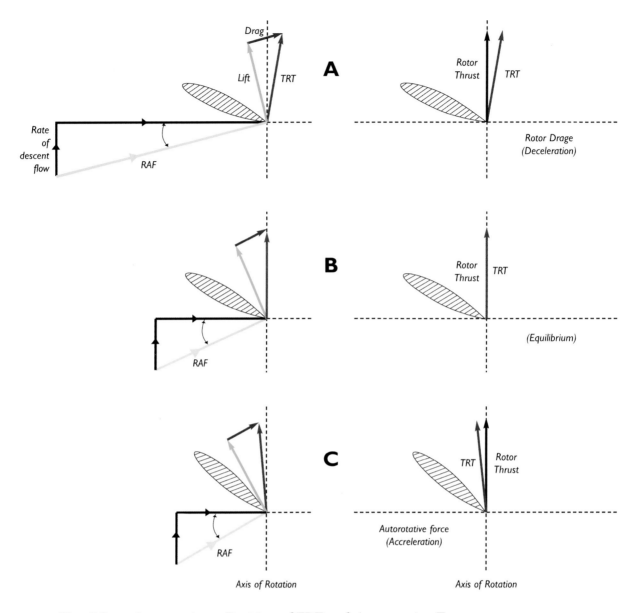

Fig. 7.3   *Autorotation – Position of TRT and Autorotative Forces.*

7.3.4   Referring to fig.7.3 A. and relating the total reaction to the axis of rotation. Notice that the total reaction is positioned behind the axis of rotation. In B it is on the axis, and at C is positioned behind. It is now possible knowing the position of the total reaction to relate this in terms of thrust and drag.

7.3.5   In figure 7.3 A. Total reaction, drag and thrust is the same as in powered flight. However, the total reaction in the plane of rotation is attempting to slow the rotor blade down. In figure 7.3 B. Total reaction is not having any effect in the plane of rotation, ie., it is all rotor thrust. In figure 7.3 C. Total reaction is acting in the plane of rotation and thus enhancing rotation the blade. With these conditions, rotor drag is now described as AUTOROTATIVE FORCE.

7.3.6   It can be seen now that the section of blade producing the autorotative force is accelerating the blade, and the section producing the drag will attempt to slow it down. These two parameters must be in balance to maintain a constant rotor RPM. It must also be remembered that the drag is enhanced by other equipment in the drive chain like ancillary equipment, tail rotor shaft, the tail rotor itself. All this will continue to operate in autorotation.

7.3.7   Assuming an adequate rate of descent exists, in normal conditions with the collective lever lowered, the configuration of the blade will see the autorotative RPM within the correct operating range. Raising the collective lever will see all sections of blade increase in pitch. See again figs. 7.2 & 7.3. The conditions at section C will tend to move towards B, and the conditions at B will tend to move towards A. **So, the autorotative section moves outwards towards the tips.**

7.3.8   When this takes place, the section at D, the root, becomes stalled. The additional drag thus generated causes the RPM to decrease; the autorotative section will also decrease. It will however stabilise at a new value but the helicopter is descending more rapidly. Further raising of the collective lever will result in the blade no longer able to autorotate.

7.3.9   When the helicopter is at a high all up weight, or operating at higher altitudes, the autorotative descent will be also be high. The autorotating section of the blade has moved outwards, and the RPM in stabilised autorotation will be higher. However, it must be noted that when descending in more dense air the rate of descent and the RPM will decrease without any change in the collective lever position.

7.4   Rate of Descent

7.4.1   Assume a helicopter is in the hover at some safe height. In the event of engine failure, the pilot will immediately reduce the collective pitch. The helicopter will accelerate downwards until the angle of attack will produce a total reaction (producing an autorotative force) to maintain rotor RPM, which in turn will produce rotor thrust equal to the helicopter mass. In this condition, downwards acceleration will stop and the helicopter will descend at a steady rate.

7.4.2   Should there be some outside influence, which causes the angle of attack to increase, then there will be reduction in the rate of descent, and if the angle of attack should decrease, then the rate of descent will increase.

7.4.3   Assume a helicopter is in forward motion, and experiences an engine failure. The procedure being the same as in para: 7.4.1, however, the rate of descent will initially be less with forward speed. Then beyond a certain speed (depending on the type of helicopter) the rate of descent will increase again. The reason for this is the changing direction of the relative airflow which happens across the speed range when autorotating.
Note: In power-off flight, there is no torque reaction: See para: 4.1.6

7.5   Relative Airflow - Vertical Autorotation

7.5.1   For a helicopter of a given mass in autorotation, and assuming it requires a mean angle of attack of 7° to satisfy the requirements of rotor thrust and autorotative forces in a vertical autorotation. Assume also the rate of descent is to be 1800 feet/min. As the inflow angle is determined from the rate of descent and the mean rotational velocity, then it will have a value of say 9°, see fig.7.4A.

7.5.2   The action of the blades slows down the airflow coming from the disc, so the actual inflow angle will be less, probably only 5°. See fig 7.4B. If the mean pitch angle of the blade is 2° then the angle of attack will be 7°. This is what is required for an 1800 feet/min rate of descent, and inflow angle of 5° for this particular helicopter characteristic and mass.

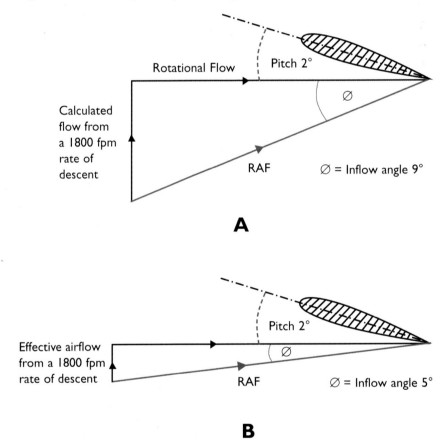

Fig. 7.4   *Inflow angle and rate of descent relationship.*

7.6   Autorotation with Forward Speed

7.6.1   **Introduction.**   There are three factors which need to be considered in determining the direction of the relative airflow when a helicopter is in forward autorotation. Each one will be examined individually first of all then a collective examination.

7.6.2   **Individual Effect:**

1.   **Factor A.** Because the disk must be tilted forward to achieve forward autorotation, and assuming the effective airflow from the rate of descent remains unchanged (see fig. 7.4), then it follows that the inflow angle must decrease, see fig. 7.5. Therefore the angle of attack will decrease and the resulting rotor thrust will decrease. This causes an increase in the rate of descent.

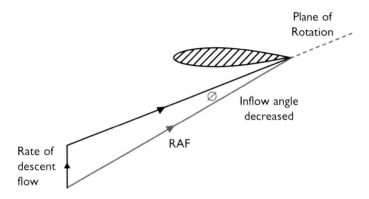

Fig. 7.5   Inflow angle – disc tilted forward.

2.   **Factor B.** In forward flight, the disc will be experiencing not only the horizontal airflow but also the descent airflow. As the disc is tilted to the horizontal flow, it further reduces the inflow angle. In fig. 7.6 it can be seen that the vectors of descent flow and horizontal airflow effect (reduce) the inflow angle. The angle of attack is further reduced which increases the rate of descent.

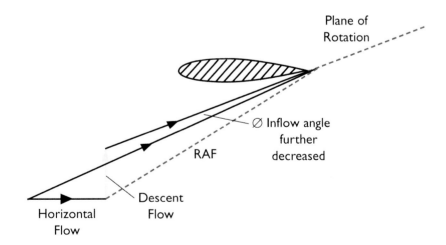

Fig. 7.6   Inflow angle – effect of horizontal airflow.

3. **Factor C.** In forward flight, the disc moves into undisturbed air, or air that has not been slowed down to the same amount by the blades as is the case with vertical descent. This means the effective rate of descent airflow will increase. The inflow angle increases, the angle of attack increases and the rotor thrust increases which decreases the rate of descent. See fig. 7.7

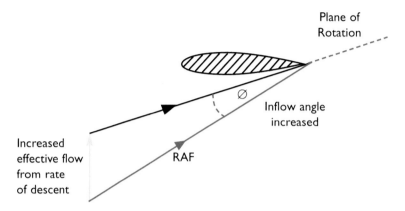

Fig. 7.7   Inflow angle – effect of forward speed.

7.7   Combined Effect

7.7.1   Only a small amount of tilt is required for low forward speed. The effect of factor C is greater than the effects of factor A and B combined. The inflow angle increases. Therefore the angle of attack increases and rotor thrust increases. The rate of descent will therefore decrease.

7.7.2   The inflow angle reduces as the rate of descent reduces. Stabilisation in the rate of descent takes place when the angle of attack is such that rotor thrust equals the helicopter mass.

7.7.3   Factor C will increase the inflow angle as forward speed increases, but as with induced flow in normal powered flight, this increase is large initially but will reduce as the forward speed increases.

7.7.4   As forward speed increases, so does parasite drag, and the tilt of the rotor to provide the speed increase. Factors A and B rapidly increase. There comes a point where the combined effects of Factors A and B equal C and balance is achieved.

7.7.5   In this condition, the resulting speed gives the minimum rate of descent. Should the speed increase then Factors A and B will increase and imbalance with factor C occurs. This will see the inflow angle reduce and rotor thrust will reduce. To achieve balance again, the required rotor thrust must be obtained with a higher rate of descent.

7.8   Rate of Descent Requirements in Autorotation

7.8.1   When autorotating, the rate of descent is required for the following:

1. Produce an autorotative force for the selected rotor RPM. (Nr).

2. Produce rotor thrust to equal the helicopter mass.

3. Produce rotor thrust component to equal the parasite drag component.

When these parameters are plotted together against forward speed, the resulting graph is similar to level flight power requirements. See fig. 7.8.

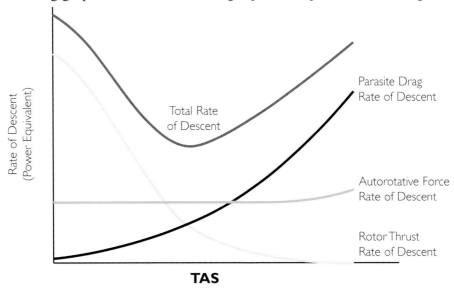

Fig. 7.8   *Autorotation combined effect of forward speed on rate of descent.*

7.9   Autorotating for Endurance and Range in Still Air

7.9.1   **Endurance.**   This means autorotating to stay in the air as long as possible. This must be done at a speed that achieves the minimum rate of descent. In fig. 7.9, this speed can be read off the graph at the LOWEST part of the rate of descent curve.

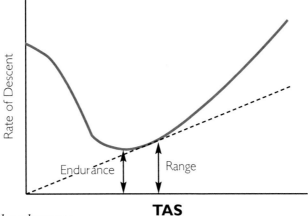

Fig. 7.9   *Range and endurance.*

7.9.2   **Maximum Rage.** This means autorotating along the shallowest flight path, or the best forward speed/rate of descent ratio. See fig. 7.9. Maximum range is found at the point where a line drawn from the zero axis of the graph is tangential to the rate of descent curve. Notice this speed is a bit higher than the best endurance speed, as too is the rate of descent helicopter operations manual.

7.9.3   Range and endurance information including rotor RPM would be found in the helicopter operations manual.

7.10   Flare

7.10.1   The flare procedure is exactly the same in autorotation as it is in powered flight. During the flare the autorotative section on the blade will move outwards towards the tip and the rotor RPM will rise initially. The increase in rotor thrust reduces the rate of descent while the flare is taking effect.

7.11   Avoid Area (for Autorotation)

7.11.1   The establishment of fully developed autorotation, following an engine failure, will involve a loss of height. This loss of height will vary, depending upon the air speed at the time of the engine failure.

7.11.2   In the hover, or at low forward speed, the loss of height necessary to establish full autorotation will be considerable as it will be necessary to lower the lever fully to restore rotor RPM.

7.11.3   At high forward speed it may be possible to flare the aircraft before lowering the lever, which will help to restore the rotor RPM and may even result in a gain of height. However, as speed is reduced it will be necessary to lower the lever to prevent the rotor RPM from falling again.

7.11.4   If the engine failure occurs at or about the minimum power speed some height will be lost in establishing full autorotation, but it will be much less than that lost when in the hover.

7.11.5   For these reasons the helicopter should not be kept in the hover between approximately 10 feet and 400 feet AGL for any period longer than is absolutely necessary, and flight in the "avoid area" should be kept to a minimum. The relevant aircraft operations manual should be consulted for specific techniques. Fig 7.10 shows a typical helicopter "avoid area" diagram, sometimes called altitude/airspeed diagram or dead man's curve!!

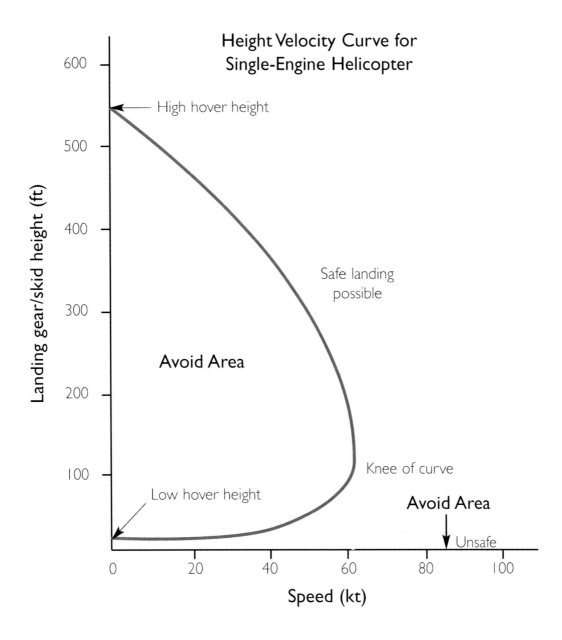

Fig. 7.10   Helicopter autorotaton avoid areas.

7.12   Autorotative Landing

7.12.1   Should an engine failure at height take place, then the helicopter has potential energy that can be converted to kinetic energy in the rotor during autorotation and landing.

7.12.2   The kinetic energy stored in the rotor as a function of its RPM can be converted into WORK when near the ground by careful use of the collective lever. A large increase in rotor thrust can be achieved as the kinetic energy is converted, but the there will be a rapid decay in rotor RPM (Nr).

7.13 Entry Into Autorotation

7.13.1 During the period between an engine failure and a fully established autorotation, the airflow around the helicopter, and the control conditions, pass through a series of transient stages. Depending on the helicopter type and the conditions, the following problems may be encountered:

1. Rapid yaw: caused by the unbalanced tail rotor thrust.
2. Pitching: nose up or down caused by airflow changes over the stabiliser.
3. Rapid decay of rotor RPM (Nr): caused by rotor drag before the collective is lowered.
4. Possible tail strike: by the main rotor blades if the lever is lowered rapidly and cyclic aft control is made.

7.14 Autorotation at High AUM and High Density Altitude

7.14.1 The problems on entry detailed above are aggravated at high density altitudes AUM and IAS. Also rotor RPM (Nr) is large when autorotation is established, and these conditions could exceed the limits if collective pitch were reduced to a minimum.

7.14.2 Therefore, the lever should not be fully lowered immediately following an engine failure in these conditions. Nr is more sensitive to small changes of pitch at high density altitude and high AUM and especially to "G" in turns. Therefore, rotor RPM (Nr) must be monitored closely to avoid exceeding the limits.

7.14.3 When autorotation is established at high density altitude, pitch is large and the autorotative section is small. If improved range is sought by increasing pitch and decreasing rotor RPM (Nr) the autorotative section may become too small to balance the rotor drag and there will be a rapid and uncontrollable drop in rotor RPM (Nr). Therefore, the lower limit in autorotation is higher at high density altitudes. Note: Rotor RPM and Nr are terms which are both used in these notes. See fig 7.11 for theoretical airflow pattern in autorotation.

Fig. 7.11   Theoretical airflow pattern for a helicopter in autorotation.

8   GROUND RESONANCE, VORTEX RING, POWER SETTLING AND BLADE SAILING.

8.1   Ground Resonance, Introduction

8.1.1   Ground resonance is normally defined as being a vibration of large amplitude resulting from a self-induced or forced vibration of a helicopter when in contact with or resting upon the ground.

8.1.2   Ground resonance can be recognised by a rocking motion or oscillation of the fuselage, and if corrective action is not taken at an early stage, the amplitude may increase to the point where it will become uncontrollable and the helicopter will roll over.

8.2   Origins of Ground Resonance

8.2.1   Vibration which can be the cause of ground resonance may be present in the rotor head before the helicopter comes into contact with the ground. Ideally the centre of gravity of the rotor disc should be over the centre of rotation, if however, for any reason this is not so, in that its position is displaced, a "wobble" will develop, the effect being similar to an unbalanced flywheel rotating at high speed.

8.2.2   Ground resonance can also be induced by the undercarriage being in light contact with the ground, particularly if the frequency of oscillation of the oleos and /or tyres is in sympathy with the rotor head vibration

8.2.3   Wheel brakes, AUM and ambient temperatures are further factors which can affect the onset of ground resonance.

8.3   Types of Ground Resonance

8.3.1   Essentially there are two primary origins of ground resonance:

1. Rotor Head Vibration

2. Fuselage Vibration

8.4   Rotor Head Vibration

8.4.1   The origins of rotor head vibration can be:

1. Blades of Unequal Weight or Balance. During manufacture blades are weighed and balanced to a degree of accuracy which usually, on most modern helicopters, allows them to become totally interchangeable. In flight, however, an imbalance of a rotor blade can be caused by a number of conditions, such as an uneven accumulation of ice or absorption of moisture.

    The nature of the collection of moisture or water in a blade may take the form of accumulation within individual blade pockets, therefore creating considerable imbalance conditions, causing severe vibration. Blade damage through structural failure or foreign object damage will also cause vibration due to imbalance of the blade.

2. Faulty or Unserviceable Drag Dampers. As an example, with a three bladed rotor system the blades should be equally spaced 120° apart. If a drag damper is sticking or is in any way permitting uneven spacing of the individual blades, the centre of gravity of the rotor assembly will be displaced away from the axis of rotation, thereby causing vibration. When these movements are in phase with the natural lateral oscillations of the fuselage about the undercarriage or tyres, then they will increase in amplitude and if uncorrected, will reach the critical point where damage is caused. See fig 8.1.

    Longitudinal oscillations do not generally occur because the fore and aft pitching moments of the fuselage are too slow to be in phase with the rotor speed.

87

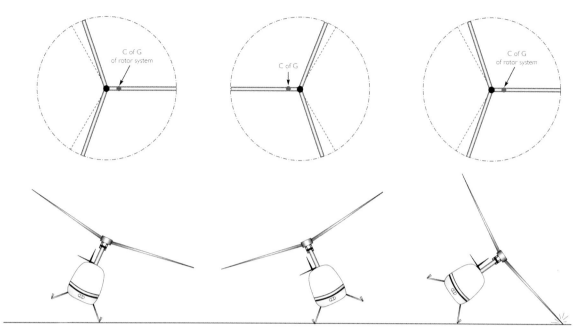

Fig. 8.1   Faulty drag dampers.

3. Faulty or Incorrect Tracking. A rotor which is greatly out of track may set up an imbalance condition which will be transmitted through the helicopter. This type of imbalance usually results in a rough running helicopter and the pilot will feel a positive "beat" in the cyclic stick. This "beat" is sometimes referred to as a "wumper" which is a nickname for one beat per revolution. If enough track imbalance exists, it is possible that a combination of factors may be encountered that would result in ground resonance being induced. See fig. 8.2.

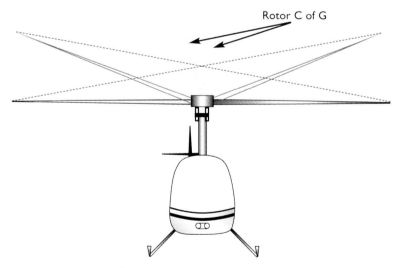

Fig 8.2   Faulty or incorrect tracking.

4. Faults in the Automatic Stabilisation Equipment (ASE) could generate control inputs in sympathy with natural undercarriage frequencies which would result in the onset of ground resonance. For this reason, it is normally preferable to disengage the ASE when on the ground.

8.5 Fuselage Vibration

8.5.1 There are a number of causes of fuselage vibration, the following being the most common:

1. Pilot mishandling, exacerbated by continued lateral movement of the cyclic control.
2. Unequal tyre pressures, or unequal oleo pressures.
3. Uneven or rough ground for a taxying take off, or run on landing.

8.6 Additional Operational Hazards

8.6.1 When operating the helicopter under certain conditions such as loading or unloading with the helicopter in a semi-hover, and the undercarriage in light contact with the ground and one wheel dropping into a hole or depression. Such hazards can induce ground resonance.

8.7 Recovery Action

8.7.1 Recovery from ground resonance can be achieved by eliminating the forces inducing the resonant frequency. Therefore as soon as resonance is recognised, either ground contact must be broken or the rotor RPM changed. The more appropriate of the following actions must be taken as quickly as possible.

1. Lift-off immediately, if lift-off rotor RPM are available. In order to recover from ground resonance and other such emergencies, rotor RPM should always be maintained in the operating range until the final landing has been completed.
2. Shut down immediately if lift-off rotor RPM are not available, or if lift-off is not practicable because there is reason seriously to doubt the serviceability of the aircraft or the power margin is insufficient for a vertical takeoff.
3. Make specific shut-down checks.

8.8 Vortex Ring

8.8.1 There are always vortices presents in the neighbourhood of the rotor periphery, similar to wing-tip vortices with a fixed-wing aircraft. There are conditions where these vortices will intensify. If a stall condition of the rotor happens, the stall spreads out from the root towards the rotor tip. This will result in a sudden loss of rotor thrust, and a rapid descent.

8.8.2   When this occurs, the helicopter is descending in a Vortex Ring state. This state can be entered from various in-flight manoeuvres, but the airflow characteristics that set off a Vortex Ring State are basically the same. This state will occur when any or all of the following are in place:

1. Normal induced flow through the rotor disc is present, as in powered flight.
2. There will be an external airflow opposing the induced flow, as in a powered descent or high rate of descent.
3. Low indicated airspeed.
4. As a result of applying power to recover from a low forward airspeed autorotation without first increasing the airspeed.

8.8.3   One flight manoeuvre from which vortex ring state can develop is when the helicopter enters a power-assisted descent with low or zero indicated airspeed. The manner in which it can develop is discussed later.

8.9   Development of Vortex Ring State

8.9.1   Referring to figures 8.3, 8.4A and 8.4B a helicopter is hovering in still air conditions. The direction of the relative airflow is a function of the speed of rotation of the blades and the induced airflow. See figs. 8.4A and 8.4B. Notice the greatest value of each is near the blade tip.

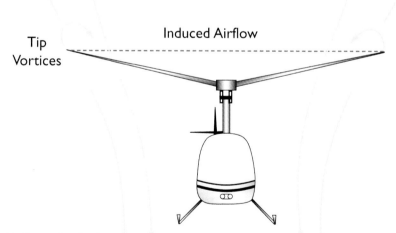

Fig. 8.3   *Airflows in the hover.*

8.9.2   Assume now that the pilot reduces collective pitch in order to start descending.

8.9.3   The ratio of the rotational velocity to induced airflow is assumed to be the same along the length of the blade. Then the direction of the relative airflow along the length of the blade will also be the same. However, because the blade has washout, the angle of attack will increase towards the blade root. See fig. 8.4B.

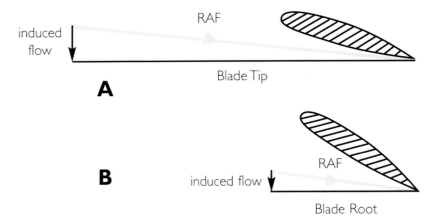

Fig. 8.4   Washout or blade tip effects.

8.9.4   When the descent is established, a new component of airflow will exist directly opposing the induced flow, which in turn will alter the direction of the relative airflow along the blade. If, at the root end of the blade, the airflow from rate of descent is equal to the induced airflow, then the relative airflow will be in the plane of rotation causing the angle of attack to increase, see fig 8.5C.

8.9.5   In the area of the tip, the conflicting airflow outside and inside the disc will intensify the tip vortices, further increasing the induced airflow, see fig 8.5B.

8.9.6   If the increase in induced flow has the same value as the airflow from the rate of descent, a change will take place in the direction of the airflow relative to the blade but, because the collective pitch has been lowered, the angle of attack in the area of the tip will have actually decreased. See fig 8.5B.

8.9.7   If the collective pitch is lowered further, the rate of descent will again increase, see fig 8.6A.

8.9.8   The process will be repeated, and eventually a condition will be reached where the root end of the blade will reach its stalling angle, see fig 8.6C.

8.9.9   At this stage, rotor thrust is decreasing both at the tip of the blade, due to the vortices, and at the root of the blade, because of its stalled condition, leaving an area in between to produce the rotor thrust necessary to balance the weight.

8.9.10   Any further increase in rate of descent resulting from lowering the lever will further reduce the area of the blade that is effectively producing rotor thrust and once a condition is reached where the rotor thrust becomes insufficient to balance the weight, then the rate of descent will rapidly increase, being as high as 6000 feet per min on some types of helicopter. See fig 8.7.

A   Rate of Descent Flow

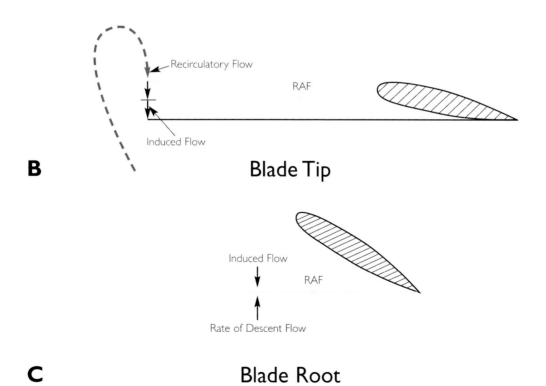

Fig. 8.5   *Slow descent.*

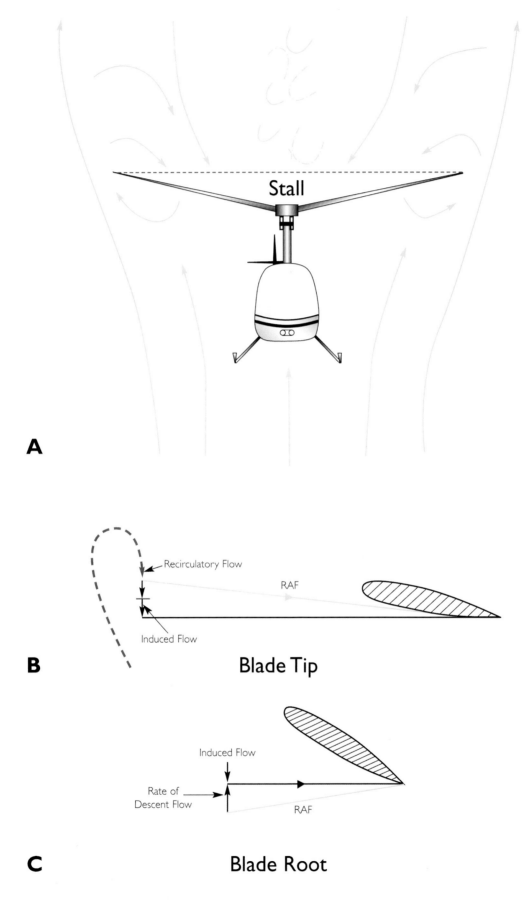

Stall

A

Recirculatory Flow

RAF

Induced Flow

B   **Blade Tip**

Induced Flow

Rate of
Descent Flow

RAF

C   **Blade Root**

Fig. 8.6   Vortex ring state.

Fig. 8.7   Theoretical airflow pattern for a helicopter in a vortex ring state.

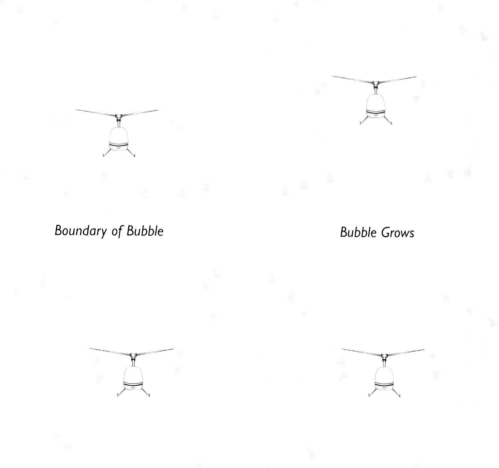

Boundary of Bubble

Bubble Grows

Bubble Bursts

Bubble Reforms

Fig. 8.8   Vortex ring: Air pattern configurations, from wind tunnel experiments. (After Prouty 1985. Helicopter Aerodynamics: Rotor & Wing International; PJS Publications pp 8).

8.9.11   Wind-tunnel experiments indicate that the vortices form and intensify in a most erratic manner, subjecting each blade in-board from the tip to large and sudden variations in angle of attack. See fig 8.8.

8.9.12   In fig. 8.8 can be seen the results of wind-tunnel tests and outlined by smoke visualisation. According to these results, the rotor is continuously "pumping" air into a big bubble under the rotor. This bubble fills up and bursts every second or two, causing large-scale disturbances in the surrounding flow field. The bubble appears to erupt first from one side and then the other so that not only does the rotor thrust vary, but the rotor flaps erratically in pitch and roll, requiring prompt action by the pilot.

8.9.13   Furthermore, dissymmetry of rotor thrust occurs and the helicopter will pitch, roll and yaw to no set pattern making control of the helicopter extremely difficult. In the fully developed vortex ring state, raising the collective pitch lever will only serve to aggravate the condition and instead of checking the rate of descent, it will cause it to increase. The higher the all up weight of the helicopter for a given rotor RPM the higher the collective pitch setting necessary to maintain the hover at the given rotor RPM. Consequently, vortex ring state can occur at an earlier stage in a heavily laden helicopter than it would in a lightly laden one, under the same conditions.

8.10   Vortex Ring State Symptoms and Recovery Action

8.10.1   **Symptoms of the Vortex Ring State.** The onset of vortex ring state can be identified from the following symptoms:

1. Judder and stick shake
2. Random yawing
3. Rapid increase in rate of descent
4. Cyclic stick less effective
5. Random rolling and pitching

Note: (1) and (2) can occur in turbulent air conditions on a steep approach, a cross check should therefore be carried out between airspeed and rate of descent to differentiate between turbulence and the onset of incipient vortex ring state.

8.10.2   **Avoidance of Vortex Ring State.** Every effort should be made by the pilot to avoid situations which are likely to cause the vortex ring state, or, if it is impossible, the rate of descent should be limited to a low rate of descent such as 200 feet per min when the airspeed is low, say 15 kt. The most likely flight conditions occur when within 500 ft of the ground where recovery techniques are unlikely to be successful.

8.10.3   **Recovery.** To recover from a state of vortex ring, it is necessary to change the airflow conditions, which are the cause of it. The method most commonly adopted is to change the rotor disc attitude to achieve forward flight. When in forward flight, the induced flow no longer opposes the airflow from the rate of descent. It is then necessary to wait until the airspeed has increased to a safe figure before increasing power.

8.10.4   An alternative method of effecting recovery is to enter autorotation. It may be impossible, however, to prevent the rotor over speeding and a full recovery will result in a considerable loss of height. The recommended recovery actions are:

1. Stick forward to tilt the rotor disc.
2. Wait - to gain forward speed above 20 kt.
3. Apply power when a safe airspeed is reached.

8.11   Power Settling

8.11.1   Besides the unsteadiness, one of the most unusual characteristics of the vortex ring is the high power required to maintain rotor thrust. This is called "Power Settling" based on observation that in some cases the helicopter keeps coming down even though full engine power is being used. Fig 8.9A & B shows the power and the collective pitch required to maintain constant rotor thrust in a vertical descent for a typical helicopter.

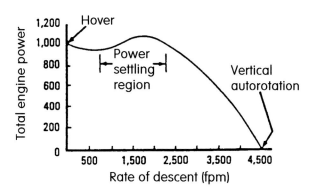

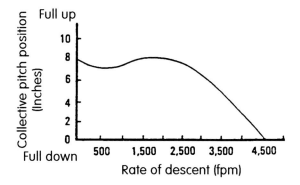

Fig. 8.9   Power and pitch required in vertical descent for a typical helicopter.

96

8.11.2 Not only does the power required increase in the vortex-ring state, but so does the collective pitch due to local blade stall during flow fluctuations. The range between 750 and 2300 feet per min for the helicopter shown in fig 8.9 is the power settling condition. This situation can become a problem when making a nearly vertical landing approach with a heavily loaded helicopter on a hot day when the power available is low.

8.11.3 *(For interest)*. Another scary scenario is an engine failure on a multi engine helicopter making a takeoff from a rooftop. In this operation, the prudent takeoff path is vertical, or even slightly backward, so that in case of an engine failure the helicopter can either return to the rooftop or (if high enough) go into forward flight without descending below the level of the roof, according to FAA rules. It is obvious that if the rate of descent back to the roof with one engine inoperative puts it into the vortex ring state, then the landing may be more traumatic than the pilot might have anticipated.

8.11.4 Power settling has also been experienced during the downwind flare used for a quick stop or during a crop dusting turn. In any case where the helicopter catches up with its own wake, the power required to keep from falling out of the sky will suddenly increase.

8.12 Tail Rotor Vortex Ring

8.12.1 The problems of operation in the vortex ring state were first discovered on main rotors, but tail rotors may get their share in conditions such as right hover turns and left sideways flight (for helicopters with main rotors turning counter clockwise). Not all helicopters experience these troubles, but for those that do, a common symptom is a sudden increase in the turn rate. This is due to the collective pitch characteristics shown on fig 8.9. See also fig 8.10.

8.13 Blade Sailing

8.13.1 Blade sailing describes a condition that can take place in starting up a helicopter or shutting one down in strong windy conditions during the period when the blades are accelerating or slowing down. Particularly relevant when shutting down.

8.13.2 Assume a helicopter is facing into wind. When shutting down or starting up, the blades are receiving a low power input and thus have a low value of centrifugal force. The blade that is advancing is subject to an increase in lift and will flap up excessively. The maximum height in front of the helicopter. As the blade continues its path to the rear of the helicopter, it experiences a sudden loss of lift and will flap down rapidly. As the blade exhibits flexing, the rapid drop reaches its lowest point to the rear over the tail assembly.

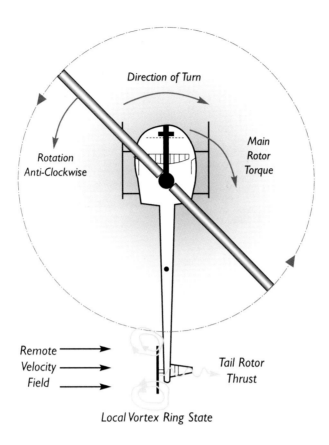

Direction of Turn

Rotation
Anti-Clockwise

Main
Rotor
Torque

Remote
Velocity
Field

Tail Rotor
Thrust

Local Vortex Ring State

Fig. 8.10 Conditions in a right hover turn.

8.13.3   This situation could see the sudden blade dropping go low enough to
strike the helicopter tail assembly. With low RPM and poor cyclic stick
response the pilot has almost no control of blade sailing. The situation can
be minimised by holding the cyclic stick forward and slightly into wind,
or the helicopter facing slightly out of wind in order that the lowest point
in the blades orbit is not over the tail assembly.

8.13.4   As this condition occurs at low rotor RPM in strong or gusty wind
conditions, efforts should be made to slow the rotor down as quickly as
possible on shut-down by using the rotor brake. On start-up, the rotor
RPM should be increased at a faster rate than normal.

8.14   Static and Dynamic Rollover

8.14.1   Static rollover is caused by a helicopter achieving an angle on a slope
steeper than it can negotiate, such that a vertical line from the aircraft's C
of G falls outside the down slope skid, (or landing wheel) see fig 8.11.
Some helicopters can withstand slopes up to 40°. Dynamic rollover on the
other hand, means that the helicopter may be irreversibly committed to
rolling over at angles less than 10° (depending on the rate of roll). It is
clear therefore that static and dynamic rollover are quite different.

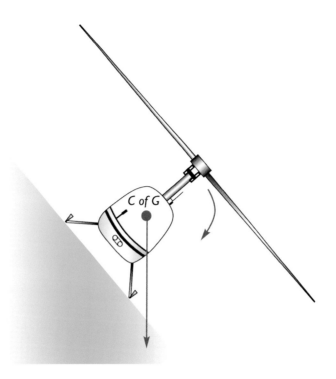

Fig. 8.11 Static rollover – C of G falls outside the downslope skid (or landing wheel).

8.14.2   Dynamic Rollover, is not simply a function of slope angle, or lateral control authority. While these can be aggravating factors, a more direct contributor is build up of angular velocity of the mass of the helicopter about the skid or wheel in contact with the ground. Thus a pilot encountering dynamic rollover may not recognise it as such, because the roll rates which precipitate it are within a range which he would normally deem acceptable.

8.14.3   Two other factors which affect the likelihood of dynamic rollover are total mass of the helicopter, and the distance the C of G is from the landing gear. The three factors combined produce angular momentum.

8.14.4   **Dynamic rollover, therefore, is simply the result of the helicopter developing excess angular momentum about the skid (wheel) in contact with the ground.**

8.14.5   To explain how dynamic rollover can take place, a sequence of actions and events will be described. The following figures shows a helicopter on a sloping landing site, but it should be emphasised that conditions such as cross-wind take offs, or take offs where one skid (or wheel) is stuck to the ground (ice, lashing etc) may cause dynamic rollover to occur.

> ***Note:***   *By convention, take-off means the transition and climb. Lifting off and alighting are: Lift-off and Touch-down.*

8.14.6   In fig 8.12, the aircraft is on the ground with the cyclic stick central. The C of G is within the landing wheels, and there is a small tail rotor force acting up the slope.

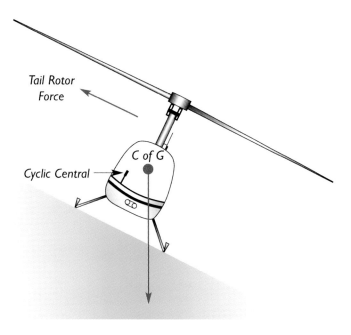

Fig. 8.12   Aircraft on the ground.

8.14.7   In fig 8.13, the disc attitude is levelled by use of the cyclic stick and, as the aircraft has offset flapping hinges, (more about this in section 9.8), there is a centrifugal loading even without rotor thrust, that tends to roll the aircraft up the slope.

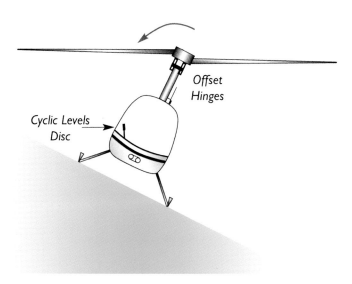

Fig. 8.13   Pilot levels the disc with the cyclic stick.

8.14.8   In fig 8.14. As the pilot applies the collective pitch lever the aircraft pivots about the up-slope skid (wheel). The C of G moves in space, creating angular momentum. If the pilot has not maintained a level disc attitude (has not centralised the cyclic as the down hill skid (wheel) leaves the ground) this will enhance a rapidly deteriorating condition.

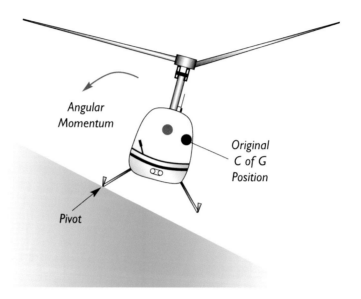

Fig. 8.14   Lift-off.

8.14.9   In fig 8.15, the pilot realises that he has a problem and adjusts the cyclic in the opposite direction. The angular momentum is greater than the available control power, so the aircraft continues to roll.

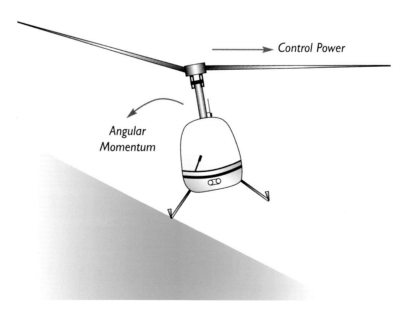

Fig. 8.15   Development.

8.14.10   In fig 8.16, the pilot may (in desperation) apply full collective pitch lever to "yank" the aircraft off the ground, and this is the last "fatal" step. By this time, the aircraft attitude is such that maximum opposite cyclic cannot level the disc, and further application of the pitch lever will simply accelerate the aircraft into the slope.

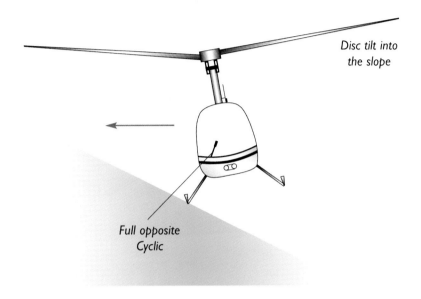

Fig. 8.16   Finally.

8.14.11   **Recovery action.** It is essential that the pilot recognises the symptoms of the condition at the stage shown in fig. 8.13, and prevents dynamic rollover by lowering the collective pitch lever. Rapid lowering of the lever should be avoided as this may lead to the helicopter bouncing off the downslope skid (wheel) and tipping the other way. The lever should be lowered swiftly but gently.

8.14.12   It was mentioned earlier, that the primary helicopter upsetting moments are the build up of angular momentum of the mass of the helicopter about the skid or wheel in contact with the ground, and the resultant tilted rotor thrust and hub movements. Sometimes tail rotor thrust and wind on the fuselage also contribute.

8.14.13   The moment that keeps the helicopter from tipping over comes from the weight acting between the two wheels or skids. If the helicopter rolls on its landing gear, this stabilising moment diminishes; it goes to zero if the helicopter ever rises on one wheel far enough to put the C of G right over that wheel.

8.14.14   As already described, it is seen that if the helicopter is on sloping ground, it already has a reduced restoring moment and a lateral C of G position (perhaps caused by fuel sloshing). A narrow landing gear width compounds the problem.

8.14.15   A rollover can happen in calm air on level ground if the cyclic stick is held off-centre enough during Lift-off, but a cross-wind can make it even more likely. In a normal lift-off of most single rotor helicopters, one landing gear comes off the ground first but, since this happens just as the aircraft becomes airborne, this action is not associated with a rollover. If however, one landing gear comes off the ground with only partial thrust on the rotor, a rollover may be starting. See fig 8.17.

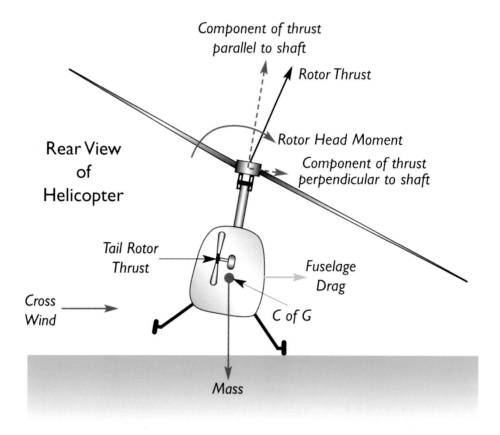

Fig 8.17   Everything in place to start a possible rollover.

8.14.16   In this situation, the pilot might try to hurry the lift-off by raising the collective. As seen earlier, this is usually a mistake since the increased thrust in the same direction results in an increase of the upsetting moment.

8.14.17   Another choice is to apply lateral control to put the gear back on the ground, but this action may be too late, especially if the initial motion came as a surprise !! If an appreciable rolling velocity has developed, it will take a second or two to stop the motion and by this time the helicopter may have tilted irrevocably beyond its critical tip-over angle.

8.14.18   A reduction of collective pitch to get both landing gears firmly on the ground is the accepted cure for an incipient dynamic rollover, but should be done gently, as (already described in the sloping ground case) if the helicopter is dropped too fast it might bounce on the gear that was in the air and start rolling in the other direction.

9 STABILITY

9.1 Principles - Introduction

9.1.1 If a helicopter is disturbed from a given path of flight by some outside influence, to be considered stable it should endeavour to return to its original state without any action on the part of the pilot. Stability can be explained under two primary classifications, Static Stability and Dynamic Stability.

9.2 Static Stability

9.2.1 It can be said that if an object is disturbed from a given position and then on its own returns back to that original position it is STATICALLY STABLE. If following the original disturbance it continues to move further away from its original position it can be said to be STATICALLY UNSTABLE and if it then takes up a new position some distance from its original position then it can be said to be STATICALLY, NEUTRALLY STABLE. See fig. 9.1.

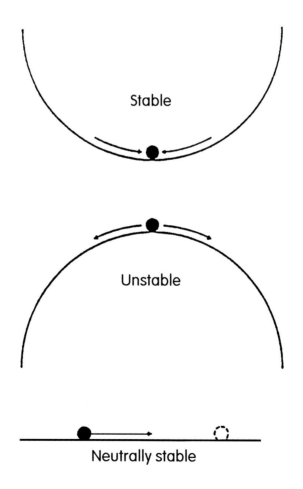

Stable

Unstable

Neutrally stable

Fig. 9.1   Diagrammatic illustration of three conditions of stability.

9.3 Dynamic Stability

9.3.1 If an object is statically stable it will return to its original position, however in doing so may initially overshoot. If the amplitude of the oscillations die out it can be said to be DYNAMICALLY STABLE. If the amplitude of the oscillations increases then it can be said to be DYNAMICALLY UNSTABLE and if the oscillations continue but at a constant amplitude it is said to be DYNAMICALLY NEUTRALLY STABLE.

9.4 Helicopter Stability - Hover

9.4.1 Consider a helicopter in the hover position in still air and a gust of wind affects the rotor disc from the side. The disc will tend to flap away from the wind and if no corrective action is taken by the pilot, the helicopter will move away from the gust. When the gust of wind then dies out the helicopter is still moving sideways and will now experience an airflow coming from the opposite direction.

9.4.2 The helicopter's sideways motion will now slow down as the disc begins to flap away from the new airflow, in addition the fuselage will tend to follow through, and as a result, the disc will tilt further than it was tilted before and the helicopter will now move sideways back towards its original position faster than it moved away.

9.4.3 The movement of the helicopter will result in continually experiencing sideways changes in the airflow affecting the disc and although it will be STATICALLY STABLE, because the amplitude of the oscillations will be continually increasing it will be DYNAMICALLY UNSTABLE. A gust of wind from any direction will produce the effect on the disc, therefore the helicopter will be DYNAMICALLY UNSTABLE in the pitching and rolling planes.

9.4.4 The same gust of wind will also affect the tail rotor. If, for example, on a helicopter with a port mounted tail rotor, the gust of wind from the starboard side will decrease the tail rotor's angle of attack and, assisted by the weathercock action of the fuselage, it will yaw into the gust, that is to say starboard. The helicopter will also move away from the gust, and in doing so will reduce the effect of the gust on the tail rotor. The helicopter will then experience an airflow from its own sideways movement and will yaw to port. It follows that the helicopter will alternately yaw to port and starboard with each successive sideways movement. The helicopter is therefore STATICALLY STABLE but DYNAMICALLY UNSTABLE in the yawing plane when hovering.

9.5 Helicopter Stability - Forward Flight

9.5.1 If a gust of wind strikes a helicopter in forward flight from the starboard side and the tail rotor is mounted on the port side the immediate effect is for the tail rotor's angle of attack to be decreased and the helicopter to yaw to starboard. The inertia of the helicopter will however continue to keep to its original flight path. Weathercock action will return the fuselage to its original position. In the forward flight, the helicopter is both STATICALLY and DYNAMICALLY STABLE in the yawing plane.

9.5.2 If a gust of wind affects the rotor disc from ahead, the disc will flap back and rotor thrust will be reduced. The helicopter will decelerate and as it does so the inertia of the fuselage will cause it to pitch nose up effectively tilting the disc back further and therefore decreasing speed even more. When the speed has stabilised to a lower figure the fuselage will pitch down below its original position.

9.5.3 The "pitch up", "pitch down" action is termed "pendulosity". As the helicopter pitches "nose down" the disc will flap forwards relative to the fuselage (reduced flap back due to lower speed). Now the speed will start to increase with the helicopter descending in a shallow dive, and as the speed increases the disc will begin to flap back again and the cycle will be repeated with, however, increasing amplitude. The helicopter will finally be pitching outside control limits unless cyclic correction is applied early in the cycle.

9.5.4 The helicopter is therefore STATICALLY STABLE because each oscillation will take it through its original position, but is DYNAMICALLY UNSTABLE because the amplitude of the oscillations progressively increase.

9.6 Helicopter Aids to Stability - Introduction

9.6.1 Various devices and systems are currently used to assist the stability of helicopters in all aspects of flight. Some modern helicopter types rely on stabilising systems to maintain flight without which only limited flight performance is possible. Such stabilising devices or systems vary from simple tailplanes to complex computer control.

9.7 Tail Stabiliser

9.7.1 One method of improving stability in forward flight is by fitting a stabiliser at the tail of the fuselage. The purpose of the tail stabiliser is to help prevent the fuselage from following through when a gust of wind causes the disc to flap back. As the fuselage begins to pitch up the increasing angle of attack on the stabiliser will damp down the movement and the rearward tilt of the disc will be greatly reduced.

9.7.2   The reverse effect takes place when the fuselage pitches down. It should be noted, however, that the stabiliser will produce adverse effects if the helicopter is moving backwards. Following a gust of wind which causes the disc to flap forwards, the fuselage will slow down and the tail will "pitch up", this will increase the angle of attack on the stabiliser, thereby increasing the pitch-up movement of the tail. Not all helicopters have this device fitted. See fig. 9.2.

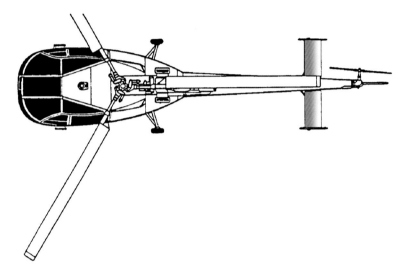

Fig. 9.2   Tail stabilizer as fitted to the SA 316B Alouette Mk 111.

9.8   Offset Flapping Hinges

9.8.1   By setting the flapping hinges away from the axis of the blade's rotation a turning force will be created if the disc flaps back which will resist the tendency of the fuselage to pitch up. See fig. 9.3A & B.

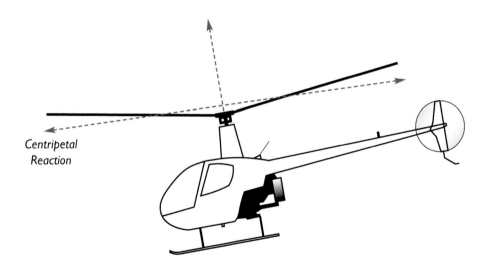

*Centripetal
Reaction*

Fig. 9.3 A

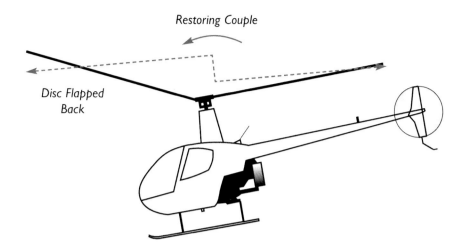

Fig. 9.3B   *Offset flapping hinges.*

9.8.2   In Fig. 9.3(A) the centripetal reaction affecting the blades at the front and rear of the disc are in the same plane. If the disc flaps back (fig. 9.3(B)) the centripetal reaction will no longer be in the same plane and a couple will exist which will automatically reduce the pitch-up tendency of the fuselage which would have otherwise occurred.

9.9   Stabiliser Bar

9.9.1   The stabiliser bar is weighted at the ends and is positioned about the rotor mast at 90° to the blades. It is connected through a variable pivot coupling to the pitch operating arms and to the cyclic controls. If there is a change in pitch on the blades caused by flapback or a gust, the point of action (POA) will act on the stabiliser bar and try to move it, the rigidity of the bar resists this movement and therefore pitch changes are dampened. Dampers on the bar also control the rate of movement of the bar (it is therefore a Rate Gyro).

9.9.2   Action of the stabiliser bar. The Bell stabiliser bar is fitted to teetering type rotor heads (more later) on single rotor helicopters eg., Bell 47 helicopter. The stabiliser bar is mass weighted and acts gyroscopically; it has the properties of a gyroscope, rigidity and precession. Any tilt of the rotor disc tends to be corrected automatically by a system of mixing levers leading from the bar to the cyclic pitch mechanism of the blades. Similarly, a tilt of the fuselage is initially prevented from being transmitted to the rotor disc. See fig 9.4.

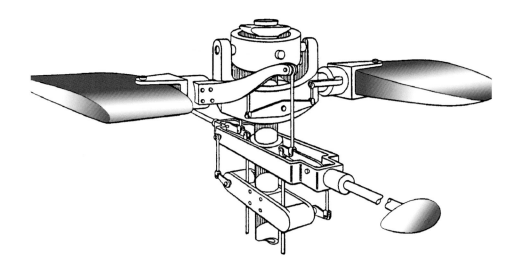

*Fig. 9.4   The Bell system, note the weighted stabilisation bar mounted at 90°
to the rotor.*

9.10   C of G Position (pendulosity)

9.10.1   The limit of control in a helicopter is determined by the amount by which
it is possible to tilt the disc. This determines the tilt of the rotor thrust line.
For a condition of equilibrium, the C of G of the helicopter must align
itself with the total rotor thrust line.

9.10.2   The greater the distance between the rotor head (centre of thrust line) and
the C of G of the helicopter, the greater the movement of C of G possible,
or conversely the more the attitude of the helicopter can change before
reaching the control limit, see fig 9.5.

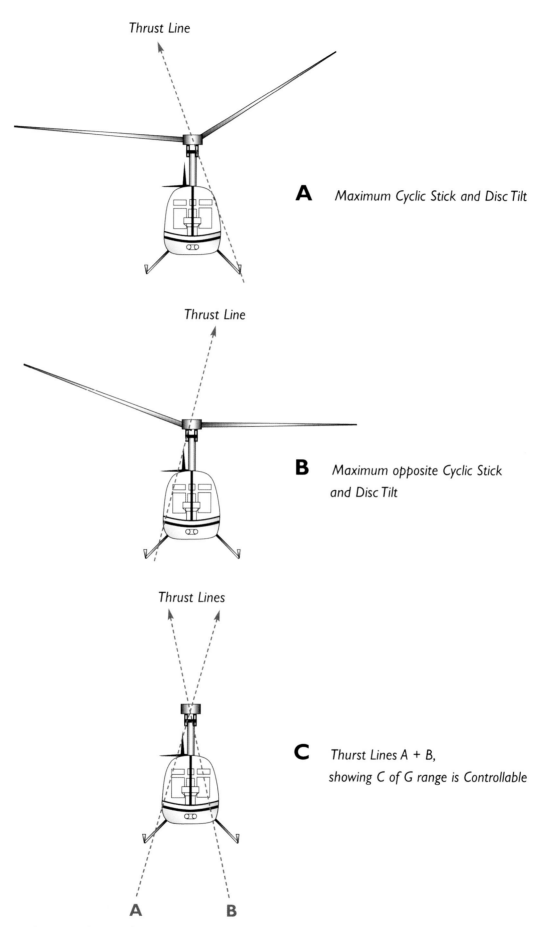

Thrust Line

A Maximum Cyclic Stick and Disc Tilt

Thrust Line

B Maximum opposite Cyclic Stick and Disc Tilt

Thrust Lines

C Thurst Lines A + B,
showing C of G range is Controllable

A   **B**

Fig 9.5   The C of G position (pendulosity)

9.11 Automatic Stabilisation Equipment (ASE)

9.11.1 Unlike the fixed wing aircraft, it has proved very difficult to design inherent stability into a helicopter. Various aids have been devised but have achieved only limited success.

9.11.2 Electronic stabilisation is becoming increasingly employed in the modern helicopter, where the helicopter movement is sensed about a gyro-controlled reference and a correcting input is applied to the helicopter controls.

9.12 Control Power

9.12.1 Control power can be defined as the effectiveness of the cyclic control in achieving changes in fuselage attitude. The main factor determining the degree of control power is the distance from the main rotor shaft at which a cyclic force is effective. This in turn depends upon which of the four basic types of rotor is being considered. The four types of rotor systems are:

1 The teetering head (Bell 47 and 206 series). See fig 9.4.
2 The fully articulated head (Whirlwind, Wessex). (Very complex)
3 Semi-rigid rotor. See fig. 9.6.
4 Rigid rotor.

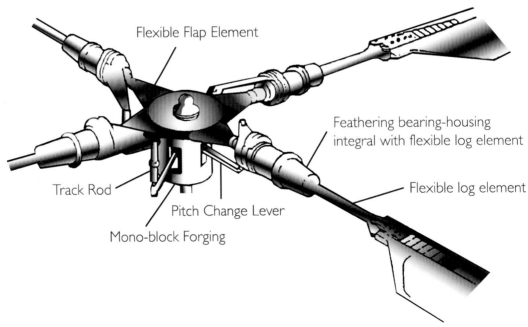

Fig. 9.6   Semi-rigid rotor.

111

9.12.2   **The Teetering Head.** The gimbal mounted, or teetering rotor head has
two blades which are rigidly connected to each other with a fixed, built in
coning angle, and is in turn gimbal mounted to the rotor shaft. It does
suffer from inherent vibration problems which are the result of the
teetering action of the blades in flight. To minimise this, the weighted bar
below the rotor acts like a gyroscope, it tends to maintain a given plane
and through a system of levers and hydraulic dampers the collective and
cyclic control levers are linked to the bar. Any tilt of the rotor disc tends
to be corrected automatically by the system of levers.

9.12.3   When a cyclic pitch change is made on a teetering head, the plane of the
disc will alter. The Total Rotor Thrust (acting through the rotor shaft) is
also tilted. It is the moment set up about the C of G that causes the attitude
to change. See fig. 9.7.

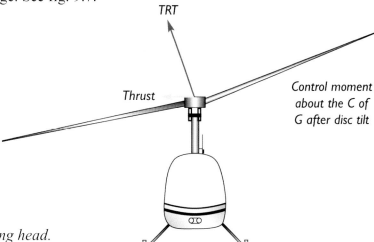

Fig. 9.7   *Teetering head.*

9.12.4   **The Fully Articulated Head.** Allows the rotor blades to move about three
hinges. Each individual blade is allowed to flap vertically about a
horizontal hinge (flapping hinge) and to move in the plane of rotation
about a vertical hinge (drag hinge).

9.12.5   These hinges consist of trunnions mounted in bearings. The blade is also
allowed to change pitch about the feathering hinge which is usually
outboard of the flapping and drag hinges.

9.12.6   When a cyclic pitch change is made with a fully articulated head, the
plane of the disk will alter and tilts the total rotor thrust vector. The point
where the cyclic force acts when changing the fuselage attitude is not only
the shaft, but the plus and minus inputs of cyclic pitch. This not only
changes the plane of the disc but are sensed at the flapping hinges.

9.12.7   See fig.9.8. The single force vector is augmented by a couple set up about
the flapping hinge geometry. It is therefore very effective. However, there
is still a lag in fuselage reaction to cyclic input changes. It can be seen
from fig.9.8 that if the flapping hinge positions are further away from hub,
then the couple would be even more effective.

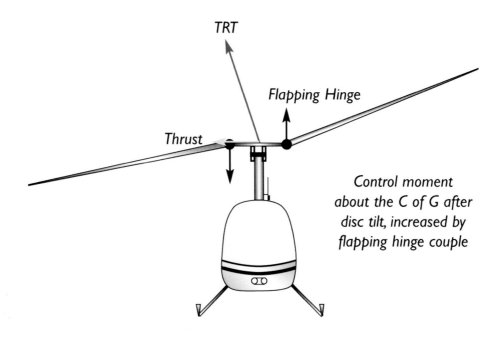

Fig.9.8   Fully articulated rotor head.

9.12.8   **The Semi-Rigid and Rigid Rotor**. Improved performance, better handling, simplified construction and in some cases less maintenance can be achieved with the use of the semi-rigid rotor over the fully articulated type.

9.12.9   In place of the flapping and drag hinges the semi-rigid rotor head employs the use of a hub assembly which comprises a flexible flapping element and a flexible drag element. The hub, and the flexible flapping and drag elements, are normally manufactured from a number of forged titanium components. Titanium has been used in manufacture due to the very high stress loads experienced in this type of construction, which could result in subsequent fatigue problems. The flexible portions or elements of the hub assembly allow the blade to move in the flapping and dragging planes but are more rigid than conventional hinges.

9.12.10   The rigid rotor is similar to the semi-rigid rotor but the rotor blades are less flexible and the rotor hub is rigidly constructed. The natural frequency of the rigid rotor is very high and as a result, air and ground resonance effects are less of a problem.

9.12.11   The control loads with a rigid rotor are very high, and stability is difficult to achieve. One system in use to resolve the stability problem is where a gyro is mounted on the rotor hub, so that with suitable linkage, the pilot controls the gyro, which in turn stabilises and controls the rotor head.

113

9.12.12　In the rigid rotor case, cyclic pitch changes set up a powerful aerodynamic couple which alters the fuselage attitude almost instantaneously. The couple is estimated to be the equivalent of placing flapping hinges on an articulated head at 17% rotor radius from the shaft. Flexing properties of the blade account for the insignificant lag that does exist. To generalise, it can be said the rigid rotor type is more rigid than the semi-rigid rotor. See fig 9.9.

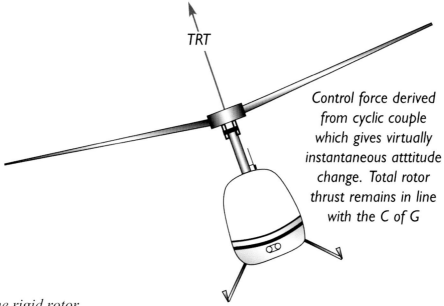

TRT

Control force derived from cyclic couple which gives virtually instantaneous atttitude change. Total rotor thrust remains in line with the C of G

Fig. 9.9　The rigid rotor.

9.12.13　**The Hiller system**. Two "paddles" are mounted at right angles to the rotor blades and rotate with them, see fig 9.10. Cyclic pitch control is affected by changing the pitch angles of the paddles. The resulting flapping motion of the paddles will apply a cyclic-pitch change to the rotor blades and the disc will tilt in the usual way.

9.12.14　If a rotor blade should flap up due to a disturbance, the linkage to the paddles is such that a change in pitch angle of the paddle, and its resulting flapping, will give the required pitch correction to the offending blade.

9.12.15　**The Delta Three Hinge**. Instead of the flapping hinge being mounted at right angles to the span of the blade, it is set at an angle, see fig 9.11. When a blade flaps up, the pitch angle of the blade is reduced. This tends to reduce the angle of flap of the blade.

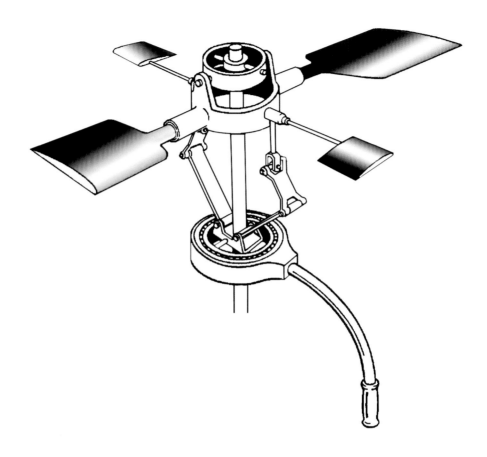

Fig. 9.10   The Hiller system. Two "Paddles" mounted at 90° to the main rotor.

9.12.16   The intention is that stability of the helicopter will be assisted because dissymmetry of lift will not cause such a large inclination of the disc due to flapping. The straightforward hinge as shown is not practical to use in a helicopter because the pitch-change mechanism will be affected.

9.13   Comparison of Control Forces

9.13.1   If the same cyclic force were applied to the three main rotor systems, the rigid rotor would be the most effective in changing the aircraft attitude, the fully articulated rotor less effective and the teetering head rotor least effective in terms of control power. Therefore, control power determines the aircraft manoeuvrability and, to some degree, speed range.

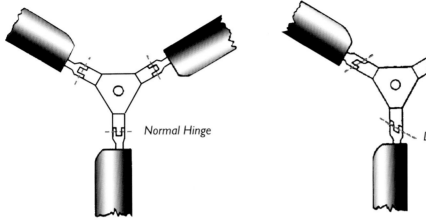

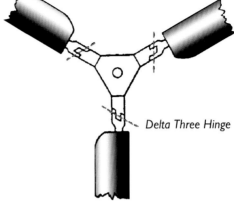

Normal Hinge

Delta Three Hinge

When a flade flaps, the pitch
angle remains the same.

When a flade flaps up,
the pitch angle is reduced.

Fig. 9.11   Normal and Delta-Three hinges.

10 DESIGN, CONSTRUCTION AND DEVELOPMENT

10.1 Introduction

10.1.1 In general terms the helicopter is a low speed aircraft, but, because of its ability to hover and to take off and land vertically, it is particularly suitable for many unique roles. This chapter deals generally with the design of helicopters in common use in civil aviation today.

10.2 Types and Configurations

10.2.1 There are four main types of rotorcraft which may be categorised according to the methods used to provide lift and propulsion.

1   Gyroplane. The gyroplane or "auto gyro" has a freely rotating wing supplying the aerodynamic force for lift; all forward thrust is supplied by a separate propeller as in a conventional aircraft.

2   Pure Helicopter. The pure helicopter has powered rotating wings supplying all necessary aerodynamic forces for lift and propulsion.

3   Compound Helicopter. The major part of the lift of a compound helicopter is supplied at all times by the rotor, but supplemented by power units or stub wings, mainly at high speed.

4   Convertible Helicopter. The convertible helicopter is capable of modifying its configuration during flight so that lift is transferred from rotating wings to other fixed wings, and vice versa.

10.3 Engine Mounting Position

10.3.1 Most current helicopters have the engine power unit mounted on top of the fuselage, or within the fuselage behind the pilot. Some early models had the engine mounted in the nose. There is a mechanical transmission system to drive the rotors. An alternative method of drive is to duct hot or cold air from the power unit to the blade tips. Although this latter method simplifies the transmission, it results in an excessively high noise level and creates problems of sealing and cooling of the blades.

10.3.2 If a power unit of a very high power/weight ratio is used, such as the ram jet, it can be mounted at the rotor tips. This method has the advantage that it requires no transmission and there is no torque reaction on the fuselage. However, it results in very high blade loading and noise levels.

10.3.3   The most common configuration is a single main rotor with a separate tail rotor to balance torque reaction. Sometimes however, two main rotors are used which contra rotate to balance torque reaction. These are normally arranged in tandem, but can be arranged co-axially with some loss of efficiency, or side by side intermeshing.

10.4   Pilot's Controls

10.4.1   The helicopter pilot's main controls are as follows:

1   **Collective Pitch Lever**. This is usually operated by the pilot's left hand and controls the total lift produced by the rotor. Movement of the collective pitch lever simultaneously alters the pitch of all the blades by the same amount.

2   **Cyclic Pitch Control Column**. This is usually operated by the pilot's right hand and varies the pitch of each blade cyclically, so tilting the rotor disc and enabling the helicopter to move horizontally. In forward flight, the effect of moving the cyclic pitch control is similar to that of a fixed wing aircraft control column.

3   **Yaw Pedals**. The yaw pedals are operated by the pilot's feet and vary the force produced by the tail rotor to oppose torque reaction, thus controlling the movement of the helicopter about the vertical axis. The sense of movement is identical to that of the rudder pedals of a conventional aircraft. Yaw pedals are sometimes referred to as anti-torque pedals or simply rudder pedals even though this latter title can be misleading on most helicopter types.

4   **Throttle**. Most modern helicopters do not have a pilot-operated throttle; the engine speed is controlled by the variation in pilot demands of the rotor. Where a throttle is used, it is mounted on the end of the collective pitch lever and usually takes the form of a twist grip.

10.5   Control/Rotor RPM

10.5.1   Movement of the collective pitch lever will require changes of power because of the variation of lift, and, therefore, the induced drag on the rotor blades. An interconnecting linkage is normally fitted between the collective pitch lever and the power unit so that when collective pitch is varied the power setting is varied by a corresponding amount to keep the speed of rotation of the rotor essentially constant. In most modern free turbine-engined helicopters, rotor RPM is maintained by centrifugal governors or by computer control of the fuel flow.

11   HELICOPTER ENGINES

11.1   Introduction

11.1.1   Most civil training helicopters are powered by piston engines. See fig 11.1 for examples of piston engine installations. However today, with the exception of these light helicopters, the majority are powered by gas turbines. Although the piston engine can be said to be economical on fuel and relatively cheap to maintain, the gas turbine engines designed for use in helicopters give a much higher power/weight ratio coupled with greater reliability.

Robinson R22

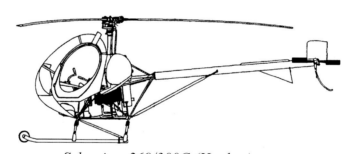

Schweizer 269/300C (Hughes)

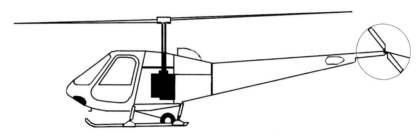

Enstrom F-28

Fig. 11.1   Piston engine installations

11.2   Piston Engines

11.2.1   Helicopter piston engines are normally constructed making wide use of light alloys in order to save as much weight as possible. Almost all modern aircraft engines are of the air cooled type and helicopter engines are no exception to the rule, however, due to the installation requirements it is usually necessary to employ the use of a large fan to assist in cooling the engine. On most helicopters using such a fan, 10% of engine power is devoted to its drive whilst in the hover. Fig. 11.2 shows a piston engine and drive chain to the rotors.

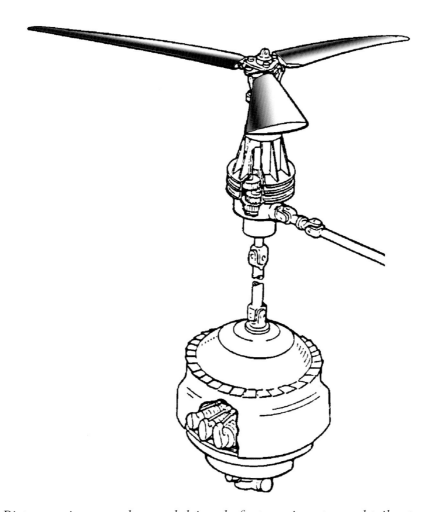

Fig. 11.2   Piston engine, gear box and drive shafts to main rotor and tail rotor.

11.3   Gas Turbines

11.3.1   Gas turbine engines designed for use in helicopters are usually of the free turbine or turboshaft type. The essential difference between a conventional gas turbine and the free turbine or turboshaft type is that the latter has a one, or two stage turbine devoted to providing a power take-off to the helicopter main rotor gearbox. Generally the free turbine engine has a gas generator of one or two spools and both axial and centrifugal compressors are used in different designs.

120

11.3.2   Free turbine engines were used as a direct replacement, with modifications, for the piston engines that were fitted. As a result most were fitted in the nose of the helicopter, however, more modern installations have placed the engine or engines on top of the airframe adjacent to the main rotor gearbox. This type of installation has helped to simplify the design and fitting of transmission systems to the airframe and leave the cabin clear of major obstructions below. See fig. 11.3.

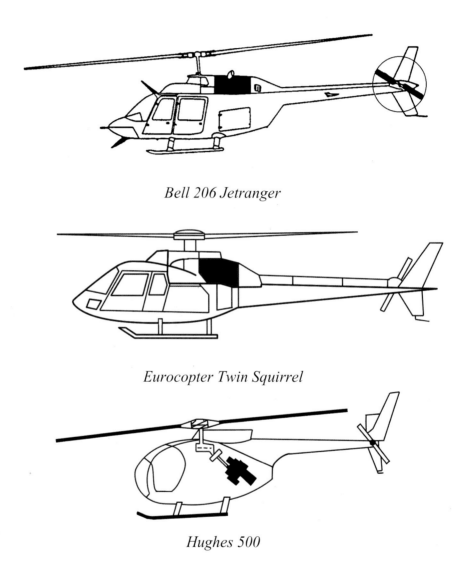

Bell 206 Jetranger

Eurocopter Twin Squirrel

Hughes 500

Fig.11.3   Gas turbine engine installations.

11.3.3   The modern generation of engines are compact, light-weight, highly reliable, easily maintainable and have a relatively low specific fuel consumption. They are supplied complete with built-in torque meter and engine reduction gearbox, and the power take-off can be from the front or the rear of the engine.

11.3.4   An important feature of modern engines is the use of a modular concept; his permits the replacement of major assemblies without the need for highly specialised equipment, and in some cases, without the need for performance checking.

11.3.5   From the maintenance and service aspects, the adoption of condition monitoring is becoming more widespread. In addition to normal flight instruments, modern engines have provision for accelerometers to measure incipient vibrations and provision for internal inspection by introscopes. Provision is also made for self-sealing magnetic chip detectors and oil sampling for spectrometric oil analysis.

11.3.6   These facilities permit regular monitoring and enable incipient defects to be recognised and rectified before damage occurs. Engine control systems are normally mechanical, or hydro-mechanical coupled electrically and electronically with safety and indication systems.

11.3.7   Some modern engines are equipped with computer-controlled automatic fuel systems. During normal operation the engine is automatically controlled to give constant speed of the engine and rotor system. The optimum engine/rotor speed is selected by a speed select lever, and the varying power demands made by change of rotor pitch are accommodated by the automatic fuel control computer.

11.3.8   The computer varies the rate of fuel flow to suit the engine power demands. The computer works in conjunction with a collective pitch anticipator unit and a throttle actuator. Provision is made in some systems for rapid change-over to manual control in the event of failure of the electrical or computer systems.

12 TAIL ROTORS AND ANTI-TORQUE DEVICES

12.1 **Introduction**. The tail rotor has been the universal anti-torque device for single rotor helicopters. There are several other devices introduced in recent years, one is the "Fenestron", which will be described briefly, and although anti- torque jets have been used experimentally, more recently, an anti torque jet system is now available on a production helicopters, the McDonnell Douglas MD 600N and 902 (Notar) (No tail rotor).

12.1.2 A typical tail rotor system is shown in fig. 12.1. The movement of the spider is controlled by a screw jack (not shown) which is rotated by cables on a pulley, the cables leading to the yaw pedals.

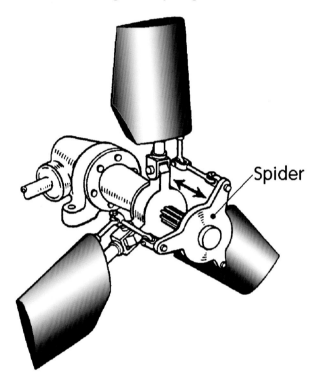

Fig. 12.1   The tail rotor blades are controlled by the spider moving in or out.

12.1.3 **The Articulated tail rotor.** The tail rotor hub is similar in construction to the fully articulated main rotor hub, but only flapping and feathering hinges are necessary. See fig 12.2.

12.1.4 There are similarities in this rotor to a main articulated rotor. There are feathering hinges to control thrust, and flapping hinges to minimise dissymmetry of tail rotor thrust by advancing and retreating blades when in forward flight. The geometry of the flapping hinge even applies the concept of the DELTA THREE principle (see para. 9.12.15) in overcoming the dissymmetry problem. Drag hinges are not normally fitted to tail rotors as blades are relatively short and the amount of drag does not justify the mechanism.

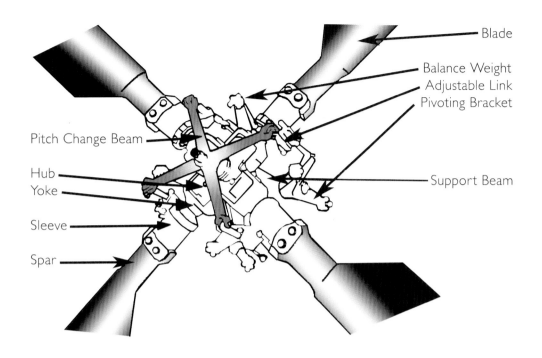

Fig. 12.2   *Conventional tail rotor (Articulated type).*

12.1.5   The hub is splined and secured to the horizontal drive shaft of the tail rotor gearbox, and pitch changes are accomplished through the pitch change beam and pitch control shaft which is located in the centre of the tail rotor gear-box. Each blade is counterbalanced by weights attached to the hub to assist the pilot to increase pitch.

12.1.6   **Teetering type tail rotor**. The teetering type tail rotor is gimbal mounted in a similar manner to a gimbal mounted teetering main rotor. Its drive is achieved through a tail rotor gear-box in the same way as an articulated type, but is simplified by the blades requiring only a feathering hinge, see fig 12.3.

12.1.7   Dissymmetry of thrust by advancing and retreating blades in forward flight is overcome by a Delta-Three hinge effect being incorporated in its construction.

12.1.8   **Tail rotor blade**. The tail rotor blade is normally of all metal construction. The leading edge and spar section is formed of a light alloy extruded section. The light alloy sheet skin is reinforced internally by a honeycomb core and bonded to the spar.

12.1.9   A polyurethane or stainless steel strip is bonded along the leading edge of the blade to prevent erosion. The blade is also balanced chordwise and spanwise.

124

12.1.10   **Shrouded tail rotor (Fenestron).** The conventional tail rotor operates in difficult vibratory and aerodynamic conditions due to its position at the rear of the fuselage and the very severe interference with the main rotor stream, the fuselage wake and the fin. See figure 12.4.

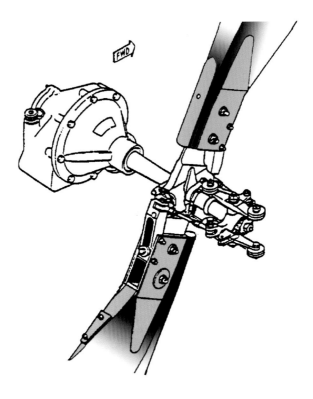

Fig. 12.3   Conventional tail rotor (Teetering type).

12.1.11   Due to these severe operating conditions, the conventional tail rotor is submitted to considerable stresses which impose a limit to the service life of its components and also generally demand a rugged design. Further disadvantages are its susceptibility to foreign object damage and its danger to ground personnel.

12.1.12   One solution to the disadvantages of the conventional tail rotor is the shrouded tail rotor or "Fenestron". It consists of a rotor with several small blades hinged about the feathering axis only, and rotating within a shroud provided in the tail boom or fin of the helicopter, see fig 12.4.

12.1.13   This system is light and less vulnerable to damage by either loose objects or obstructions, and is very much less of a hazard to ground personnel. However, a servo unit is required for pitch control because of the high and variable aerodynamic forces encountered in the hover. There is also a structural problem in finding the space for the shroud within the tail boom or fin.

12.1.14   Fins are also fitted to some helicopters to maintain directional control. Those helicopters that do not have torque reaction, ie., counter rotation sets of main rotor blades. Also, a fin is fitted to helicopters that use the "Fenestron" system to give additional stability and in some cases camber is provided on one side of the fin (see fig 12.4) to produce a side force to assist in counteracting main rotor torque. This results in a reduction of drag in forward flight that would otherwise be generated by the action of the "Fenestron" or tail rotor.

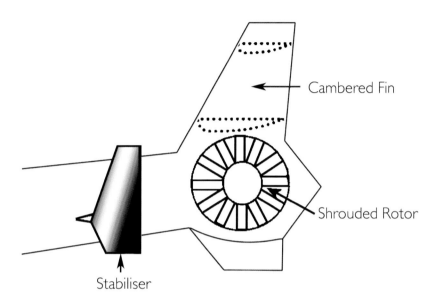

Fig. 12.4   Shrouded tail rotor (Fenestron).

13   HELICOPTER TRANSMISSION SYSTEMS

13.1   Introduction

13.1.1   The transmission system (or chain) is the means by which power from the engine is applied to the rotors. The difficulty with helicopters is that the rotors are mounted on the top of the helicopter fuselage, and the engine must be located where the drive chain is not too long. Mounting engines on top of the fuselage keeps the drive chain short, it also raises the helicopters C of G, but reduces the number of gearboxes, with the exception of the tail rotor. In fig.13.1 is shown a drive chain as fitted to a gas turbine powered helicopter.

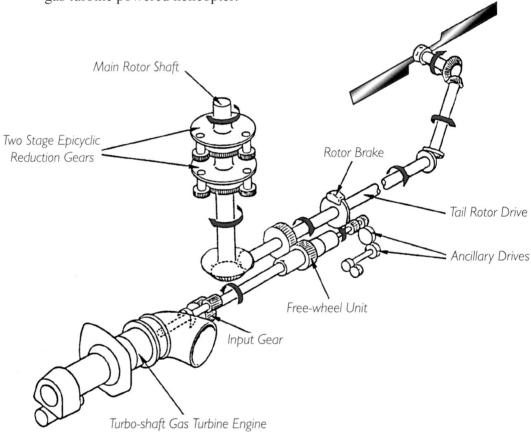

Fig. 13.1   Helicopter transmission system. Turbo-shaft gas turbine engine.

13.1.2   **Components.** The main components in a drive system are: Output Drive Shafts and Reduction gear/s, Free Wheel Unit, Main Rotor shaft and Gear box, Tail Rotor Drive Shaft and gear box/es, Rotor Brake, and a number of ancillary drives. See fig. 13.1

13.1.3   **Free Wheel Unit.** The free wheel unit automatically disengages the drive in the drive chain to the rotor. This is a safety feature in the event of engine failure. This means that the drag of a dead engine and ancillaries does not impose drag on the rotor.

127

13.1.4   One type of free wheel unit employs a coiled spring, which increases in diameter in the direction of the drive, and decreases in diameter in the reverse case. This provides a drive against a sleeve in normal power, but should the engine fail, the drive does not operate in the overrun condition. There are other types of mechanical systems used in free wheel units.

13.1.5   **Main Rotor Gearbox.** This is a substantial gearbox. It takes the engine drive through epicyclic gears to the main rotor shaft. There are other take-offs to provide a drive to the tail rotor, alternators or generators, oil pump, hydraulic pump, also tachometers for engine/gearbox monitoring. The main gearbox is housed in an alloy casting with steel liners for bearings and bolt threads. The gearbox is pressure lubricated by a spur gear oil pump. The base of the gearbox is usually bolted to the airframe. There is an oil cooler radiator, which is fan assisted, as the helicopter not always has ram air available.

13.1.6   **Main Rotor Brake.** The rotor brake is necessary to hold the main rotor stationary. This is used to allow the main power unit to run up to operating speed. Also, it is used to stop the main rotor on shutting down. There are a number of braking methods; the simplest on small helicopters are operated by a cable. The actual brake could be like a car type drum brake, or a disk brake, mounted up near the main gearbox. On some helicopters, the brake is mounted on the intermediate drive shaft to the tail rotor. See fig. 13.1.

13.1.7   **Intermediate Drive Shaft.** This is another drive shaft from the main rotor gearbox that exits at right angles to the main rotor shaft. This drive shaft is positioned along the fuselage to drive the tail rotor. There is a tail rotor gearbox, and some helicopters have a further gearbox in this chain. As this shaft is quite long, it is mounted in anti vibration bearings, and flexible couplings to allow for fuselage flexing.

13.1.8   **Intermediate and Tail Rotor Gearboxes.** These gearboxes allow for a tail rotor drive shaft to follow the geometry of the helicopter fuselage. The drive shaft may have to change direction more than once in large helicopters, and this is where a gearbox is necessary. However, the final tail rotor gearbox is a reduction gearbox, and also changes the direction of the drive 90° to the tail rotor. The gears are spiral bevel gears. The pitch control mechanism is also accommodated in the tail rotor gearbox. See fig. 13.2. . The tail rotor gearbox is immersion and splash lubricated.

13.1.9   The pitch of the tail rotor is controlled by the pilot's yaw pedals. A pitch changing control shaft passes through the centre of the gearbox. (See section 12 on tail rotors). Movement in and out of the control shaft actuates a control beam, which changes the pitch angle of the tail rotor blades. The pitch control shaft is splined onto the rotor output shaft, and therefore rotates with it.

13.1.10   **Torque meter Transducer.** It is important that the pilot is able to monitor the torque on a suitable display in the cockpit, and check that torque is maintained at the proper level in the transmission chain. Early helicopter engines using piston engines, when converted to turbine power were not able to display the increased torque that was now available. Furthermore, twin turbine installations enabled the helicopter to operate on one engine, so power output had to limited. Torque is measured by the use of strain gages positioned in the drive chain. Referred to as Transducers.

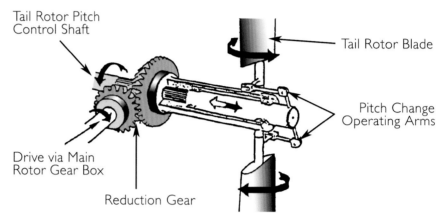

Fig. 13.2   Tail rotor gearbox.

13.2   Gearbox Condition Monitoring

13.2.1   The use of magnetic chip detectors are used in gear boxes similar to engines. The chip detector is mounted usually in the sump. Ferrous particles are collected on the magnet, and would be checked periodically. Only ferrous particles are collected this way, non ferrous particles are found (if any) by spectrometric oil analysis, although this will also detect non ferrous particles in suspension. This is an efficient method of detecting incipient gearbox failures.

13.3   Conformal Gears

13.3.1   As helicopter gearboxes are subjected to large and continuous loads, the conformal gear mesh offers a better load transmission through the gear contact than the involute gear mesh. There is a bigger area contact between the gear teeth and thus higher loads can be accommodated than the involute gears, which have only a line contact between teeth. See fig. 13.3A and 13.3B.

13.3.2   A further advantage of a gearbox using conformal gears, is that a reduction is possible in the number of teeth. This means a greater gear reduction in each stage for the same load, and fewer gears. This is important as it enhances reliability.

13.3.3   Conformal gears allow a smaller size and weight of the main gearbox. Efficiency is improved as fewer gears and bearings are used, so less overall friction. However, a conformal gearbox is manufactured to close tolerances and requires a heavier gearbox casting. It must be remembered that gearboxes can distort under load, so the housing has to be very rigid and is heavier.

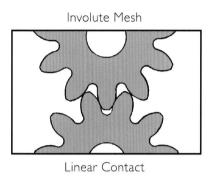

Fig. 13.3A Involute mesh gears.

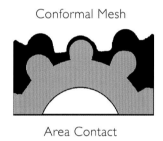

Fig. 13.3B   Conformal mesh gears.

14   LIMITS TO HIGH SPEED FLIGHT

14.1   **Introduction**. The designer has a number of factors to take into account when trying to design a helicopter that can fly fast, but whatever are his solutions, there remain problems for the pilot. A brief discussion is now presented to familiarise the private pilot with some of the more important limitations.

14.2   **Power Available**. In level flight V_{max} (maximum speed) is limited by the Power Available. A higher speed is possible in the descent.

14.3   **Structural Strength**. As speed increases, both the forces on the Rotor and Transmission and the levels of vibration increase. Apart from the limitation of the strength of the airframe and other components against these forces, the combination of stress and vibration causes **Fatigue.**

14.3.1   Fatigue is a weakening of metal over a period of time, with possible eventual failure. There is a level of stress and vibration below which there will be no fatigue, but increases above this level cause the time to failure to decrease very rapidly.

14.3.2   Because of their greater weight, it is usually impractical to make components so strong that they do not suffer fatigue. Therefore, the level of vibration must be kept below a limit chosen by the designer and components are replaced before their fatigue life expires. This sets a limit to the very maximum speed.

14.4   **Cyclic Control**. As airspeed increases the rotor disc flaps back relative to the cyclic control position, and the attitude of the disc is maintained by moving the cyclic stick forwards. There will be a speed at which the cyclic is fully forward and no further acceleration is possible (except outside the safe flight envelope). The amount of forward cyclic control is reduced if the helicopter is loaded with the C of G aft, see fig 14.1.

Fig. 14.1   Centre of gravity (C of G) aft of the rotor shaft axis.

14.4.1   Although as forward speed increases, the fuselage pitches nose down, the amount of pitching down is limited by the horizontal stabiliser at the tail. See fig 14.2. The helicopter hangs tail low with aft loading, limiting the amount of available forward cyclic control.

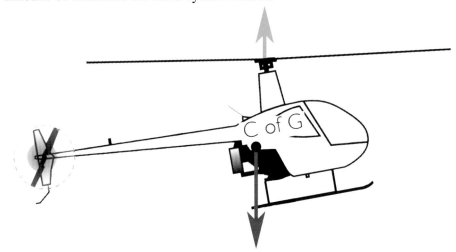

Fig. 14.2   Helicopter hangs tail low with aft loading, limiting forward cyclic control, and hence maximum speed.

14.5   **Airflow Reversal**. Flapback is caused by the difference in the relative velocities of the advancing and retreating blades in forward flight. The velocity of the retreating blade is reduced and there is an airspeed where the root of the blade, which is the slowest part, has zero relative velocity and no thrust is produced. As airspeed is increased, the airflow is reversed to greater distance from the blade root. This results in a loss of rotor thrust. See fig 14.3.

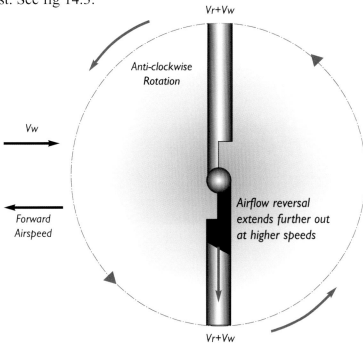

Fig. 14.3   Airflow reversal on retreating blade.
(Vr = Velocity of rotator, Vw = free air velocity).

14.5.1   The reduction of rotor thrust on the retreating blade by **Airflow Reversal** is countered by greater cyclic control and hence, the retreating blade operates at an increasingly higher pitch angle and consequently, at a higher angle of attack.

14.6   **Retreating Blade Stall**. Due to airflow reversal, the retreating blade will be operating at a higher angle of attack, the angle of attack being maximum when the blade is half-way round on the retreating side. As the forward speed of the helicopter increases, the greater must become the retreating blade's angle of attack, and eventually a forward speed will be reached where the retreating blade will stall.

14.6.1   The large sudden loss in rotor thrust will cause the blade to flap down, but instead of flapping to equality, the effect will be simply to stall the blade even further. The stall starts at the tip first and spreads inboard as shown in the pattern in fig 14.4.

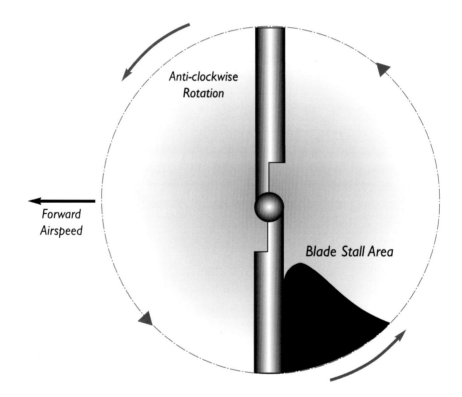

Fig. 14.4   Retreating blade stall.

14.6.2   In figure 14.5 can be seen the reason why the stall commences at the blade tip. Despite washout, which will to a degree offset the angle of attack along the blade length, the highest angle of attack will be at the blade tip in forward flight.

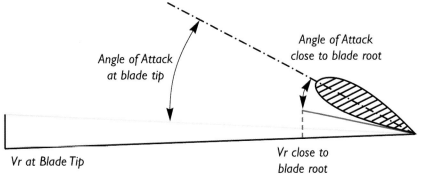

Fig. 14.5   Stall at the tip and not at the root.

14.6.3   The onset of retreating blade stall will display the following characteristics:

1.   Cyclic stick shaking
2.   Erratic stick forces
3.   Roughness of the rotor

Note: *If these initial conditions are ignored, the next stage is a pitch-up tendency, and the helicopter will roll over towards the retreating blade side.*

4.   If the stall is severe then there is a substantial loss of control, if not complete loss of control.

14.7   Causes of Retreating Blade Stall

1.   Pulling high "G" forces
2.   Flying at high forward speed
3.   Flying in turbulent air
4.   Using abrupt or excessive control excursions
5.   A high AUM/High density altitude will also aggravate the situation

14.8   **Recovery**. The recovery action will depend upon which of the above in-flight conditions are prevailing when the stall symptoms are recognised. Recovery will normally be made by reducing forward speed, reducing collective pitch, reducing the severity of the manoeuvre or combining these recovery actions together.

14.9   **Compressibility**. In developing the formulae for lift and drag on an aerofoil, it is assumed that the air is incompressible. However, at high relative airspeeds, approaching the speed of sound, the character of the airflow is changed and account must be taken of compressibility.

14.9.1   In the hover, the tip of a characteristic turbine powered single rotor helicopter is travelling at about 210 m per sec. In forward flight at 150 kt, the advancing blade tip has a relative velocity of 295 m per sec. The velocity of sound at sea level is 340 m per sec and it can be seen how close this margin is, and therefore, compressibility is significant.

14.9.2   The main effects are:

1.   To reduce the Lift Drag ratio (L/D ratio), requiring more power for the same TRT.
2.   To increase the pitching moment on the aerofoil which is normally very small. This requires greater control forces and leads to vibration.
3.   To produce shock waves which increase vibration and noise.

14.9.3   These effects can be reduced by using a high speed aerofoil section or sweep back at the blade tips. Any such solutions have penalties however at low speeds.

14.10   **Avoiding Mast Bumping.** Mast bumping is where the clearance between rotor head and the mast decrease and meet, and this could result in the rotor separating from the mast. Clearly, the answer to mast bumping is to avoid flight conditions that produce this situation. This can take place under conditions of reduced or negative-g. If a pilot inadvertently finds himself in a zero or negative-g state he must react with the correct instincts and particularly resist the natural tendency to move cyclic left when right roll starts.

14.10.1   Total rotor thrust must be restored. To do this, the pilot must reload the disc by either moving the cyclic aft or increasing collective. Of the two techniques, increasing collective is less desirable because the associated increase in power tends to produce more yaw problems, particularly under low-g conditions. Also, tests have shown a tendency for main rotor underspeed or gearbox overtorque when the collective recovery technique is used.

14.10.2   **Recovery from Low and Zero-G.** The most effective recovery technique from a low or zero-g condition is: apply gentle rearward cyclic to reload the rotor (reintroducing a positive-g situation), then use left cyclic to roll the aircraft level.

14.10.3   **Mast Bumping-Summary**

1.   Avoid, low, zero or negative-g situations especially when flying teetering-hinge helicopters.
2.   An unintended right roll may commence during low, zero or negative-g conditions.
3.   Left cyclic will not stop a right roll under low, zero or negative-g conditions and can rapidly lead to mast bumping.
4.   Total rotor thrust must be restored before lateral cyclic becomes effective.
5.   Aft cyclic, applied gently, is the most effective way to reload the disc.

15   AERO ENGINES

15.1   Principle

15.1.1   The piston engine produces power by converting fuel (petrol) into heat, and heat into energy. The energy is harnessed by mechanical means and the resultant power is then transmitted by a rotating shaft, which is made to rotate the propeller or rotor/s of an aircraft. It is self evident that when ignited a liquid fuel will burn and produce heat but how the heat is able to provide mechanical energy will be less obvious until it is realised that heat can be applied to air, and heated air will expand very considerably exerting great pressures if contained in some way. Aero engines are "internal combustion engines" which describes engines where energy is provided by burning fuel inside the engine, in contrast with such things as steam turbines where combustion of the fuel takes place outside the engine in a steam boiler.

15.1.2   The basic components of an engine consist of a number of cylinders and pistons with connecting rods to a crankshaft. One end of the connecting rod is attached to the base of a piston, and the other end to the crankshaft, which converts the straight up and down action of the piston into a rotary motion which turns a propeller or rotor.

15.1.3   To enable the necessary cycle of events to occur, an induction and carburation system, an ignition system, and an exhaust system are required. These systems respectively control the air and fuel supply, provide a spark to ignite the fuel, and guide the exit of the expelled products of combustion. Due to the relative movements of many of the engine components, a lubrication and oil cooling system will also be needed to reduce friction, and disperse heat created between the moving parts.

15.1.4   **The four stroke cycle**. Piston engines used in aircraft operate on the principle of the "Otto" cycle, a name derived from the inventor Nicholas A. Otto who built the first successful engine operating by means of pistons moving back and forth within cylinders (reciprocating). This cycle comprises four strokes to complete one cycle and it can be used with one or more cylinders.

15.1.5   With helicopters, conventional aero engines (adapted from fixed wing aeroplanes), have been used, and this is still very much the case with small piston powered helicopters, but the mountings are often vertical with special ducting to assist in engine cooling. Only with turbine power can it be said that power units have become specialised units for helicopters.

15.1.6   The four stroke piston engine must be understood by PPL students. The four strokes are termed Intake (or Induction), Compression, Expansion (or Power) and Exhaust. See fig 15.1 which illustrates these four strokes.

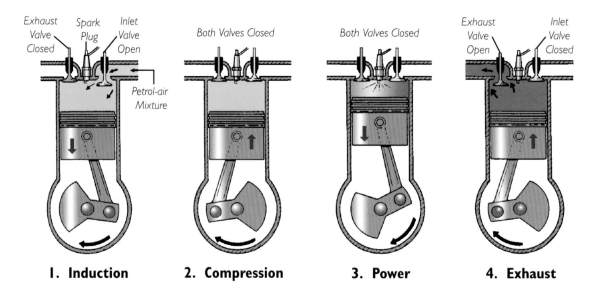

| 1. Induction | 2. Compression | 3. Power | 4. Exhaust |

Fig 15.1   The four stroke cycle

15.1.7   The four strokes of a petrol engine are now described:

1.   In (1) the Induction stroke, fuel/air mixture enters the cylinder by atmospheric pressure (unless the engine is supercharged and the pressure would then be above atmospheric) as the piston moves downwards. Notice that the inlet valve is open.

2.   In (2) the Compression stroke, the fuel/air mix is compressed and a spark generated by the spark plug ignites it just before the top of the stroke. Notice that the inlet and the exhaust valves are closed.

3.   In (3) the Power stroke, the fuel/air mixture burns and expands, releasing energy to push the piston downwards. Notice that both valves are still closed.

4.   In (4) the Exhaust stroke, the burnt gases expelled through the exhaust port. Notice that the exhaust valve is open.

15.1.8   This cycle then continues to repeat itself throughout the period the engine is running. It should be noted that the power stroke occurs once, and the crankshaft revolves twice, for every four strokes of the piston.

15.1.9   To increase the engine power developed by this cycle and create more smoothness in operation, more cylinders are added with the power strokes being timed to occur at different but successive intervals during the revolution of the crankshaft. Fig. 15.2 shows the arrangement of cylinders and other components in a horizontally opposed 4 cylinder aero engine.

137

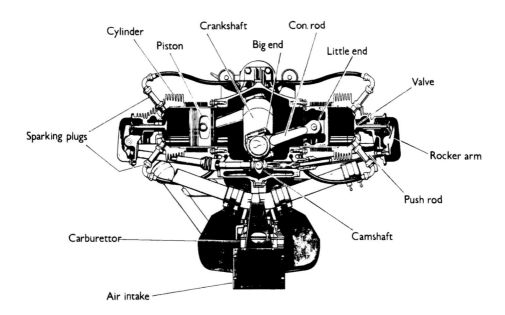

Cylinder
Piston
Crankshaft
Big end
Con. rod
Little end
Valve
Sparking plugs
Rocker arm
Push rod
Carburettor
Camshaft
Air intake

Fig. 15.2   Section through a typical air-cooled horizontally opposed engine.
***Note**: for helicopter use, the cooling air is often fan assisted to improve the cooling air circulation, as there is little ram air available, unlike a fixed-wing aeroplane.*

15.1.10   The inlet and exhaust valves through which the fuel/air mixture is introduced and the exhaust gases expelled from the cylinders of the engine, slide rapidly to and fro in their guides during the operation of the engine. These valves are usually activated by rocker arms driven either directly from a camshaft or indirectly from the camshaft via push rods.

15.1.11   As the power developed by the engine is a function of the amount of fuel/air mixture which can be forced into the cylinder during the intake stroke, it can readily be appreciated that the amount of power developed depends among other things, on the size of the intake port and the length of time the inlet valve is open.

15.1.12   Because the inlet stroke occurs once for every two revolutions of the crankshaft, it can be seen that when the engine is running at 2500 revolutions per minute (a typical high cruising RPM), the intake valve will open 1250 times per minute or some 20 times per second. Therefore it is clear that a major problem in obtaining a given power output is in getting sufficient mixture into the cylinder during each intake stroke, i.e. to improve its volumetric efficiency.

15.1.13   **Valve Timing.** One way in which this can be improved is to arrange the valve cycle so that the inlet valve opens just before the piston reaches the top of its stroke (Top Dead Centre or TDC) and closes just after it reaches the bottom of its stroke (Bottom Dead Centre or BDC). This is technically known as **Valve Lead and Valve Lag.**

15.1.14   In fig 15.3 it is shown diagrammatically how this is arranged. Notice that the exhaust valves open just before the exhaust stroke commences and also close later. As the pressure from the burning gases have done most of its useful work, opening the valve just before BDC means that what pressure is left can be used to help evacuate the burnt gases. Also, it increases the time available for the cylinder to be scavenged of the burnt gases.

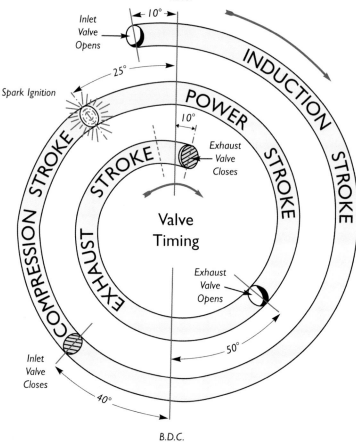

Fig. 15.3   Valve timing in the four stroke cycle.

15.1.15   The less the volume of burnt gases remaining, the greater will be the amount of fuel/air mixture introduced into the cylinder during the inlet stroke. The time when both inlet and exhaust valves are open in conjunction is known as the **Valve Overlap, or Valve Overlap Period.**

15.1.16   It can be observed that the moment when the sparking plug is activated is just prior to the commencement of the downward movement of the piston (power stroke). This is to give the burning gases a chance to expand and create maximum pressure on the crown of the piston at the moment it commences its downward stroke.

15.1.17   Although it would appear that the effect of valve overlap can at best give only a slight improvement to the power output of the engine, it should nevertheless be appreciated that in view of the minute period of time that the valves are open during each cycle, any increase in this period will produce a significant increase to the amount of fuel/air charge induced into the cylinder.

15.2   Ignition Systems

15.2.1   The purpose of the ignition system is to provide a high tension spark to each cylinder of the engine in the correct firing order and at a predetermined number of degrees ahead of the top dead centre (TDC) position of each piston in its cylinder.

15.2.2   **Principles**. Regardless of the type of engine the basic requirements for reciprocating engine ignition systems are the same. The most common system used in light aero engines is the dual ignition type, consisting of two high tension magnetos linked by an electric cable harness to two sparking plugs in each cylinder.

15.2.3   **Magnetos**. The magneto is a type of self contained engine driven generator which is not connected in any way with the aircraft's main electrical system but uses a permanent magnet as a source of initial energy. Nevertheless, the aircraft battery is used initially to activate the rotating element of the magneto via the starter system.

15.2.4   Once the engine has been started, the starter system is disengaged and unlike a car ignition system, the aircraft battery has no further part in the operation of the engine, i.e. if the battery master switch were to be turned off, the engine will continue to run normally. Naturally, with the engine turning, the alternator or generator will ensure the battery is charged.

15.2.5   The magneto develops the high voltage needed to force a spark to jump across a gap in the sparking plug. This spark ignites the fuel/air mixture and is arranged to occur in each cylinder at a specific moment in the four stroke cycle.

15.2.6   **Dual Ignition**. With few exceptions, even the most expensive motor cars run on one set of sparking plugs and a single ignition coil. For reasons of safety all aircraft engines are required to have two separate ignition systems, i.e. two magnetos feeding two sets of sparking plugs through separate ignition leads. See fig 15.4.

15.2.7   There is, however a less obvious reason for Dual Ignition. It will be remembered that the aircraft engine is designed to develop its power at relatively low RPM. Because of this it is invariably a large engine relative to power output so that large pistons and cylinders are used in conjunction with a combustion chamber of considerable volume. While the large volume of compressed mixture could be ignited by a single sparking plug, better combustion and therefore more power results from having two sparking plugs positioned one either side of the cylinder head.

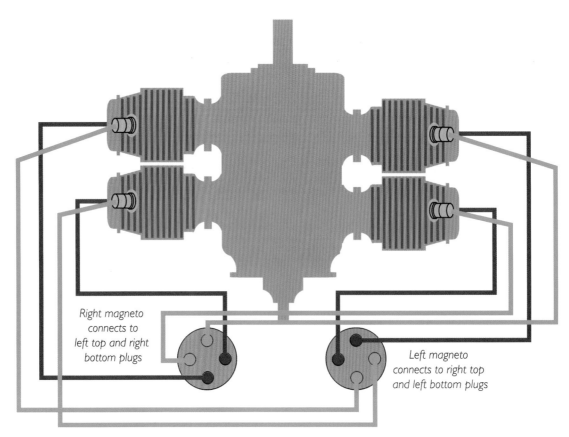

Right magneto
connects to
left top and right
bottom plugs

Left magneto
connects to right top
and left bottom plugs

Fig. 15.4 Typical ignition system – plan view of a 4 cylinder horizontally opposed engine.

15.2.8   It is part of a pilot's pre-flight checks to run up the engine, testing each ignition system in turn, and noting the decrease in RPM or Mag Drop as each switch is turned off. The maximum permitted drop in RPM per magneto, and the maximum difference in mag drop that may be allowed between magnetos will be listed in the helicopter manual. A serious drop in RPM could be caused by a defective magneto, a faulty plug lead or an unserviceable sparking plug.

15.2.9   When the switches are both in the ON position an increase in RPM will be seen on the engine speed indicator thus demonstrating that dual ignition increases power on a large slow running engine.

15.2.10   With the exception of low powered engines installed in simple light aircraft, starting is performed electrically. Even so the engine is turned over very slowly during starting and one of the following methods has to be adopted to ensure that, although the magneto is rotating slowly, a high intensity spark is provided for starting:

1.   **Impulse Starter.** A form of magneto which is driven by the engine via a spring. As the engine is turned over for starting, the spring, on becoming fully wound, flicks the magneto shaft at sufficient speed to generate a spark. To prevent "kick back" during starting the spark is retarded, ignition occurring after TDC. When the engine is running at some 700 RPM, bobweights built into the impulse device fly outwards locking the spring drive in the correct position for

141

advanced ignition. The Impulse starter is fitted to only one of the magnetos, and is the one that is selected when starting the engine. When the engine has started, the magneto switch is moved to "BOTH" and both magnetos are then working.

2. **High intensity Magneto**. The method favoured by most American manufacturers is to provide magnetos of large capacity which are capable of generating a spark at low rotational speeds.

15.2.11 **Ignition switches**. The ignition switches are different in at least one respect from all other types of electric switch in that when the ignition switch is in the OFF position, the circuit is "closed" from the switch to the ground. In other electrical switches, the OFF position normally "opens" the circuit. It is for this reason that propellers on aeroplanes must be treated as live at all times, because if a "ground" connection is broken for any reason, the circuit becomes live. Whereas this is a good safety factor during flight, it can clearly be seen that an inherent danger will exist when the engine is switched off on the ground, and a fault develops in the circuit.

15.2.12 **Spark plugs**. Like valve timing the precise moment when the mixture is ignited is all-important. The spark has to be of sufficient intensity to ignite the fuel/air mix, and the sparking plug must provide the spark under conditions of high pressure and great heat. Length of spark is governed by the Gap between the Central Electrode of the plug and the Side Electrode (sometimes called the Earthed Electrode). See fig 15.5 which shows a typical sparking plug.

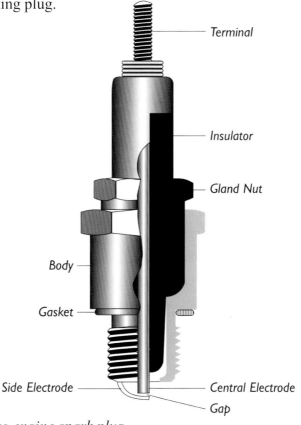

Fig. 15.5 A typical aero engine spark plug.

15.2.13 High tension current for the spark is generated by a magneto on aero engines (an ignition coil is used in most cars) and provision is made for precise emission of the spark by a switching device (Distributor) operated by rotation of the magneto shaft. The device incorporates a pair of platinum Points which is accurately adjusted to ensure that the spark occurs at the right time.

15.2.14 It would be expected that ignition is timed to occur just after the piston has compressed the mixture and started to descend, but it should be remembered that combustion in a piston engine is a progressive burning of the fuel which commences gradually (relatively speaking) building up as the flame spreads across the combustion chamber.

15.2.15 Time is therefore required for full combustion to develop so that the spark is arranged to occur 10-15° before TDC. The higher the operating RPM the more must the spark be advanced (in cars it is the practice to fit an automatic advance/retard control which caters for various engine speeds and load conditions).

15.3 Carburation

15.3.1 Petrol and other hydrocarbon fuels will not burn at all unless they have a correct supply of oxygen. This oxygen supply is provided by mixing the fuel with air, and in order that this mixture can burn properly within an engine cylinder, the ratio of fuel to air must be maintained with certain limits.

15.3.2 The chemically correct ratio is 15 parts of air to 1 part of fuel, but in small engines, which use a float type carburettor to produce the required mixture, this ideal ratio may not be achieved for various reasons.

15.3.3 One reason is that it is not always possible to deliver the same mixture strength to each cylinder due to their different positions relative to the carburettor and the resultant variation in the length of piping from the carburettor to the inlet valves at the cylinder heads.

15.3.4 **Carburation Principles**. On small aero engines a carburettor assembly is used to meter the airflow through the engine's induction system and to regulate the amount of fuel discharged in the induction airstream. Basically it utilises the principle of a venturi inside a cylinder which causes a drop in pressure, resulting in fuel from the adjacent float chamber being sucked into the induction airstream. The amount of air permitted to pass through the induction system is controlled by a butterfly valve connected to the pilot's throttle twist grip on the collective lever in the cockpit.

15.3.5 Fuel jets are positioned in the venturi to meter the correct fuel amount and are fed from the adjacent float chamber. Fig 15.6 shows a diagrammatic illustration of a carburettor assembly.

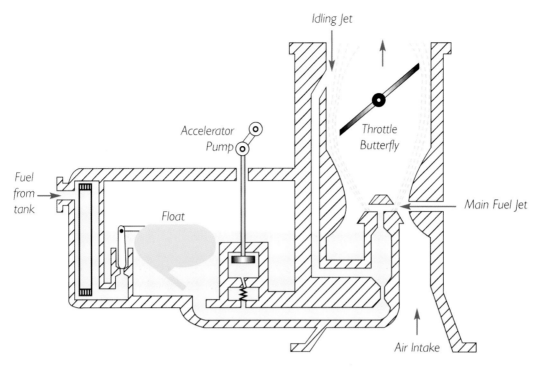

Fig. 15.6   Section through a simple float type carburettor.

15.3.6   As the pressure surrounding the discharge nozzle is lowered, a differential pressure is created between that in the float chamber and that in the venturi. This results in fuel flowing from the chamber to the fuel jets. As fuel leaves the chamber, the float lowers, lifting a needle in the inlet orifice permitting a continuous replenishment of the chamber from the aircraft fuel tanks.

15.3.7   The size and shape of the venturi passage depends upon the size of the engine and where the carburettor is positioned so for example, if the air passes through it in an upwards direction to the cylinders, it is known as an up draught carburettor, the converse of this arrangement is called a down draught carburettor. The up draught type is the one most commonly used in small aero engines.

15.3.8   Apart from the main metering jet, each carburettor has certain other fuel control units to provide for operating under various conditions and power settings. These units normally consist of at least the following:

1   Idling jets
2   Accelerator pump
3   Idle cut-off valve
4   Mixture Control system

15.3.9   These different units operate to meter the fuel flow at different power outputs and may act alone or in conjunction with each other. These four units will now be described.

15.3.10 **Idling jets**. At low engine speeds the throttle is nearly closed, as a result, the velocity of the air through the venturi is also low and there is little drop in pressure. Under these conditions, the differential pressure between the float chamber and the venturi section is insufficient to operate the main metering system (main jet). Therefore, most carburettors have an idling system, which normally consists of one or more small orifices adjacent to the throttle butterfly. Refer back to fig 15.6. It can be seen that as the throttle is closed, a depression or venturi effect is created at the idling jet allowing a sufficient rate of flow of fuel for the idling condition.

15.3.11 **Accelerator pump**. When the throttle is opened, the airflow through the carburettor increases. Unless the throttle is opened very slowly the initial increase in rate of airflow is more rapid than the increase in fuel flow. This creates to a delay before the engine power increases. See again fig 15.6.

15.3.12 The accelerator pump system which normally consists of a plunger assembly in the carburettor attached to the throttle linkage provides extra fuel during that period in which the throttle is being opened. This provides a more balanced fuel/air ratio and consequently smoother engine acceleration.

15.3.13 **Idle Cut-off valve**. This system is normally incorporated with the manual mixture control system and is provided so that the engine can be stopped without leaving a combustible mixture in the induction passages, cylinders, and exhaust system. This is a situation, which could easily occur if the engine were stopped by turning off the fuel or ignition switches.

15.3.14 The idle cut-off system normally utilises a tapered needle which moves into the fuel passage between the float chamber and the carburettor when the mixture control lever is moved to the position marked "Idle cut-off". In light piston engine powered helicopters, flight is normally conducted with the mixture control at fully rich.

15.3.15 **Fuel Injection Systems**. Direct fuel injection systems meter fuel directly into the cylinder and have many advantages over a conventional carburettor system. They reduce the possibility of induction icing since the drop in temperature due to fuel vaporisation (which causes approximately 70% of the temperature drop during mixing of air and fuel at cruise power setting. (More later). In addition to this, a direct fuel injection system provides better engine acceleration and improved fuel distribution, leading to greater economy of operation.

15.3.16 Each cylinder has its own individual fuel line and thus overheating problems caused by uneven fuel distribution to the cylinders, associated with the normal carburettor systems are reduced. This reduces the need to provide a richer mixture than necessary so that the cylinder receiving the leanest mixture will operate properly.

15.3.17   Fuel injection systems vary in detail but basically they consist of a fuel injector, flow divider and fuel discharge nozzle. The fuel injector monitors the volume of air entering the system and meters the fuel flow. The flow divider keeps the fuel under pressure and distributes the fuel to the various cylinders at the rate required for different engine speeds. It also shuts off the individual nozzle lines when the Idle Cut Off control is used.

15.3.18   A fuel discharge nozzle is located in each cylinder head and incorporates a calibrated jet. The fuel is discharged through this jet into an ambient air pressure chamber where atomisation occurs.

15.3.19   Although fuel injection systems have many advantages, their expense is not normally warranted with smaller aero engines, and they are rarely used in typical training aircraft. Nevertheless, their use is becoming quite common with the higher performance aircraft available to private pilots after training.

15.3.20   **Detonation and Pre-ignition**. Normal combustion within the cylinder occurs when the mixture ignites and burns progressively. This produces a normal pressure increase forcing the piston smoothly towards the bottom of the cylinder.

15.3.21   There is, however, a limit to the amount of compression and degree of temperature rise that can be tolerated before the fuel/air mixture reaches a point at which it will ignite spontaneously without the aid of the sparking plug. This causes an instantaneous combustion, i.e., an explosion, and when this occurs, an extremely high pressure is created within the combustion area. This is called detonation and it is very damaging to the piston top and valves.

15.3.22   In automobile engines, detonation can be identified by a "Pinking" noise and the driver can take action to eliminate this by reducing power or changing gear. In aero engines, this characteristic pinking noise cannot be heard, and therefore, the engine designer arranges for the mixture to be richer than normally necessary. This acts as a coolant to prevent the mixture reaching a critical temperature.

15.3.23   When the engine is operating at below approximately 70% power, detonation will not normally occur, but it should be borne in mind that the use of a lower grade fuel than recommended, or if the mixture is weak, can produce detonation under most power conditions.

15.3.24   **Pre-ignition,** as the name implies, means that normal combustion takes place but before the sparking plug fires. This condition is often due to localised hot spots e.g. carbon deposits becoming incandescent and igniting the mixture. Although pre-ignition can be the result of detonation it can also be caused by high power operation in lean mixture. Pre-ignition is usually indicated by engine roughness, back firing or a sudden increase in cylinder head temperature.

15.3.25   The best "in flight" measure for correcting detonation or pre-ignition should it occur, is to ensure the mixture is rich and to decrease the power.

15.4   Carburettor Icing

15.4.1   Under certain atmospheric conditions when the air humidity and temperature are within a particular range, ice will form in the induction system and affect the carburettor operation. This will take the form of a reduction in power, rough running, or both, and in severe cases the engine may stop.

15.4.2   It is important that pilots know about induction icing and the manner in which it is formed as well as the precautions to be taken to avoid it and the remedial measures which can overcome the problems.

15.4.3   There are 3 types of induction system icing, these are:

1.   Impact Icing
2.   Fuel (or Refrigeration Icing)
3.   Throttle (or Venturi Icing.)

15.4.4   **Impact Ice**. Impact ice is formed by super cooled water droplets striking against the external induction aperture or filter and freezing on impact. It can also occur inside the induction channel to the carburettor. This type of icing can also affect fuel injection systems as well as those using a normal float type carburettor.

15.4.5   **Fuel Ice**. Fuel ice can form at and downstream from the point where fuel is mixed with the incoming air. (In some texts, fuel icing may be called "refrigeration icing" as it is caused by the vaporising of a liquid absorbing latent heat from the surroundings as is the case in a refrigerator). It occurs if the entrained moisture in the air (and sometimes in the fuel) reaches the icing range (usually 0°C down to –8°C) as a result of the cooling which takes place when the fuel is vaporised. If the temperature drops below –8°C, the moisture precipitates out directly into ice crystals which pass through the system with little or no effect on the engine power, but if the temperature in the system drops to between 0°C and –8°C water will be precipitated from the incoming air and freeze on the walls of the induction passages, throttle butterfly, or any other protrusion in the carburettor passages. See fig 15.6.

15.4.6   This will effectively reduce the size of the carburettor passage, causing a change to the fuel/air ratio, leading to loss of power and rough running. If the build up of ice is allowed to continue, the rough running will worsen and the engine may stop. Fuel icing is rare in fuel injection systems as the fuel/air mixture is injected directly into the cylinders, which have a considerable heat content.

15.4.7 **Throttle Ice**. This is caused by the sudden drop in temperature as the air pressure drops when passing the venturi and butterfly section of the carburettor passage. (Adiabatic temperature drop). In conventional float type carburettors, throttle icing usually occurs in combination with fuel icing which serves to compound the rate of ice accretion.

15.4.8 **Recognition**. In all forms of induction icing, the main recognition features are, a drop in engine power, followed by rough running. However, because a pilot monitors the RPM less frequently than the ASI or altimeter, he may more quickly recognise the presence of induction icing when in level flight, by noticing a decrease of airspeed for a constant altitude, or a loss of altitude for a constant airspeed.

15.4.9 **Remedial Actions**. Impact ice, which forms around the engine air intake will normally only occur during flight in cloud or heavy rain at freezing temperatures. (Super-cooled water drops). The ambient temperature at which impact ice can be expected to build up ranges between 0°C and –7°C in layer type cloud, but can be experienced at temperatures as low as –18°C in cumulus cloud.

15.4.10 Pilots should be particularly alert for this type of icing whenever flying in rain, sleet or snow, especially when ice deposits are seen building up on the windscreen or any part of the fuselage. It should also be understood that impact ice can occur to the same extent with fuel injection or float type carburation systems. However, most fuel injection systems are equipped with an alternate intake air source situated within the engine cowling, and this should be used according to the aircraft manufacturer's recommendations.

15.4.11 **Types and Effects of Carburettor Heating Systems**. Fuel and throttle ice can occur whether the aircraft is in or clear of cloud and this is an important point to bear in mind. To combat fuel or throttle icing, it is now normal to equip helicopters with a carburettor hot air system.

15.4.12 With hot air systems application of carburettor heat will almost always raise the carburettor air temperature well above that at which freezing can occur and can therefore be used either as a precaution against ice formation, or, as a very effective remedy to clear any ice which has already formed.

15.4.13 The most common type of hot air system utilises a heat exchanger incorporated with the exhaust assembly. In some aircraft the carburettor heat is supplied from the same heat exchanger unit as the cabin heat system. The exact form and operation of hot air systems will be particular to the aircraft make and the Aircraft Manual should be studied carefully to obtain a precise knowledge of its operation.

15.4.14   The use of hot air will automatically reduce the engine power by a small amount, due to it being less dense than cold air. It should be appreciated that the use of full heat can increase the fuel consumption by as much as 20% which means that the aircraft's range and endurance would also be drastically reduced. On long flights, this could result in a significant reduction to operational safety margins.

15.5   Oil Systems

15.5.1   The primary purpose of engine lubricating oils is to reduce friction and remove heat from between the moving parts. In principle, oil prevents metal to metal contact; and provided that the oil film remains unbroken, metallic friction is replaced by fluid friction.

15.5.2   Oil also acts as a cushion and reduces shocks between metal parts. This is particularly important for such components as the engine crankshaft and connecting rods which are subject to high loads when the engine is running.

15.5.3   Additionally, as oil circulates through an engine, it absorbs heat and this is particularly important in the case of the pistons and the internal walls of the cylinder. The oil film between the piston and cylinder wall also produces a seal to prevent gases leaking from the combustion chamber. Finally, during its circulation, oil collects dirt introduced into the engine from the atmosphere and also the carbon particles produced by combustion, these are collected by the oil filter thereby reducing abrasive wear on the internal parts.

15.5.4   **Properties of Oil.** There are several important properties which an engine oil must possess. It must flow freely over a wide range of temperature yet not become so fluid at high temperatures that its viscosity breaks down resulting in too thin a film of oil between moving parts.

15.5.5   It must therefore remain viscous enough to withstand high operating temperatures and high bearing pressures. It must also have a high flash and fire point, that is to say, the temperature at which it will produce ignitable vapours and support a flame.

15.5.6   Aviation oils are classified numerically, and the numbers used indicate the degree of viscosity. A high viscosity oil flows slowly and a low viscosity oil flows freely. It is important that the correct grade of oil as recommended by the engine manufacturer is used throughout the life of an engine. Further to this, it should be appreciated that different grades are recommended for the same engine dependent upon the average climatic temperature. i.e. in winter or cold climates, a grade of lesser viscosity will be recommended.

15.5.7   **Lubrication Methods**. Piston engine lubricating systems are of two specific types, those which use a wet sump and those which have a dry sump. The wet sump type stores the oil as an integral part of the engine casing, and the components are lubricated by a pressure pump or simply by splashfeed. The dry sump type has a separate oil tank located in a convenient position adjacent to the engine. Oil is supplied from the tank by a pressure pump, and having passed through the engine is returned to tank by a separate scavenge pump.

15.5.8   **Pumps, Sumps and Filters**. Apart from the differences involved in having a sump located at the lower portion of the engine or a separate tank installation, oil systems generally incorporate a supply pump, which forces oil from the sump or tank into and around the moving parts of the engine via drilled passages.

15.5.9   Because it is essential to keep the oil as clean as possible, filters are fitted into the system and these absorb the dirt, carbon particles and other foreign matter. Normally the elements of these filters are replaced at regular maintenance intervals and the condition of the engine can often be determined by the type and amount of particles they collect.

15.5.10   Apart from absorbing foreign matter, two important chemical changes take place in the oil during use. These are firstly, Oxidation which occurs due to contamination from corrosive lead salts produced during combustion, and secondly, the Chemical effect of Water Vapour condensing inside the engine as the oil cools after the engine is stopped. These effects cannot be removed by any system of filters, and for this reason alone, it is important to adhere to the oil change periods recommended by the manufacturer.

15.5.11   **Typical Systems**. Apart from the method of storing oil, the wet and the dry sump systems are similar, and the wet sump type will be described.

15.5.12   The oil is collected and stored in a sump which forms the lower end of the engine casing. An oil pump driven by the engine draws oil out of the sump through an oil screen. See fig 15.8.

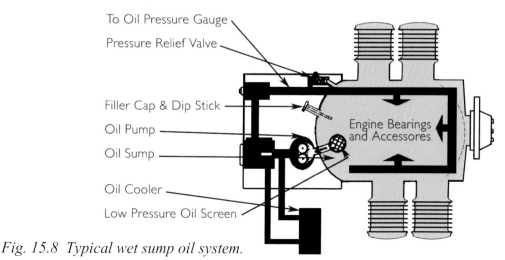

Fig. 15.8 Typical wet sump oil system.

15.5.13   The oil flows through to the pressure side of the pump and then to the engine. It should be appreciated that the oil pump has to provide the correct oil pressure over a range of RPM settings, therefore a relief valve is integral with the system. If the pump pressure is too high it is relieved by allowing some of the oil to flow directly back into the sump, whilst the remaining oil travels through an oil cooler (on most lower power engines the oil cooler is an optional item) and then via galleries and passages into the engine.

15.5.14   **Recognition of Oil System Malfunction.** Two gauges are usually mounted in the cockpit which show the pilot the temperature of the oil and the oil pressure being maintained in the system. It should be noted that the oil temperature shown on the gauge is the temperature of the oil as it leaves the oil cooler, however, some low horsepower engines are not equipped with an oil cooler, and in this case the oil temperature gauge reflects the oil temperature immediately the oil is drawn out of the sump, where it has had time to cool before redistribution.

15.5.15   On most systems the oil pressure gauge indicates the pressure at which oil enters the engine from the pump. The most common pressure gauge used with small aero engines utilises a Bourdon Tube system which measures the difference between oil pressure and atmospheric pressure. It has a simple dial presentation and is normally colour coded to show the safe pressure range (green) and a red segment either side of the green band shows when oil pressure is too high or too low.

15.5.16   The oil temperature gauge measures the temperature of the oil by means of a temperature sensitive probe. There are many types of probe in use, but one common type is filled with a volatile liquid which is then connected to a bourdon tube. As the oil temperature increases, the vapour pressure inside the probe increases, and this is then displayed on a gauge in the cockpit. Although the gauge is actually indicating vapour pressure, it is calibrated in degrees of temperature and the face of the instrument is usually colour coded.

15.5.17   If low oil pressure is indicated at cruising power or above, it is a sign of likely engine failure resulting from too little or no oil available, leaking oil lines, burned out engine bearings or failure of the oil pump. However, because it is possible for an oil pressure or temperature gauge itself to fail, it is advisable to note carefully the readings from the oil temperature gauge in order to decide whether it is the oil system or the gauge which is at fault. For example, if the quantity of oil in the system is low, or if it is not being properly circulated, a rapid rise in oil temperature will result.

15.5.18   If, on the other hand, the oil temperature gauge continues to give a normal reading whilst the oil pressure gauge indicates a low pressure it will be a fairly good indication that the oil pressure gauge has become unserviceable.

15.5.19 Finally, the modern aero engine is extremely clean in operation, and, if during a pre-flight inspection, oil is seen coating parts of the engine or cowlings, the flight should be cancelled and the fact reported to an engineer.

15.6 Fuel Systems

15.6.1 The aircraft fuel system is designed to store fuel and deliver it to the carburettor in the correct quantity and at sufficient pressure to meet the demands of the engine in all normal flight conditions.

15.6.2 A properly designed fuel system ensures a positive and continuous flow of fuel throughout changes in altitude, or sudden acceleration and deceleration of the power plant.

15.6.3 **Fuel Tanks**. Generally, there are one or more fuel tanks (or fuel cells as they are sometimes called) incorporated into even the simplest fuel system. Some tanks are constructed of metal and are known as rigid tanks, others are constructed of non rigid material and depend upon the structure of the helicopter cavity into which they are inserted to support the weight of the fuel within them. Another method of storing fuel in aircraft structures is a cell constructed integrally within, and this is therefore part of the aircraft structure.

15.6.4 The materials used in tank construction can be aluminium alloy, synthetic rubber, nylon etc. Regardless of the material used, it must be one, which does not react chemically with aviation fuel.

15.6.5 Normally, a sump and drain is provided at the lowest point of the tank and the fuel supply line, which is fitted with a filter, is arranged to terminate at some point higher than the sump. This latter arrangement reduces the possibility of any sludge or sediment, which may be present, from blocking the filter.

15.6.6 The top of each tank is vented to the outside air so that atmospheric pressure can be maintained in the tank as the fuel is used up. If this vent becomes blocked for any reason, a suction (reduced pressure) will be created in the area above the head of the fuel and reduce the normal rate of fuel flow. Such a reduced pressure area can eventually cause the flow to cease completely and the engine will stop.

15.6.7 In order to resist fuel surging about in the tank, due to changes of attitude during flight, the tanks are normally fitted with baffles. An expansion space is also designed into the top of the tank to cater for the expansion of fuel volume whenever the temperature increases. Aircraft Certification requirements demand that the fuel caps or the areas adjacent to them be clearly marked with the fuel capacity and fuel grade designation.

15.6.8   **Fuel Distribution**. The basic components of a typical fuel system consists of a fuel tank or tanks, fuel lines, selection valves, filters, pumps, quantity indicators, and fuel pressure gauges. See fig 15.9.

15.6.9   An electric pump is fitted to pump fuel from the tanks, through the lines to the carburettor or fuel injector. In this system, a fuel pressure gauge is a normal requirement in order that correct functioning of the fuel pump can be monitored. Starting an engine requires priming the fuel lines. In general, this is done by operating the fuel pump, which will pressurize the fuel line up to the mixture control, or some helicopters use a throttle twist grip which can also prime fuel lines. Some have a priming pump. Specific starting procedures vary, and pilots must refer to the aircraft operating manual for correct procedures.

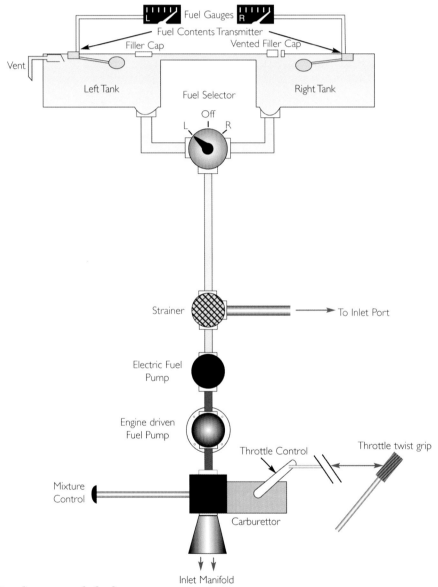

Fig. 15.9   A simple two tank fuel system.

15.6.10   **Fuel Selection Methods**. From each tank, a fuel line leads to a selector valve in the cockpit. This valve is used by the pilot to either select fuel from the appropriate tank(s) or to shut off the supply.

15.6.11   The fuel valve passages and fuel lines must be of sufficient bore to accommodate the maximum flow demand required by the engine when operating at full power. It is vital when selecting the appropriate tank, to ensure the selector valve is positively seated in the correct position, otherwise the pipe bore will be partially obstructed and only a reduced rate of flow will be possible.

15.6.12   This reduced flow could be such that the engine will operate normally at low to cruising power but will be insufficient to meet the engine demand at high power such as at lift-off. In this case, a marked loss of power and possible engine stoppage will occur.

15.6.13   **Fuel, Pumps (Mechanical and Electrical).** A mechanical fuel pump is fitted to those systems in which the fuel tanks are positioned at or below engine level. The pump is used to provide a continuous supply of fuel from the tank to the carburettor and it is normally mounted on the accessory section of the engine.

15.6.14   For safety reasons, engine driven fuel pumps are normally designed to be capable of supplying more fuel than the particular engine requires. They are therefore fitted with a relief valve system which permits unused fuel to return to the inlet side of the pump, or alternatively to be returned directly to the tank.

15.6.15   The electric pump is usually also used on other occasions such as during tank re-selection, and when flying above a certain altitude. At high altitudes, the air pressure acting on the fuel in the tank is low. This lowers the boiling point of the fuel and causes vapour bubbles to form. If this vapour becomes trapped in the fuel lines, a **VAPOUR LOCK** may occur and restrict or even prevent any fuel flow.

15.6.16   High outside air temperatures can also cause the same effect and the possibility of vapour lock can be substantially or completely reduced by operating the electric pump and so increasing the fuel pressure within the tanks and fuel lines.

15.6.17   **Fuel Grades and Colouring**. Aviation gasoline (AVGAS) consists almost entirely of hydrocarbons, that is, compounds composed of hydrogen and carbon. Even though great care is taken during the refining of fuel, some impurities in the form of sulphur, and absorbed water will always be present. This water content cannot be avoided because fuel is exposed to the moisture contained in the atmosphere and which enters the tanks via the vent openings.

15.6.18   The volatility of fuel (its tendency to vaporise) is controlled during manufacture. If fuel vaporises too readily, it can cause vapour locks in the fuel lines and so decrease the rate of fuel flow. If this fuel does not vaporise readily it can cause difficult engine starting, uneven fuel distribution to the cylinder and retarded engine acceleration.

15.6.19   During compression and combustion it is possible under certain conditions for detonation to take place. Detonation is an uncontrolled rate of burning which is akin to an explosion, therefore to reduce this possibility, AVGAS incorporates a fuel additive known as Tetraethyl Lead (TEL).

15.6.20   This TEL nevertheless has certain corrosive properties which can lead to chemical deposits on the sparking plug electrode, valves, and pistons, and therefore its use has to be kept to a minimum.

15.6.21   **Fuel grades**. Aero engines vary widely in the power they can produce. Some aircraft use small engines as low as 65 HP (48 kW), whereas others have HP outputs which run into thousands. Because of the markedly different requirements and performance of these various engines, it is necessary to produce varying grades of aviation fuel, and these are identified by a numerical code system. This grading system differentiates between fuels which have low or high anti-knock (anti-detonation) qualities.

15.6.22   The higher the grade or octane, the greater the compression the air/fuel mixture can stand without detonating, and therefore it is particularly important for a pilot to see that his aircraft is provided with the correct grade of fuel recommended by the manufacturer.

15.6.23   To assist in identification, all aviation gasoline contains a coloured dye and the allocation of different colours to different fuel grades is standardised throughout the world. Small aero engines now operate on AVGAS Grade 100LL (the LL stands for low lead content) which is coloured blue, and is easily recognisable by looking into the tank through the filler orifice.

15.6.24   **Inspection for Contamination and Condensation**. Fuel contamination occurs when any material other than that provided for in its specification is introduced into the fuel. This material generally consists of such items as, water, rust, sand, dust or micro-organisms (microbia).

15.6.25   Although rigorous precautions are taken to ensure that fuel pumped into an aircraft contains as little water as possible, an aircraft fuel containing no water is almost an impossibility. This is due primarily to the affinity which hydrocarbon fuels have for water. (Hydrophilic).

15.6.26   All aviation fuels absorb moisture from the air and contain water in liquid form. Whenever the temperature of the fuel is decreased, some of the condensed water comes out of solution and falls slowly to the bottom of the tank. Whenever the temperature of the fuel increases, water is drawn from the atmosphere to maintain a saturated solution. Therefore changes of temperature result in a continuous accumulation of water. In temperate climates the rate of this accumulation is fairly low, but it will be accelerated during aircraft operation due to the significant change of temperature with altitude.

15.6.27　Additionally, and during changes of ambient temperature, water can condense out as liquid droplets on the inside walls of the tank and then settle into the fuel. Keeping the aircraft tanks topped up particularly overnight when temperature changes are usually most rapid or on those occasions when the aircraft is not being used for several days will greatly reduce this condensation effect.

15.6.28　Rust, from storage tanks and ground pipelines is an additional factor and requires a high degree of filtration to eliminate it. Dust and sand may accumulate in small quantities via tank openings and whenever fuel is being transferred. These particles tend to gravitate towards the lowest point in the fuel system. The entry of rust, dust and sand particles into the aircraft fuel line is normally reduced by the fitting of filters at suitable points in the system.

15.6.29　Microbia, is more prevalent in unleaded fuels such as those used in turbine engines, (AVTUR) but can to a smaller extent develop in AVGAS particularly in climatic conditions of heat and high humidity. Micro-organisms tend to mat together and form a slimy brown layer in the fuel. The growth of these bacteria can cause blocking of filters and fuel screens.

15.6.30　Fuel Strainers and Drains. In order to reduce the possibility of fuel contamination, all fuel systems are equipped with fuel strainers and drain points which are easily accessible. Strainers are installed in the fuel tank outlets and sometimes in the tank filter necks. These are normally of a fairly coarse mesh and prevent only the larger particles from entering the fuel system. Other strainers which are of a finer mesh are usually provided in the carburettor fuel inlets and in the fuel lines.

15.6.31　In light helicopters, a main strainer, often called a gascolator is fitted at the lowest point of the fuel system. Fuel which has left the tank has to flow through this strainer before reaching the carburettor and its purpose is to trap water and other foreign matter.

15.6.32　The strainers usually consist of a small metal, glass or perspex bowl which can be opened during a pre-flight inspection to drain fuel and with it any water or sediment. Because it is practically impossible to drain all the water held in the tanks by straining the fuel system, it is also necessary to fit each fuel tank with a separate drain unit. These are installed at the bottom of the tank sump and when these are of the finger or quick drain type, they should be manually operated for a short while at frequent periods.

15.6.33　The particular aircraft manual will contain the operating instructions for their use during pre-flight inspections. Because fuel system designs differ significantly it is advisable to use the information contained in the particular Flight/Owners Manual/Operating Handbook rather than rely upon some generally accepted procedure.

15.6.34   It must also be appreciated that, merely opening a strainer or fuel drain and allowing fuel to flow out onto the ground will not in itself reveal any presence of water. It is only by collecting the fuel in a small glass or perspex cup or jar that the presence of water in the system be detected. Water, being heavier than fuel, will separate and settle in the lower portion of the container. If water is discovered, then the tank and/or fuel system should be drained until no indications of water are present.

15.6.35   A further point with regard to straining procedures is that after refueling, it is advisable to allow at least 15 minutes before opening any strainers or drains. This is to allow sufficient time for any water to settle down to the bottom of the tanks and the lowest point of the fuel system.

15.6.36   **Recognition of Malfunction/Mismanagement.** Any situation in which fuel is available in the tanks but is not able to reach the engine, is known as **Fuel Starvation.** The components which are most likely to malfunction and cause fuel starvation are the pumps and filters. Mechanical pump failure, although rare, is nevertheless capable of producing a hazardous situation unless the back up electric fuel pump procedures are quickly performed.

15.6.37   For example, a fuel pump failure at altitude will normally allow sufficient time for the electric pump to be switched on and take over the task of maintaining fuel pressure and an adequate supply of fuel to the engine. However, aircraft manuals recommend that electric pumps are checked on the ground and switched on prior to take-off and landing; thus permitting a supply of fuel to the engine even if the mechanical pump fails.

15.6.38   It must be appreciated that if the electric pump is OFF and the mechanical pump fails, the engine will stop only after most of the fuel has been drawn from the lines. This will therefore mean a significant delay following the switching on of the electric pump during which pressure is restored, the fuel line primed, and fuel is arriving at the carburettor. If the helicopter is at low altitude, such as, when taking-off or landing, there could be insufficient time available for the engine to restart.

15.6.39   Blocked filters will naturally starve the engine of fuel, but as most aircraft have more than one tank, the greatest hazard will occur if the carburettor filter itself becomes blocked.

15.6.40   **Fuel System Malfunction.** Sudden loss of power without any accompanying mechanical noise or vibration is usually indicative of fuel starvation or exhaustion. Indications of impending power failure due to lack of sufficient fuel can normally be obtained via the fuel contents and fuel pressure gauges.

15.6.41   When the aircraft is equipped with an electric fuel pump this should be switched on immediately if the appropriate tank gauge is still giving a positive indication of fuel in the tank. In those cases where inadvertently a tank has been run dry, the manufacturer's instructions should be followed in relation to the correct procedure to be followed when changing fuel tanks during flight, e.g. the switching on of an electric pump before tank re-selection may be recommended, or alternatively, its use may be recommended only after the tank change has been made.

15.6.42 **Fuel System Mismanagement**. By far the most common reason for engine failure is mismanagement of the fuel system. This can result in the engine stopping due to fuel exhaustion or fuel starvation. In relation to fuel exhaustion, past experience with fuel gauges in light aircraft has revealed that when the fuel contents are low, it is often impossible for a pilot to know with sufficient accuracy how much fuel is left for him to decide whether or not to continue his flight. Consequently pilots should exercise the greatest caution in fuel management.

15.6.43 A useful general rule to apply to the operation of light helicopters is that pilots should not rely on the quantity of fuel left in the tanks when the gauges indicate one third full or less in straight and level flight. The more obvious general precautions that should be taken include physical checks of the amount and grade of fuel in the tanks before takeoff, and the accurate calculation of the amount of fuel required for the intended flight including that needed for take-off, hovering, climb to cruising altitude, plus a sensible allowance to cover a possible diversion en route due to weather or other reasons.

15.6.44 The general definition of fuel starvation is, any occurrence which interrupts, reduces or terminates the correct supply of fuel to the engine, even though there is sufficient fuel in the tanks. Fuel starvation may occur as a result of a variety of reasons and it is essential that all pilots be thoroughly conversant with their aircraft fuel system and the correct fuel management procedures before take-off and during flight.

15.6.45 A summary of fuel management pointers is listed below. These should be carefully studied and applied:

1   Make adequate pre-flight preparation to ensure that sufficient clean fuel of the correct grade is on board the aircraft for the distance to be covered and the time to be flown, plus an adequate reserve.

2   Know the total usable fuel on board. Most aircraft fuel tanks carry a quantity of unusable fuel and this cannot be included when calculating the fuel amount which is to be consumed during a flight.

3   Before flight, make a visual inspection to assess the fuel quantity in the tanks. Complete trust in the fuel gauges has often resulted in fuel depletion before reaching the destination and an accident in consequence.

4   Make a thorough drain check of the fuel sumps, prior to flight following the fuel draining procedures as recommended in the aircraft manual.

5   During the pre-flight inspection, ensure that all tank vents are undamaged and clear of obstructions.

6   Positively determine that manual priming pumps are closed and in the locked position prior to flight (if fitted).

7   When practical, check fuel flow from all tanks prior to take-off. Never select a tank immediately before takeoff or landing, but always allow time after selection to ensure that the fuel supply to the carburettor is being maintained.

8   Know and understand the positions of the fuel selector valves. Markings should be clearly legible, and the valves should be easy and smooth to operate with a positive detent action.

9   Be completely familiar with the operation of the electric fuel pumps.

10   When switching from one tank to another, double check the quantity of fuel available as shown by the appropriate fuel gauge and after switching, recheck that the new position of the fuel selector valve is the correct one.

11   After switching tanks, monitor the fuel pressure (when pressure gauges are fitted) for a short while to ensure that fuel is flowing correctly from the selected tank.

15.7   Cooling Systems

15.7.1   The temperature generated in the gases within the cylinders of an aero engine during the use of maximum cruising power may be in the order of 2000°C and even greater than this at maximum power. Although the internal combustion engine is a heat machine, which converts the chemical energy of the fuel into mechanical power, it does not do so without some loss of energy.

15.7.2   **The Purpose of Cooling Systems.** This loss of energy may amount to 60 to 70% of the original energy in the fuel, and unless most of this waste heat is rapidly removed, the cylinders may become hot enough to cause damage to the engine or even complete failure of the power plant.

15.7.3   There are four main reasons why excessive heat should be avoided and these are:

1   It weakens the engine components and so shortens engine life.
2   It reduces the efficiency of the lubrication system.
3   It can cause detonation to occur.
4   It affects the behaviour of the combustion of the fuel/air mix.

15.7.4   **Methods of Cooling.** Cooling systems are therefore designed to transfer the excess heat from the cylinders to the air, however, this is not simply a matter of arranging for the cylinders to be placed in the airstream. When air passes around a cylinder, flow breakaway occurs at the rear and this portion of the cylinder will receive inadequate cooling which will lead to a localised hot spot and possible detonation and subsequent damage to the cylinder wall etc.

15.7.5   To improve the normal cooling action of the air, the external area of the cylinder barrel is fitted with fins which give it a considerable increase in cooling area and also provides for greater heat transfer by radiation.

15.7.6   Air is forced around the cylinders by the use of a powerful squirrel fan (squirrel fans are able to deliver pressure) providing a cooling air pressure system which is then ducted by baffles to achieve the maximum cooling effect on the cylinders. Increased cooling capacity and the avoidance of local hot spots is obtained by carefully designed baffles which direct air around the cylinders.

15.7.7   The cylinder baffles are metal shields designed and arranged to direct the flow of air evenly around all parts of the cylinders. This even distribution of the airflow aids in preventing local hot spots in any one cylinder, or more than one cylinder from becoming excessively hotter than the rest. The air is then expelled out of the cowled area via apertures at the bottom or rear of the engine compartment. (Fixed cowl outlets).

15.7.8   Some cooling installations use a liquid coolant to remove excess heat from the power plant, but these are not in common use with light helicopters. Glycol is the normal coolant used with this method, and after circulating around the engine, it is directed through a radiator to cool it down before it continues its cooling cycle.

15.7.9   **Operation of the Air Cooling System**. Cooling air is supplied via intake duct/s and a squirrel cage fan providing positive air pressure, which is directed by a suitably shaped shroud to the engine cylinders. Air is also directed by ducts from the shroud supply to cool the alternator and main rotor gearbox. Air is also ducted and controlled by the pilot to allow either cool or warm air, via a filter into the carburettor. Some helicopters have a carburettor temperature gauge.

15.7.10   If a cylinder head temperature gauge is fitted, pilots should be careful to monitor this gauge, particularly during extended ground operations, or when the aircraft is in the hover. The aircraft manual usually gives information on the best cylinder head temperature to maintain, and sometimes this is indicated by colour coding on the gauge.

15.7.11   If at any stage of a flight, the cylinder head temperature gauge shows excessively high readings, the pilot should take any or both of the following actions:

1   Check rich Mixture. (If manual control fitted)
2   Reduce the Power being used.

16   VACUUM SYSTEM

16.1   The power plant fitted to an aircraft is also harnessed to drive ancillary systems one of which is the suction system. See fig 16.1. This is the source of power for the operation of the gyroscopes fitted into the Attitude Indicator and Heading Indicator. Current practice is to drive the gyros of these latter instruments by electricity thereby providing a safety factor should the suction system become inoperative during flight. Fig. 16.1 shows a simple vacuum system, as fitted to a light aircraft.

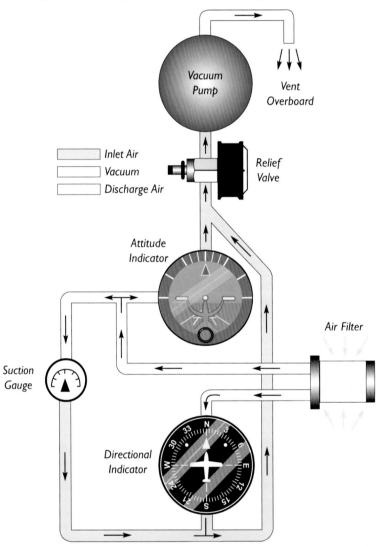

Fig. 16.1   A simple vacuum system.

16.1.1   The vacuum system of modern light aircraft is driven by means of a suction pump driven by the engine.

16.1.2   The vacuum system spins the instrument gyro by sucking a continuous stream of air against specially shaped indentations in the rotor (buckets) and so causing the gyro to spin at a very high speed. This air is drawn in through an aperture in the instrument case and then passes out via the suction pump into the atmosphere.

16.1.3   The degree of vacuum normally required to drive the gyros is between 3½ and 5½ in. Hg (Mercury) and this is usually controlled by a vacuum relief valve located in the supply line.

16.1.4   **Suction Pump**. The engine driven suction pump used in light aircraft is usually of the vane type. This can be mounted on the engine block and driven by the engine crankshaft via a pulley and belt arrangement. The size of the pump used and its capacity, varies according to the number of instruments to be operated.

16.1.5   **Recognition of Malfunction**. This will be recognised by the vacuum gauge reading too high, too low, or failing to show a reading at all. Incorrect suction will normally be caused by dirty filters or by incorrect operation of the suction relief valve. A zero reading on the suction gauge will be evidence that the vacuum pump has failed or the gauge has become unserviceable, but because the instrument gyros run down within a few minutes, a vacuum pump failure will normally be initially recognised by erratic, sluggish or incorrect readings from the gyro instruments.

17 ELECTRICAL SYSTEM

17.1   **Introduction**. Electrical energy is widely used to provide power for many of the aircraft systems. Such systems or services typically comprise: the radio, lighting equipment, navigation lights, landing lights, anti collision light/strobe lights, pitot heater, starter motor, some flight and engine instruments, and similar items.

17.1.1   Light helicopters are normally equipped with what is known as a direct current single wire, negative ground electrical system. The circuit commences through a single wire carrying the positive current and is completed by grounding each electrical service to the airframe structure. In the wiring diagram (see fig 17.1), the ground or earthing connections are shown at the left of the diagram. The BUS BAR is used to connect the supply to the aircraft services as listed in para. 17.1.

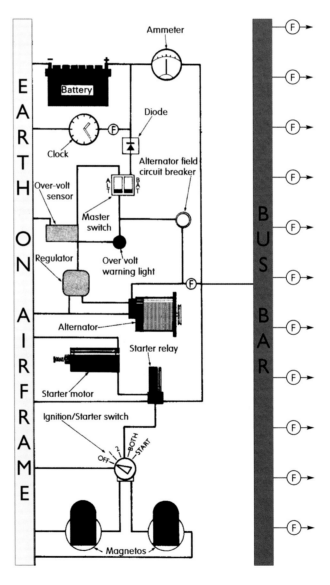

Fig. 17.1   *An electrical circuit fitted to a light helicopter. The connections to the aircraft services are made to the BUS BAR on the right of the diagram through fuses or circuit breakers marked "F".*

17.1.2   The circuit is powered by an electric current obtained from either a generator or an alternator. Older aircraft use generators, but alternators which are more efficient at low RPM than generators, are normally fitted to all new aircraft. A battery supplies power for engine starting and acts as a reserve source of supply should the generator or alternator fail. During normal operation of the engine the generator/alternator charges the battery as required.

17.1.3   Other components are the Master Switch which is used to bring the electrical power on line and a voltage regulator which controls the rate of charge from the generator to the battery. An Ammeter is fitted to the system to indicate the rate of current flowing either to or from the battery. Voltmeters which measure the electrical force which is available to deliver the current are sometimes included in the system.

17.1.4   An optional component is an external power source socket, which can be used to plug an external power supply into the electrical system during periods of ground maintenance when the engine is not running or to conserve the aircraft battery when starting the engine.

17.1.5   As a precaution against fire risk or damage to equipment from overloading, each electrical circuit is normally provided with a fuse or thermal trip contact breaker. The type of fuse or contact breaker most commonly used in light aircraft systems is either in the form of a cartridge or a reset circuit breaker.

17.1.6   Types of Fuses. The cartridge type is simply a wire strand passing between two terminals and enclosed by a glass tube. The wire burns out if the circuit overloads. The cartridge fuse usually fits into a cap which is screwed or slotted into the fuse mounting. A minimum number of spare fuses of the correct type and rating must be carried in a convenient place in the cockpit.

17.1.7   The circuit breaker fuse is normally of the "press to reset" type. If the electrical circuit overloads, the push Button pops out and isolates the circuit from the electrical supply.

17.1.8   Basically, there are two types of circuit breaker, one has to be re-set manually by pressing the push button which protrudes out from its mounting. This type is known as a manual reset circuit breaker. The other method known, is an automatic reset circuit breaker, which uses a bimetallic strip consisting of two metals of dissimilar thermal expansion which are bonded together and attached to a fixed base. If the circuit becomes overheated the effect is to cause the strip to curl back from the contact point, and the circuit is broken.

17.1.9   When the strip cools down, the strip straightens again and presses against the contact point reactivating the circuit. This type of device is often used in the case of fuel gauges or turn and balance indicators, the readings from which could be vital to a pilot during flight.

17.1.10   Whenever a fuse burns out or a manual circuit breaker trips, and there are no indications of damage to the system e.g. odour or smoke, allow at least 2 minutes for the circuit to cool down before replacing the fuse or resetting the circuit breaker. After this, if the fuse again burns out or the circuit breaker trips, the pilot should switch off the services supplied through the circuit and report the unserviceability after landing.

17.2   Alternators/Generators

17.2.1   The alternator or generator will normally supply all the power needed to drive the various services incorporated in the electrical system. The electrical pressure that causes electricity to flow is measured in Volts and the rate at which electricity flows is measured in Amperes (usually shortened to amps).

17.2.2   Light aircraft normally use 14 or 28 volt systems and the current capacity of the particular generator or alternator used varies between 35 and 60 amperes. The ammeter gives an indication of the amount of electric power being used by the electrical services, and the more services in use the higher the amperage taken. For example, assume a typical light single engined aircraft which has a 14 volt system and a 25 amp hour battery with an alternator capable of generating 60 amperes. When the engine is switched off and the alternator is not charging, the battery would supply the service with 25 amps for one hour after which it would be fully discharged. Alternatively, it could supply electric current at the rate of 1 amp for 25 hours.

17.2.3   With the engine running and the alternator charging, a rate of 60 amps is supplied and therefore more than 25 amps is available with any excess power being used to charge the battery. If the rate at which current is used is more than 60 amps, the alternator supply would be exceeded and current would automatically be taken from the battery, which would eventually become discharged. It is therefore important to monitor the ammeter to ensure that the rate at which current is being used does not exceed the supply from the alternator.

17.2.4   Originally, generators (which supply direct current DC) were used in aircraft because direct current is used in most of the aircraft's electrical services. However, modern technology has produced a type of generator known as an alternator. Although this initially produces alternating current, it is internally rectified into direct current for use by the aircraft electrical system. Other advantages are that alternators are lighter, more compact and capable of functioning effectively at idle power settings, thereby preventing a current drain from the batteries during low powered settings, low powered descents etc.

17.2.5 **Batteries - Capacity and Charging**. It has already been stated that battery capacity is measured in ampere hours which in effect is a measure of the amount of electrical energy that the battery contains when in a fully charged condition.

17.2.6 Batteries are also rated by their voltage, (electrical pressure) and those used in most aircraft are either of the 12 or 24 volt type. A 12 volt battery is used with a 14 volt system and a 24 volt battery is used with a 28 volt system. The reason the battery has a slightly lower voltage than the electrical system in which it is used is related to the charging operation. For example, if 14 volts are applied to a 12 volt battery it will become fully charged, but if less than 12 volts are being supplied, the battery will resist the charge and try to send the power back to the generator or alternator. In other words, it will refuse to be charged. Therefore by having a charging system of slightly higher voltage than the battery, this situation is avoided.

17.2.7 The voltage output from the generator or alternator is kept at the correct level by a voltage regulator. This component is therefore a voltage limiting device, which is also designed to prevent the battery trying to force electricity into the generator when the generator output falls below that designated for the system.

17.2.8 Should the voltage regulator fail, the generator or alternator may supply a greater voltage than that which the system was designed for. This would result in the battery becoming overcharged, with a risk of more permanent damage. The most common battery used in light aircraft is the lead acid type which creates electricity by reaction between the lead plates and the liquid electrolyte (dilute sulphuric acid).

17.2.9 In order to protect the aircraft structure from any inadvertent spillage of acid the battery is normally housed in an enclosed compartment or box. A vent from this box to atmosphere is then arranged to exhaust the gases, hydrogen and oxygen, which form whenever the battery is being charged.

17.2.10 **Recognition and Procedures in the Event of Malfunction.** The failure of any electrical service could be an indication of an overload in the circuit causing the fuse or circuit breaker protecting the particular circuit to blow. In this case, the fuse or circuit breaker should be inspected and at least 2 minutes should be allowed before replacing the fuse with another one of the correct amperage rating or re-setting the circuit.

17.2.11 Apart from a situation in which the particular protection device fails, there is also the question of whether the generator or alternator is supplying the necessary power to operate the electrical service, or to charge the battery. This will be indicated by the ammeter, which will show a charge.

17.2.12   When the engine is not running, the electrical services will be driven by power taken from the battery and the ammeter will indicate the amount of amps being used indicating discharge. Once the engine is running, the generator or alternator will be operating and providing power for the electrical services and also to charge the battery as required, during which, the ammeter will show the rate at which the battery is being charged.

17.2.13   Ammeter presentation may vary according to whether a generator or alternator is fitted and the pilot will need to study the particular aircraft manual to interpret the ammeter readings.

17.2.14   Electrical power malfunction usually falls into two categories, i.e., insufficient rate of charge or excessive rate of charge. If the ammeter indicates a continuous discharge rate, the generator or alternator will be supplying either insufficient power, or no power to the system. In this case, the use of electric services should be reduced to the absolute minimum, and the flight terminated as soon as safely possible.

17.2.15   In the event that an excessive rate of charge is occurring, the battery will overheat and evaporate the liquid electrolyte at an excessive rate. Also, if the fault lies in the voltage regulator, the electronic components e.g. radio etc. could be adversely affected.

17.2.16   Most modern aircraft are equipped with an over voltage sensor which will shut down the alternator and illuminate a warning light in the cockpit which quickly warns the pilot of the situation.

18   AIRCRAFT INSTRUMENTS

18.1   Introduction

18.1.1   The modern light helicopter is equipped with a variety of instruments which basically fall into three groups:

1.   Flight Instruments
2.   Engine Instruments
3.   Ancillary Instruments

18.1.2   The flight instruments are those which are used in controlling the aircraft and they indicate its attitude and performance. This essentially means the airspeed, altitude, air pressure variation, aircraft attitude, direction, balance or slip. They consist of the Air Speed Indicator, Altimeter, Vertical Speed Indicator, Attitude Indicator, Heading Indicator, Magnetic Compass and the Balance Indicator. The instruments are grouped in front of the pilot on a console. See fig 18.1.

18.1.3   The flight instruments provide much essential information and the pilot will need to understand the basic principles of their operation, and to develop the ability to interpret them during flight in order to control the aircraft accurately under various conditions.

18.1.4   The engine instruments are basically designed to measure the quantity and pressure of liquids (i.e. fuel and oil) and the temperature of liquids and gases, manifold pressure, engine RPM and turbine speed (Tachometer or Tacho).

18.1.5   The ancillary instruments are all other instruments, ie., radio navigation, outside temperature, cabin air conditioning etc. In fig. 18.1 can be seen an instrument panel displaying more than the usual basic instruments.

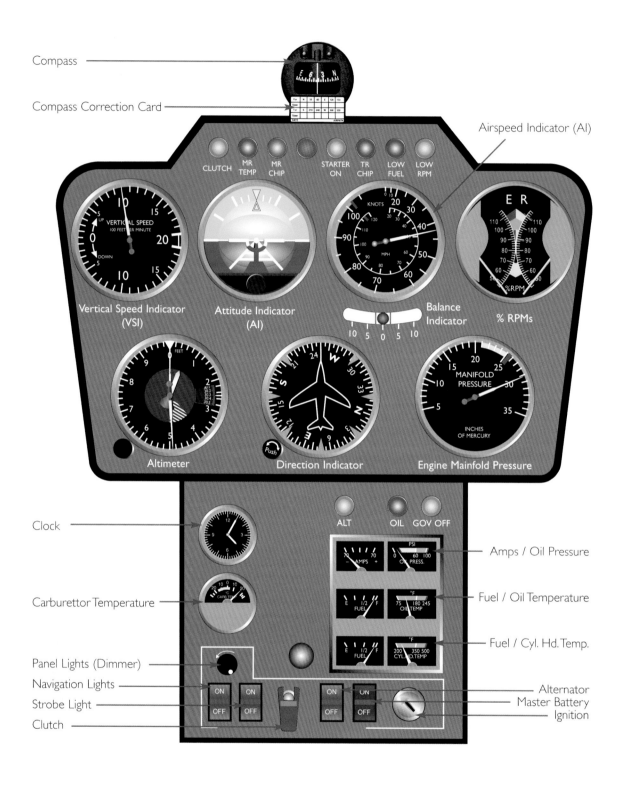

Compass

Compass Correction Card

Airspeed Indicator (AI)

CLUTCH | MR TEMP | MR CHIP | STARTER ON | TR CHIP | LOW FUEL | LOW RPM

Vertical Speed Indicator (VSI)

Attitude Indicator (AI)

Balance Indicator

% RPMs

Altimeter

Direction Indicator

Engine Mainfold Pressure

Clock

Carburettor Temperature

ALT | OIL | GOV OFF

Amps / Oil Pressure

Fuel / Oil Temperature

Fuel / Cyl. Hd. Temp.

Panel Lights (Dimmer)
Navigation Lights
Strobe Light
Clutch

Alternator
Master Battery
Ignition

Fig. 18.1   Light helicopter instrument panel (Robinson R22).

18.2   The Pitot Static System

18.2.1   To provide the airspeed indicator, altimeter and vertical speed indicator with suitable air supply careful steps are taken to obtain the sample away from airframe disturbances. The altimeter and the VSI are supplied with static air, i.e. air at a pressure not distorted by aircraft movement which represents the prevailing pressure for that altitude.

18.2.2   The airspeed indicator, on the other hand, requires two samples of air for comparison, static and the same static air that has been subjected to a rise in pressure due to the aircraft's movement (i.e. dynamic air). Because the ASI, altimeter and VSI depend for their function on air pressures they are known as Pressure Instruments.

18.2.3   **Methods of obtaining Air Samples**. There are two main pressure sensing methods used in light aircraft:

1.   **The Pitot Head,** a combined pressure/static device suitably located on the aircraft in a position away from airflow disturbance. It consists of an open-ended tube which samples pressure air. Surrounding it is a concentric tube which is blocked at the front. A series of small holes are drilled along the sides to admit air at static pressure. The pitot head often incorporates an electric element which may be switched on to avoid the build-up of ice which would result in the loss of all pressure instruments in some cases and distorted reading in others according to the extent of icing.

2.   **Pressure Head/Static Vent**. An alternative system makes use of an open ended pressure head which, like the pitot tube, may incorporate a heater. Static air is obtained from a static vent which takes the form of a small plate mounted on the side, or both sides, of the fuselage. The plate has a small hole to admit static air.

18.2.4   **Pressure Instrument System**. The pressure/static sources previously described are connected by a system of light alloy tubes to the instruments. Over a period of time moisture can collect in the system and a drain valve is often provided. In case there is a sudden blockage of the static source it is usual to have an Alternative Static Source valve which can be operated from the cabin. This will restore the altimeter and VSI following loss of readings due to a blocked static source. It may also reinstate the ASI unless its pressure source is blocked.

18.2.5   Because the static air sample is from within the cabin (in a non pressurised aircraft) it is always a little less than the static outside pressure. There are likely to be small inaccuracies in the readings of these instruments. These inaccuracies will be quite small and aircraft manuals will give information about these errors.

18.2.6   To protect the pitot/pressure head from the intrusion of water or insects, a cover is provided and this should be tied in place while the aircraft is parked for any length of time. The pitot cover is usually coloured bright red to remind pilots that it must be removed before take-off. A typical pressure/static system is illustrated in fig 18.2.

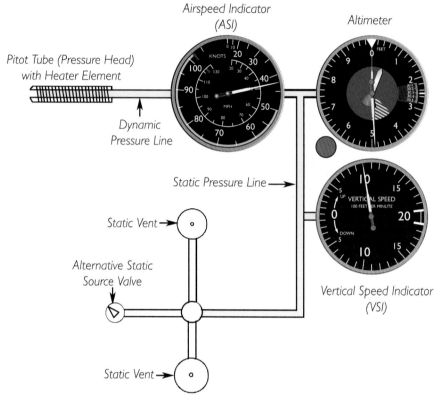

Fig. 18.2   Pressure head/Static system. The pitot tube (or pressure head) is usually positioned in front of the fuselage and the static vents are positioned on each side of the fuselage. Some aircraft have only one static vent.

18.3   The Airspeed Indicator

18.3.1   This instrument may be calibrated in knots, miles per hour (or kilometres per hour in some countries). It measures the pressure difference between static and dynamic air by employing a diaphragm or a capsule. When the aircraft is stationary both tubes transmit static pressure, but during forward movement, dynamic pressure is built up through the open-ended pitot tube and the diaphragm will distend accordingly. In effect the instrument measures the pressure difference between the two samples, the dial being calibrated in units of speed instead of pressure. Fig 18.3 illustrates the complete installation.

18.3.2   Airspeed indicator errors. While there is no lag in the instrument itself, an aircraft, like any other vehicle, requires time to change from one speed to another so that an alteration in attitude will not produce an immediate change in airspeed. The positioning of the pressure head is critical and even in the best installations errors are caused which are due to airflow disturbances.

18.3.3   This Position Error is taken into account together with Instrument Error (inaccuracies in the instrument itself) when converting IAS to RAS. A correction card will be found adjacent to the instrument except when the position and instrument error is small. For practical purposes IAS is often treated as RAS while flying training aircraft. (See also para: 18.3.15)

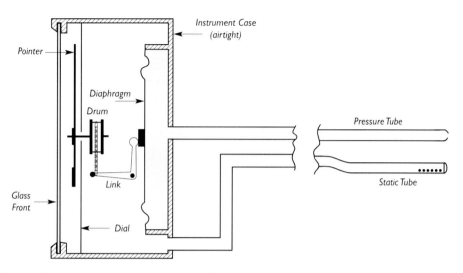

Fig. 18.3   Simplified diagram of an airspeed indicator.

18.3.4   Of more importance is the effect of varying air density which in turn is dependent upon height (pressure) and temperature. The difference between RAS and TAS resulting from these factors can be very considerable and the following examples will illustrate the importance of calculating TAS for navigational purposes. See the following tabulation.

Height	OAT°C	RAS	TAS
2000 ft	20°C	140 kt	146 kt
5000 ft	14°C	140 kt	153 kt
10000 ft	4°C	140 kt	165 kt

18.3.5   The Pooley's (CRP1) and other navigational computers will calculate a TAS when height and outside air temperature are set against the appropriate scales.

18.3.6   The serious consequences of taking off in marginal Meteorological Conditions without first removing the pressure head cover are very obvious.

18.3.7 **Calibration and Interpretation of Colour Coding.** Airspeed indicators are normally calibrated to show miles per hour or knots or both. Most indicators nowadays are colour coded so that the pilot can see important airspeed ranges or critical speeds a glance.

18.3.8 The normal operating range is shown as a green arc.

18.3.9 The red line at or near the high speed end of the airspeed scale indicates the maximum airspeed at which the aircraft is permitted to fly and this should never be exceeded. (V_{ne}). See fig 18.4.

18.3.10 Some helicopter ASI's have a blue indicator showing the maximum safe autorotation speed.

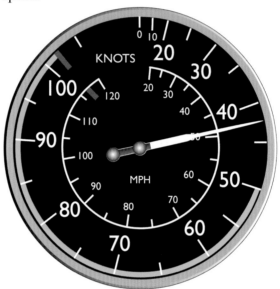

Fig. 18.4   A helicopter Airspeed Indicator

18.3.11 The manufacturer makes every attempt to minimise errors in construction and positions the pressure head where it will be largely unaffected by the disturbance of the air as the aircraft passes through it. However it is not possible to eliminate totally the errors caused by changes in the aircraft attitude. The important errors are now described.

18.3.12 **Installation Error**. It should be appreciated that even if the pressure head were in a position where no air disturbances occurred it could still only be fixed so that it meets the air directly when the aircraft is at one particular attitude. When the aircraft departs from this angle a small error will occur. This error is primarily in the static source and is variously known as installation error, pressure error, or position error.

18.3.13 The use of static vents placed in a suitable position (usually well back along the side of the fuselage) significantly reduces this error. Although the error is small at normal cruising speed, it becomes larger either side of this, and particularly in the lower airspeed range when the aircraft is flying at relatively low speeds approaching the hover.

173

18.3.14   In order that pilots appreciate the magnitude of this error throughout the speed range of the aircraft, a table or graph is normally included in the Aircraft Manual. As an example, at 100 kt, the error is very small, but in the low speed range it increases significantly, ie., when the IAS is 40 kt the installation error can increase to 11 kt or so.

18.3.15   Remember the letters CAS stand for Calibrated or Corrected Airspeed, which is the indicated airspeed corrected for installation error. In the U.K. the term RAS (Rectified Airspeed) is often used in place of CAS.

18.3.16   **Density Error**. The standard airspeed indicator is calibrated to give a correct reading when the air density corresponds to the International Standard Atmosphere (ISA).

18.3.17   This effectively means that it can only accurately measure the True Airspeed at sea level and then only when the ISA prevails at sea level. As altitude is gained, the air density reduces and therefore the effect of the impact pressure at any given airspeed is less, i.e. the IAS becomes lower than the true airspeed (TAS) at which the aircraft is flying. Although this effect may seem an added complication, the use of TAS is from a practical point of view generally only necessary during air navigation.

18.3.18   The air loads on an aircraft and behaviour (i.e. stalling in fixed wing aircraft) are directly proportional to the dynamic pressure acting on it during flight.

18.3.19   **Compressibility Error.** Since air is a compressible fluid it will compress when forced to come to rest in an impact tube. The higher pressure recorded in the ASI as a result of this is interpreted in the instrument as a higher IAS.

18.3.20   The effect of compressibility error is however not marked until reaching airspeeds of approximately 200 kt and over, and therefore it is not generally applicable to light single engined helicopters.

18.3.21   Pilot's Serviceability Checks. Before entering the cockpit the pilot should ensure that the pressure head is unblocked, secure, and that any protective cover has been removed.

18.3.22   The instrument itself is sealed and therefore it is essential to check that the front is undamaged, i.e. no cracks or looseness of the glass. The glass must also be clean and the instrument dial numerals and colour coding must be clearly legible. Further to this the pointer should be giving a zero reading when the aircraft is stationary. A small fluctuation of the pointer when the aircraft is stationary or hovering when the wind is brisk or strong may occur and this is quite normal.

18.4   The Altimeter

18.4.1   This instrument is essential to the operation of the aircraft in that its correct use ensures the pilot is able to operate at precise altitudes and flight levels as well as indicating the aircraft's vertical position in relation to the surface.

18.4.2   **Simple Pressure Altimeters**. These altimeters, through the use of a datum setting knob, provide the pilot with three basic references:

1.   Height above an aerodrome.
2.   Altitude above mean sea level.
3.   Operation of the aircraft at specific flight levels.

18.4.3   **Construction and Function**. The instrument is similar to an aneroid barometer in that it utilises a stack of two or three pressure sensitive capsules which expand or contract with the pressure changes in the atmosphere. The instrument case is sealed except for a connection with the static tube or static vent. See fig 18.5.

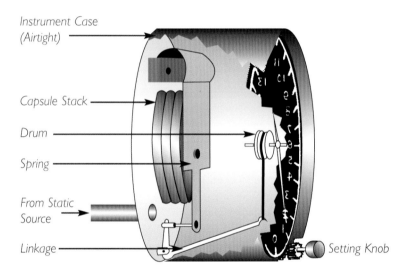

Fig. 18.5   Section through a simplified altimeter.

18.4.4   Any changes of static pressure surrounding the aircraft therefore affect the capsule stack. The expansion or contraction of the aneroid capsule actuates a linking mechanism which operates the pointers on the face of the instrument. The instrument is calibrated in feet. There are countries where altimetry is presented in metres.

18.4.5   The most common type of altimeter used in light aircraft has a dial and pointer presentation consisting of two needles. These needles sweep the calibrated dial to indicate the altitude of the aircraft. The shortest needle indicates altitude in terms of thousands of feet, and the longest needle shows hundreds of feet in 20 or 50-ft increments.

18.4.6   In fig 18.6, a simple two needle altimeter is shown. The shorter (thick) needle shows 1000's of feet, and the longer (thinner) needle shows 100's feet. The height displayed is 480 feet. On the right of the face of the instrument is the pressure setting (QFE, QNH or standard). This is adjusted by the pressure-setting knob below the instrument.

Fig 18.6 Simple two needle altimeter

18.4.7   **Effects of Atmospheric Density.** The altimeter is calibrated in the International Standard Atmosphere (ISA). Under standard atmospheric conditions each level of air in the atmosphere has a specific density, so where the real atmosphere deviates from this standard, an error will arise in the altimeter reading.

18.4.8   The practical application of this error is in relation to aircraft performance in that the performance data given in aircraft manuals is based upon the ISA. Since this performance data at any level is based upon ISA it will not necessarily correspond exactly with the actual altimeter indications.

18.4.9   **Function of the Altimeter Sub Scale**. A barometric pressure scale, which in the UK is graduated in millibars, (in American registered aircraft, inches of mercury) is located at one side of the instrument face, or at the bottom of the instrument face. This scale can usually be adjusted to give any pressure datum within a range from 950 - 1050 hPa (mb).

18.4.10   Since atmospheric pressure continually changes it will be necessary to set the required datum pressure e.g. sea level (QNH) or aerodrome level (QFE) as required in order to measure the aircraft's vertical distance from sea level or the aerodrome surface. Increasing the barometric pressure setting scale will increase the indicated altitude by approximately 30ft for every hPa. (Only applicable in the lower atmosphere).

18.4.11   **Errors**. Altimeters are subject to small mechanical errors, installation errors and those due to non-standard temperatures.

18.4.12   Mechanical errors are relatively small in a correctly functioning altimeter, and although installation error which is brought about when the static tube is not aligned directly into the airflow is not very large, it can be reduced even further by the use of static vents mounted flush with the fuselage.

18.4.13   Whenever the air temperature varies from that specified in the requirements for the ISA, an additional error will occur and the altimeter will either under-read or over-read. For example, an altimeter at sea level will be measuring the weight of a column of air above it. If the aircraft has now climbed to 5000ft, the weight or pressure on the altimeter aneroid capsule is less by that portion of the column of air below it. If under these conditions the temperature is the same as the ISA then the altimeter will read 5000ft.

18.4.14   However, if the column of air is warmer than the ISA atmosphere, the air has expanded, and the equivalent pressure level corresponding to 5000 feet in the ISA atmosphere is now at a higher (absolute) level. Therefore, 5000 feet reading on the altimeter puts the aircraft at a higher (absolute) level, in other words, the altimeter under-reads in warmer air. Conversely, the altimeter over-reads in colder air.

18.4.15   **Temperature error** is related to density error, and given the pressure altitude and the air temperature at that altitude, the error can be calculated by using a navigation computer (CRP1).

18.4.16   **Pilot's Serviceability Checks**. The pilot must ensure that the pressure head or static vents are secure, unblocked, and any protective covers or plugs are removed before entering the cockpit. As with the ASI the glass of the instrument must be clean, free of cracks and fit tightly into the casing. The numerals on the instrument dial and subscale must be clear and easily read.

18.4.17   The datum knob should be turned to ensure that it operates freely and that the needles respond correctly in conjunction with the millibar sub scale. Once the QFE or QNH setting (as required) has been obtained this should be set and the altimeter indication should not show an error of more than +30 to -50 ft.

18.5   The Vertical Speed Indicator

18.5.1   The Vertical Speed Indicator (VSI) measures rate of climb or descent and, during a letdown procedure, assists the pilot to maintain a constant known rate of descent.

18.5.2 **Construction and function.** The operation of the instrument is in many respects similar to the altimeter in so far as it consists of a capsule inside an airtight case together with suitable magnifying linkage between the capsule and the indicating pointer. The VSI is connected to the static line, which leads from the static tube or static vent to the altimeter and the airspeed indicator.

18.5.3 Inside the instrument the static line is coupled to the capsule so that its internal pressure is the same as that of the surrounding air at whatever height the aircraft may be flying. Air at static pressure is also fed into the case of the instrument via a small choke, which is finely calibrated so that pressure can change at a constant known rate.

18.5.4 When the aircraft is flown at a steady height, pressure will be the same both within and outside the capsule and the instrument will read zero. Should a climb or descent occur, pressure inside the capsule will change accordingly, whereas the restricted choke will cause the pressure outside the capsule to alter at a slower rate.

18.5.5 The capsule will contract (climbing) or expand (descending) until level flight is resumed when the restricted choke will allow the pressure within the instrument case to equal that inside the capsule. It will then return to its normal shape causing the instrument to indicate zero once more.

18.5.6 Because the restricted choke is calibrated to leak at a steady rate, a quick gain or loss of height will produce a correspondingly greater difference in pressure between the inside and outside of the capsule. This causes it to expand or contract more extensively when a high rate of climb or descent will be indicated. It takes some 5 to 10 seconds to stabilise whenever an aircraft commences to climb or descend. While the needle is "moving" it is unreliable until it stabilises.

18.5.7 A setting screw is provided for adjusting the capsule so that when static pressure is steady a zero indication is given.

18.5.8 The restricted choke is compensated for changes in air density which occur with height and which would otherwise affect the rate of flow through the orifice. Temperature changes resulting from a climb or descent distort a bi-metal strip to which is attached a small conical projection which alters the size of the choke. A simple VSI is shown in fig 18.7.

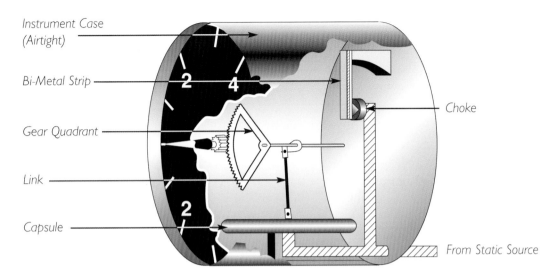

Instrument Case
(Airtight)

Bi-Metal Strip

Gear Quadrant

Link

Capsule

Choke

From Static Source

Fig. 18.7 A simple VSI.

18.5.9   **Pilot's Serviceability Checks**. During the pre-flight inspection of the aircraft, the pilot must ensure that the pressure head (or when fitted, the static vents) are unobstructed. The glass of the instrument must be checked to make sure that it is clean, fitting tightly and that there are no cracks. Any leakage of cockpit air into the instrument case will cause instrument errors during climbs and descents.

18.5.10   The instrument face must be clearly legible and the indicating needle should show zero when the aircraft is on the ground. If the instrument is showing an error of more than plus or minus 200 ft, it should be reported as unserviceable. Fig 18.8 shows a VSI indicating a climb at 1000 feet per minute.

Fig. 18.8   A VSI showing a steady climb of 1000 ft/min.

179

18.6 The Need For Other Instruments

18.6.1   The pressure instruments so far described give an incomplete picture to the pilot when flying without visual reference because their information is confined to:

1.   Airspeed (ASI)
2.   Height (Altimeter)
3.   Rate of height change (VSI).

Certain important factors are missing in the readings provided by the pressure instruments and these are:

1.   Heading
2.   Attitude in the lateral plane
3.   Slip or skid
4.   Attitude in the pitching plane.

18.6.2   In view of the relationship between pitch attitude and airspeed, to some extent the last requirement is catered for by the airspeed indicator while requirement 1 (Heading) may be obtained from the magnetic compass.

18.6.3   The Vertical-Speed Indicator together with an Attitude Indicator and a Direction Indicator, the latter two being gyroscopic driven, brings the flight panel up to the standard illustrated in fig 18.1. The flight instrument panel is mounted on flexible attachment points to prevent damage from shock or vibration.

18.7 Gyroscopic-operated Instruments

18.7.1   The behaviour of a gyroscope should be understood. When a wheel of any kind is rotated there is a tendency for the material of which it is made to fly outwards because of centrifugal reaction. Because the resultant lines of force emanate radially around its circumference, the wheel tends to remain in its plane of rotation and will resist attempts to alter its position.

18.7.2   This property is called **Rigidity** and its magnitude depends upon the speed of rotation and the mass of the wheel or other object (this is equally applicable to a propeller or helicopter rotor, or a child's top). Rigidity in a gyroscope is used to provide attitude information when no natural visual references exist. The second important property of a gyroscope is called **Precession.**

18.7.3   When an attempt is made to disturb its position, the gyroscope will resist the force at the point of application. A reaction will occur at a point 90° removed from the original force.

NOTE: *Students are directed to section 1.3, where a more detailed description of the gyroscopic precession principle is presented.*

18.7.4   The 90° shift from point of disturbance to the reaction is always in the direction of rotation. The rate at which a gyro precesses is dependent upon the degree of the disturbing movement, and this principle is employed to provide information about the rate at which an aircraft changes heading.

18.7.5   Using the properties of rigidity and precession, gyroscopes are variously mounted in instruments according to the information required. The gyroscope may be free to move in one plane only, or arranged to allow freedom around all axes. This is accomplished by suspending the gyro in one or more Gimbal Rings, see drawing number 16 in fig 1.11B.

18.7.6   Gyros are driven by air, which is directed, via jets into notches or Buckets indented around the outside edge of the gyro. See fig 18.9. In practice air is drawn out of the instrument by an engine driven vacuum pump. Replacement air flows into the instrument after passing through a suitable filter and finally discharges through jets, rotating the gyro at some 9000 - 12,000 RPM according to the type of instrument.

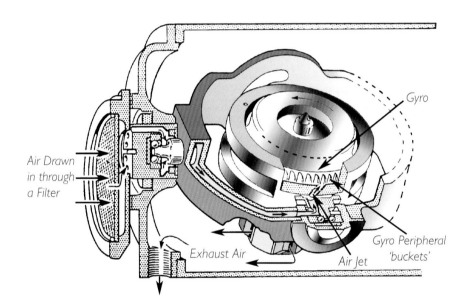

Fig. 18.9   Airflow through the gyro unit of an Attitude Indicator.

18.7.7   Because the jets of air must be directed constantly on the periphery of the gyro and as a result of certain other mechanical difficulties, angular movement of the gimbal rings is limited by stops in instruments of earlier design. Should the aircraft take up a flight attitude outside the limits of these instruments both attitude indicator and direction indicator will Topple, i.e. the gyro will cease to hold itself rigid thus causing the instrument to fluctuate violently until it has been re-set. Some modern instruments have complete freedom of movement.

181

18.7.8   Electrically rotated gyroscopes are in common use in many small helicopters. Some of their advantages being:

1. Simpler design of the gimbal rings allows the instrument to register more extreme flight attitudes before toppling (or freedom from toppling).
2. Higher rotational speeds are possible with the attendant greater rigidity of the gyro.
3. Whereas the efficiency of air-driven gyros decreases at high altitudes because of reduced atmospheric density, electrical gyros are not similarly affected.
4. Electrical instruments, being completely sealed have no contact with fine dust particles and moisture as is the case with air operated instruments, however well filtered.

18.7.9   When the flight instruments are vacuum operated it has become common practice, even in light aircraft to fit an electric turn and balance indicator as an insurance against complete loss of gyro instruments in the event of vacuum pump failure.

18.7.10   **Gyro serviceability checks.** After the engine has been started, the vacuum gauge should be checked to see that the system is operating correctly.   At low RPM however, the suction indication may be on the low side. The gauge reading should therefore be checked again during the engine power checks prior to lift-off.

18.7.11   During the hover, the gyro instruments can be checked by turning the aircraft to the left and to the right to check that each one gives correct indications.

18.7.12   In the case of a venturi operated suction system, it should be appreciated that the system cannot be properly checked until the aircraft has become airborne and a reasonable airspeed established.

18.7.13   The operation of those gyro instruments which are driven by electricity can either be checked:

1. Aurally e.g. after the master switch has been placed in the ON position it is usually possible to hear the gyroscope rotating and speeding up, or
2. Noting the instrument reaction during turns whilst hovering.

Note: *Current practice is to fit each electrically driven gyro instrument with a warning flag (normally coloured red). This comes into view on the face of the instrument whenever the electrical supply fails.*

18.8   **Balance Indicator**. The most common type of balance indicator in use today consists of a curved glass cylinder filled with kerosene in which is placed a small agate stone, or a ball bearing. The fluid provides a damping action and so ensures smooth and easy movement of the ball. A small vertical projection at one end of the glass tube (not visible to the pilot) contains a small bubble of air to compensate for expansion of the fluid during changes in temperature. See fig 18.10.

18.8.2   With the ball in a tube system, the glass container is curved so that when no yaw forces are present the ball will settle at the lowest point. During turns, the ball will also settle in the centre of the tube when the centrifugal force is equal to the horizontal component of the lift force i.e. when the forces are in balance.

Fig. 18.10 Balance indicator.

18.8.3   Helicopter pilots often fit a strand of wool on the nose of the helicopter, (if it has one) and this is very effective in showing slip or skid !!

18.9   The Attitude Indicator

18.9.1   This instrument is variously known as an Attitude Indicator, Gyro Horizon or Artificial Horizon depending upon its year of manufacture and limitations. It is used to present the pilot with a pictorial display of the aircraft's attitude. See fig 18.11 which shows the presentation to the pilot of the correct attitude, flying straight and level.

Fig. 18.11 Pilot's attitude indicator showing straight and level flight.

18.9.2   **Function.** The instrument is constructed about a gyroscope, the spin axis of which is mounted vertically, (axis ZZ in fig 18.12), and maintained in this position by a gravity sensing device in the form of a pendulous unit. Utilising the properties of a gyro to maintain a constant position in space, the rotor is mounted in a gimbal assembly consisting of an inner and outer ring. The gyro in this unit is called an Earth Gyro, because it is tied to the direction of gravity. See fig 18.12.

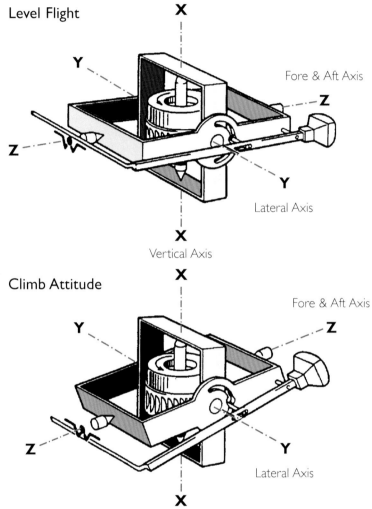

Fig. 18.12   *Principle of operation of the Gravity Controlled Earth Gyro. (Attitude indication).*

18.9.3   The inner gimbal forms the rotor casing and is pivoted parallel to the athwart ships axis of the aircraft. Axis YY. The outer gimbal is pivoted parallel to the aircraft's fore and aft axis. Axis ZZ. The pivot points of the outer gimbal are located at the front and rear ends of the instrument case, and thus the aircraft itself.

18.9.4   A change in pitch attitude of the aircraft turns the instrument case and hence the outer ring about the lateral axis YY of the inner ring or rotor case which is stabilised by gyroscopic rigidity. The pointer bar, representing the horizon, is pivoted on the side of the outer gimbal ring and engages an actuating pin on the outer case.

18.9.5 When the outer ring turns about the lateral axis YY, the pointer bar moves up or down relative to the instrument case and in particular, relative to the miniature aircraft symbol (index aircraft) engraved or fixed behind the glass bezel.

18.9.6 Rolling or banking of the aircraft turns the instrument case about the fore and aft axis (ZZ), the outer ring being stabilised by the rotor's gyroscopic rigidity.

18.9.7 There are various Attitude Indicator/Artificial Horizon models in use and, while earlier instruments have toppling limits of 110° in bank and 60° in pitch, later designs allow complete freedom in roll and 85° in pitch. Others have complete freedom in both axes.

18.9.8 When toppling occurs (when the aircraft is flown outside the bank and pitch limits ie., doing aerobatics), the instrument will re-set automatically although some ten to fifteen minutes is required for full recovery. During the resetting period the horizon screen will move random fashion across the face of the instrument, the oscillations becoming less as the automatic erecting device brings the gyro under control.

18.9.9 Earlier instruments incorporated a manual caging device which could be used to cage the instrument before carrying out manoeuvres which are known to be in excess of its limitations. It can also be used as a quick erection device should these limitations be inadvertently exceeded. When uncaging the instrument it is however necessary to ensure the aircraft is in straight and level flight, otherwise erroneous indications will be given until the normal erection mechanism has had time to act.

18.9.10 Automatic erection of the gyro is accomplished by a valve suspended below the rotor called the Pendulous Unit. The pendulous unit also maintains the rotor in its correct position when for any reason it has become displaced.

18.9.11 **Operation of erection unit.** The pendulous unit consists of a body attached to the bottom of the rotor case, and in this body there is a slot aperture on each side through which the air is exhausted into the instrument case. The slot apertures are controlled by two pairs of pendulous vanes arranged so that diametrically opposite vanes are mounted on a common spindle. (See fig 18.9 for a section through an attitude indicator and airflow passages. Air is directed at the rotor unit to spin it, and proceeds out through the pendulous unit).

18.9.12 The vanes hang vertically and are adjusted so that the vanes bisect the slots when the rotor axis is vertical, thereby producing four equal jet streams, namely fore and aft, and left and right. Should the rotor axis depart from the vertical, for example to the left as shown in fig 18.13 the correction or "erection" action will be as follows:

185

18.9.13   The vanes remain vertical and so vane A opens the slot aperture B whilst the opposite vane closes its slot aperture. Thus there will be an unequal reaction between the two slots on the fore and aft axis and there will be a force applied to the pendulous unit body which produces in effect a torque on the rotor assembly equivalent to an upwards force C or downwards force D. Precession will be introduced acting at 90° to this force which will correct the displacement of the rotor axis from the vertical.

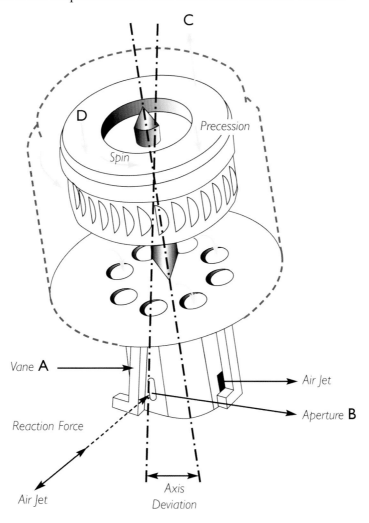

Fig. 18.13 Operation of the erection unit (Pendulous Unit).

18.9.14   **Errors**. In flight, accelerations in the fore-and-aft and lateral planes will displace the pendulous vanes so producing a 90° precessing effect on the gyro axis when the horizon screen will fail to correspond with the true horizon. Furthermore the pendulous unit is suspended below the tilting axis of the gyro so that any tendency for the assembly to swing under the influence of acceleration or deceleration will cause the gyro to precess through 90° and as a result to give an incorrect indication.

18.9.15 **Acceleration**. While the effect is of less importance in light helicopters or those of moderate performance, serious displacement of the horizon screen can occur during take-off with a high-speed aircraft capable of more rapid acceleration. The combined effect of vane displacement and pendulous unit inertia during take-off will cause the instrument to indicate a climbing turn to the right (or, in the case of electric instruments, a climbing turn to the left, because electric rotors spin in the opposite direction to air driven gyros) and while the indication is small, an attempt to correct would result in a descending turn in the opposite direction.

18.9.16 This error would be most likely to occur with a high-performance aircraft when it would be particularly dangerous. It can be overcome by monitoring the attitude indicator with the turn and balance indicator and ASI during the early stages of the take-off and climb away. (Included in illustrating errors, not of particular concern to the helicopter pilot).

18.9.17 **Deceleration**. The effects of deceleration are the reverse of acceleration causing the instrument to show a gentle descending turn to the left, although it is emphasised that such indications only occur when a high-speed aircraft reduces airspeed over a lengthy period.

18.9.18 **Turning Errors.** During a turn, centrifugal reaction will displace the two pendulous vanes which pivot on a fore-and-aft axis causing the rotor to precess through 90° in the rolling plane. Additionally the pendulous unit will be subjected to centrifugal reaction causing rotor precession in the pitching plane.

18.9.19 The combined effect of both displacements during a prolonged turn results in errors which increase until the aircraft has changed heading through 180°. Continuation of the turn beyond 180° has the effect of progressively cancelling these errors until 360° is completed when accurate indications will be given again.

18.9.20 These inaccuracies, which are not of great magnitude, show themselves as incorrect nose up or down indications coupled with too large or too small a degree of bank, according to the direction of turn and the number of degrees change of heading. The errors are partly compensated for by arranging the gyro to run at a slight angle so that during a rate 1 turn errors are very small, increasing slightly when heading changes are made above or below that rate.

18.9.21 **Pilot's Serviceability Checks**. After starting the engine, the instrument should be checked to see that it has erected properly and that the artificial horizon is laterally level. Some instruments have an adjustable index (miniature aircraft) which can be raised or lowered by a setting knob. When this facility is fitted, it is important to align the index aircraft over the artificial horizon bar so that a presentation of level flight is more clearly shown when airborne.

18.9.22　The normal suction required for this instrument is between 4½ to 5½ inches of mercury and this can be checked from the vacuum gauge. It takes about 4 minutes to bring the rotor up to speed. Whilst hovering, the aircraft should be turned left and right during which, the artificial horizon line should remain stable. On earlier instruments, the action of turning the aircraft will affect the pendulous vanes which are part of the pendulous erection device and it will be normal to note a slight change in the lateral level of the artificial horizon line.

18.10　The Heading Indicator

18.10.1　This instrument, also known as the Directional Gyro (DG) or Directional Indicator (DI) was designed to give the pilot dead beat indications of the aircraft's heading. See fig 18.14 for the instrument presentation in the cockpit. The "Lubber Line" is the fixed heading index at the top of the instrument, against which heading is measured.

Fig. 18.14　Cockpit presentation of a Heading Indicator.

18.10.2　Although the magnetic compass is the master instrument for determining the heading of an aircraft, it oscillates and cannot be damped sufficiently to overcome the fluctuations and erroneous readings arising from air turbulence and the errors associated with turning and changes of airspeed.

18.10.3　**Function.** The construction and operation of the heading indicator is based upon the principles of gyroscopic rigidity. The rotor is mounted vertically and is normally driven from the suction created by the vacuum system. See fig 18.15. This is a tied gyroscope (but not an earth gyroscope).

18.10.4   Air enters the instrument case, passes through channels in the vertical gimbal ring and impinges upon buckets cut into the periphery of the rotor. The rotor is enclosed in a case and supported in an inner gimbal ring which is free to turn about a horizontal axis. This inner gimbal is mounted in an outer gimbal, the bearings of which are located at the top and bottom of the instrument case, permitting the gimbal to pivot about a vertical axis.

18.10.5   The rotor is maintained in vertical alignment by arranging for the air jets which strike against the rotor grooves, to apply a precessional force whenever the rotor starts to tilt from the vertical. This precessional force automatically re-aligns the rotor into a vertical position with its axis horizontal.

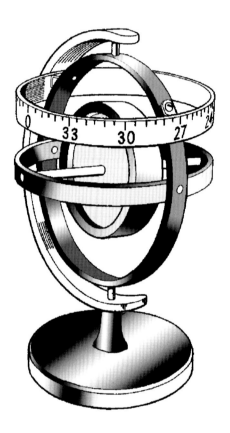

Fig. 18.15   The arrangement of the gyro unit in a Directional Indicator.   (Heading Indicator).   This arrangement shows the old style scale mounted horizontally, although this presentation is still in use, a more modern display is shown in fig. 18.14.

18.10.6   A second type of erection device is incorporated in the mechanism which is used to set the instrument's heading to that of the magnetic compass. This mechanism which is operated by an external knob below the glass case of the instrument is also used to cage and uncage the gimbal assembly. Whenever the knob is pressed in, it operates a caging arm which re-erects the rotor to its correct position should it have toppled due to the limitations of the gimbal assembly being exceeded.

18.10.7 There are two fundamental characteristics of all directional gyroscopes regardless of whether they are vacuum driven or electrically driven, namely **DRIFT in azimuth and TURNING or GIMBALLING errors during a banked turn**.

18.10.8 **DRIFT**. A directional gyroscope over a period of time will fail to agree with the reading of the magnetic compass, the difference becoming larger as time advances. This drift from the correct setting emanates from three sources, **Mechanical Drift, Apparent Drift and Transport Error.**

18.10.9 **Mechanical Drift**. Although the directional gyroscope is manufactured to high standards, bearing friction, imperfect balance of the gimbal rings and severe turbulence in flight will cause the gyro to precess. Furthermore the erecting action of the double jet supplying the rotor tends to displace the outer gimbal ring so that up to 4°drift may occur in a 15 minute period.

18.10.10 **Apparent Drift**. Apparent Drift is non-existent at the equator. In the extreme case of an aircraft flying over the North or South Pole, the scale of the directional gyroscope will remain rigid while the earth rotates at its rate of 15°/hour and the DG will appear to have wandered off setting by that amount.

18.10.11 As an aircraft flies towards the equator, apparent drift decreases accordingly and in proportion to the latitude. The instrument is compensated by employing a Drift Nut which applies a precessing force to the inner gimbal ring so balancing apparent drift. The drift nut completely balances apparent drift at one latitude only and when an aircraft moves to another base some distance north or south of original, the instrument should be adjusted. This is of particular importance when a change is made from the northern to the southern hemisphere or vice versa since apparent drift is reversed in sign in each case.

18.10.12 **Transport Error**. Yet another error results from convergence of the meridians towards the poles. In northerly or southerly latitudes an aircraft flying in a straight line on an easterly or westerly heading would cut successive meridians at different angles because they are not parallel. In consequence there will be a changing relationship between magnetic north as indicated on the compass and DG reading which remains fixed in space. This is known as Transport Error; it is at its maximum at the poles and does not exist at the equator where, for practical purposes, the meridians run parallel to one another.

18.10.13 **Gimballing or Turning Error**. The mechanical limitations imposed by the inner and outer gimbal system cause the scale to rotate past the lubber line at an uneven rate when the aircraft is banked, but as the wings become level the gimbal system aligns itself and the correct heading will be indicated. While this Turning Error is noticeable at fairly steep angles of bank, it is of little importance in instrument flying when turns are limited to a Rate 1 or less.

18.10.14   **Operating Limits**. Earlier models had a geometric limitation to the gimbals which caused the instrument to topple when 55° of pitch or bank were exceeded. Later models, of improved geometric gimbal design permit the instrument greater freedom in pitch and bank and like certain attitude indicators some of these models are considered as "topple free".

18.10.15   **Caging and Resetting Procedure.** The earlier models of this instrument are equipped with a caging knob below the instrument face, which can be pushed in locking the whole gyro assembly until pulled out again. This facility can be used to avoid strain and wear on the gimbal bearings when carrying out manoeuvres known to be in excess of the gyro's limitations. The same caging mechanism is also used to re-synchronise the heading card with the magnetic compass.

18.10.16   Later instruments incorporate a spring loaded knob which when pushed and held in this position can be rotated to re-synchronise the instrument with the magnetic compass.

18.10.17   **When re-synchronising any type of heading indicator it is important to maintain an accurate heading with the aircraft level fore and aft, and in unaccelerated flight before noting the compass heading and setting it on the heading indicator. Failure to do this will result in an erroneous reading from both instruments.**

18.10.18   Pilot's Serviceability Checks. Prior to starting up the engine, the instrument should be checked to see that the glass front is intact and the numerals are clearly legible. The power source supply should be checked after engine starting to ensure that it is functioning correctly and when a vacuum operated instrument is used, the correct minimum amount of suction must be obtained.

18.10.19   During the hover, the heading indicator should increase its heading reading when the aircraft is turned to the right and decrease its reading when turned to the left. The heading card should also give a dead beat reading.

18.10.20   The instrument should be synchronised with the magnetic compass before leaving the parking area and re-checked again during the pre-take-off checks. Small errors of 5° to 10° incurred during hovering will normally be acceptable but larger errors will indicate a faulty instrument.

18.10.21   During normal flight, errors of up to 3° every 15 minutes is considered normal, but anything larger may mean the instrument is suspect.

19 ENGINE INSTRUMENTS

19.1   In addition to the flight instruments previously described are those provided to allow proper management of the engine. It is usual to group these together in one area of the instrument panel. Note that the term aeroplanes is used in these notes as the instruments are universal in light piston engine fixed wing aeroplanes and light piston helicopters.

19.1.1   In light aeroplanes many of the engine instruments are supplied by the motor industry and a typical complement of engine readouts to be found in a light aeroplane would be as follows:

19.1.2   **Engine Speed Indicator**. Sometimes known as a Tachometer, this instrument reads engine RPM. It is usually calibrated at intervals of 100 RPM and the dial will have a red line at the maximum permitted engine speed. Some engines have a small range of RPM within which vibration can be harmful and, in these cases, the manufacturers recommend that such power settings must be avoided. The engine speed range to be avoided will be marked with a coloured arc.

19.1.3   The normal range of engine speeds is often marked with a green arc. Many RPM indicators incorporate a small window through which mileometer-type numbers indicate total engine hours, a useful check on servicing intervals.

19.1.4   **Oil Pressure Gauge**. This is similar to a car-type oil pressure gauge except that it is marked with a minimum idling pressure (red line), a normal operating sector (green) and a maximum pressure red line.

19.1.5   **Oil Temperature Gauge**. Within the engine oil system is an electrical resistance-type temperature sensor which is coupled to a temperature gauge on the instrument panel.

19.1.6   Like most modern engine instruments the oil pressure gauge is usually marked with a green arc for normal operating temperatures and a red line to denote maximum. Ideally, the engine should not be run at more than 1000-1200 RPM until the oil temperature is in the green sector. However, on a cold day it is sometimes not possible to achieve this temperature without idling for a long time and the aircraft manual usually advises a minimum warm-up period before opening the throttle for the power checks.

19.1.7   **Cylinder Head Temperature Gauge**. In many respects this instrument is the equivalent of a car water (cooling) temperature gauge. Most aero engines are air-cooled and, since there is no water, temperature is measured at the cylinder heads.

19.1.8   A cylinder head temperature gauge like other engine instruments is colour coded to assist the pilot in instant recognition of what is normal and what is abnormal.

19.1.9   **Fuel Contents Gauge.** Light aircraft fuel gauges are similar to those fitted in most cars. In the tank, a float mounted on a hinged arm adopts the level of fuel at the time. As the float arm takes up its position according to the amount of fuel in the tank it alters a rheostat (variable electric resistance) which adjusts readings on the pilot's fuel gauge by altering the balance between two electric currents.

19.1.10   The instrument is based upon a potentiometer - a form of electric circuit which, because it measures differences between currents is therefore little affected by the state of the battery unless it is so undercharged that it cannot work the instrument.

19.1.11   When more than one tank is fitted each will have its own fuel gauge although in some larger aircraft a single gauge reads the contents of fuel in the tank selected. Alternatively, there may be a single gauge with a tank selector switch. Rheostat/potentiometer based fuel measuring systems vary in accuracy. Furthermore, today's accurate gauge could prove untrustworthy tomorrow. Therefore, before any flight the pilot must visually check fuel contents (and colour) by looking into the tank through the filler cap.

19.1.12   **Fuel Pressure Gauge**. An electric fuel pump is normally fitted as a back-up in case of mechanical pump failure. In such cases a fuel pressure gauge is provided and when the electric pump is turned on prior to engine starting, it will indicate that fuel pressure exists, thus confirming that the carburettor is being supplied.

19.1.13   In the event of engine failure the fuel pressure gauge should form part of the "cause of failure" checks. Lack of fuel pressure could indicate malfunction of the engine-driven fuel pump, a situation that can be rectified by turning on the electric fuel pump.

19.2   Instruments in More Advanced Aircraft

19.2.1   Engine instruments so far described are fitted to most light training aircraft however, many aircraft have certain additional instrumentation related to the engine, and these are:

19.2.2   **Exhaust Gas Temperature Gauge.** To assist the pilot in setting the most economical mixture for best fuel economy an Exhaust Gas Temperature Gauge (EGT Gauge) is often fitted. It functions by measuring the temperature of the exhaust gas, there being a direct relationship between this and fuel/air ratio. A weak mixture burns hot while rich mixtures burn at lower temperatures.

19.2.3 **Manifold Pressure Gauge.** To provide the pilot with a suitable means of setting the throttle a manifold pressure gauge is provided. This measures the pressure within the induction manifold and the instrument is calibrated in inches of mercury.

19.2.4 **Fuel Flow Indicator.** Fuel injected engines are provided with fuel flow indicators which, as the name implies, measure the flow of fuel in gallons per hour. Since most light aero engines are of American manufacture these instruments are calibrated in US gallons.

19.2.5 Fuel burns for normal cruising are usually marked with a green sector. When the aircraft engine is fuel injected, it is the practice to house both the manifold pressure gauge and the fuel flow indicator within one case.

19.3 Ancillary Instruments

19.3.1 **Ammeter/Voltmeter.** Most light aircraft are fitted with an Ammeter which indicates current flow (in amperes) from the alternator to the battery or from the battery to such electric services as the radio or pitot heat when the alternator has failed or current demand exceeds the output of the alternator.

19.3.2 Engine starting demands a heavy current and immediately after the engine is running a high charge will be indicated as the alternator charges the battery. Gradually the charging rate will decrease as the battery is replenished.

19.3.3 **Outside Air Temperature Gauge.** So that the pilot may make both airspeed and altimeter corrections in flight, and be aware of icing risks, an Outside Air Temperature Gauge (OAT gauge) is fitted, usually high up on the windscreen behind the temperature probe which measures the temperature of the outside air.

19.3.4 An alternative type of OAT gauge is mounted on the instrument panel, some distance from the probe and linked to it electrically. Although this instrument is regarded by most manufacturers as an optional extra it is nevertheless important for safe operation of the aircraft. In a helicopter, it affords the pilot the means to calculate the maximum power and maximum 5 minute continuous power settings.

19.3.5 **Vacuum Gauge.** To operate the attitude indicator and the direction indicator vacuum is supplied by an engine-driven pump. Satisfactory performance of these instruments depends, among other factors, on their being supplied with vacuum sufficient to spin the gyros at the correct speed.

19.3.6 In most light aircraft the vacuum system operates in the range of 4½ to 5½ in. of mercury and a small vacuum gauge is provided on the instrument panel so that the pilot can check that this is being delivered.

19.3.7 Usually normal suction is marked on the vacuum gauge by a green sector and the instrument should be checked during the engine run up. Low vacuum could be caused by a blocked filter or an unserviceable vacuum pump. In either case readings of the gyro-operated instruments could be suspect.

19.3.8 **Hydraulic Pressure Gauge.** This instrument is only fitted in aircraft of more advanced design that have hydraulic systems. Its purpose is to enable the pilot to ensure that the hydraulic system is being supplied with sufficient pressure to operate the services.

19.3.9 **Warning Lights**. It is common practice to fit warning lights in aircraft. These draw attention to such matters as low oil pressure, alternator failure, electric fuel pump on, low fuel pressure, low RPM, main and tail gear box chip lights and main gear-box over temperature. The low RPM caution light and horn indicates rotor RPM at 95% or below. The oil pressure and low fuel warning lights are actuated by sensors in those systems and are independent of gauge indicators.

19.3.10 The main and tail gear box chip detectors are magnetic devices located in the drain plugs of each gear box. When metallic particles are drawn to the magnets they close an electrical circuit turning on the warning light. The metal particles could be caused by a failing bearing or gear, thus giving the pilot warning of impending gear box failure. The main gear box over-temp warning light is actuated by a temperature switch located on the box near the input pinion bearing (typical system).

19.3.11 Usually the various warning/advisory lights are grouped together. In a light aircraft there will be a strip of such lights along with a "Press to Test" button for checking that all bulbs are functioning. A more complex aircraft will have a large cluster of these lights. Such an arrangement is known as an **Annunciator Panel.**

19.3.12 Fixed Notices. On the instrument panel and elsewhere in the aircraft are a number of fixed notices giving limitations (weights, speeds and such matters that may affect the safe operation of the aircraft). All notices, which are often known as **Placards,** are listed in the aircraft manual.

20 FIRE EXTINGUISHERS

20.1   Pilots should be aware of the types of fire extinguishers available, their identification and particular application.

20.1.2   **Water**. These are suitable for most fires except those involving flammable liquids or live electrical apparatus. When operating a water fire extinguisher, the jet should be directed at the base of the flame and should be kept moving across the area of the fire. After the main fire has been extinguished, hot spots should be sought out and dealt with. A fire spreading vertically should be attacked at its lowest point and followed upwards. This type of extinguisher is identified by a **RED coloured label** on the container.

20.1.3   **Foam**. This type is used mainly for fluid fires, for example, fuel spilt on the ground, paint, oil and coolants. This is now a pre-mixed extinguishant, normally consisting of bicarbonate of soda soap extract, sulphate and water. The jet of the extinguisher should NOT be aimed at the liquid, but should be aimed just above the liquid fire and allowed to settle onto the liquid. The jet from one of these extinguishers is about 7 metres. The foam extinguisher is identified by a **CREAM coloured label** on the side of the container.

20.1.4   **Chemical Dry Powder**. This type is suitable for flammable liquids and electrical apparatus, but is mainly used for aircraft wheel brakes. It consists of approximately 25 lbs of bicarbonate of soda dry powder. The dry powder extinguisher is recognised by a **BLUE coloured label** on the side of the container.

20.1.5   **Carbon Dioxide (CO$_2$).** Although not to be used in confined spaces where the fumes can be inhaled, the carbon dioxide extinguisher is used in aircraft engine bays. This type is suitable for fires involving flammable liquids or electrical apparatus. The jet or horn of the extinguisher should not be touched by hand as adiabatic cooling cause a dramatic drop in temperature when the CO$_2$ is released. Although these types of extinguishers are normally identified by **BLACK steel cylinders with a SILVER painted top**, the only positive way to identify a CO$_2$ extinguisher is by a BLACK label on the side of the cylinder.

20.1.6   **BCF. This is a RED bottle** containing Bromochlorodifluormethane which is under pressure of dry nitrogen. These fire extinguishers are used for **all** classes of fire in an aircraft, including pressure cabins. This is a non toxic fire extinguishant although it is advisable to ventilate the compartment after use. Its identification is by reference to the label on the extinguisher.

20.1.7   No harm is normally caused to an engine where a CO_2 or BCF fire extinguisher has been used, provided the engine is run or turned over adequately within the following few hours. These types are therefore the most suitable and ideal fire extinguishers for engine fires, both internal and external.

20.1.8   A lesser used extinguishant known as **Methyl Bromide** is sometimes used for engine fires, however, if allowed to remain in the engine, it will be necessary to strip the engine to ensure that corrosion has not occurred, (particularly at temperatures below 4°C when it is in liquid state.

20.1.9   **Mechanical foam extinguishants**, formed by mixing air, water and foam-making liquid, are a greater corrosion danger to the engine, and therefore should not be used especially for engine intakes. If this foam enters the engine it will leave deposits which will require an engine strip.

CAUTION:

In the UK, many fire extinguishers are still coloured for identification, however, this should not be considered the standard method of identification. The only safe form of identification of a fire extinguisher is by the specifications on the label, which is attached to the side of the container. This is the only positive method.

Self Test Questions for Part 1
Aircraft General & Principles of Flight

1   Why is it usual that helicopter rotor blades have symmetrical aerofoils:

    (a)   In order that the centre of pressure is at the same point as the centre of gravity.

    (b)   To allow the centre of pressure to move more freely.

    (c)   To avoid the introduction of dangerous forces.

    (d)   Allows linear movement of the angle of attack.

2   Which of the following is correct regarding Angle of Attack and Pitch Angle of a helicopter rotor blade:

    (a)   The Angle of Attack is greater than the Pitch angle in a forward going blade when a helicopter is moving forward.

    (b)   The Pitch angle is greater than the Angle of attack in a retreating blade when a helicopter is in forward flight.

    (c)   The Angle of Attack and the Pitch Angle will be the same in the fore and aft position, but only in the hover in zero wind.

    (d)   The Angle of Attack is smaller than the Pitch Angle in a forward going blade when a helicopter is moving forward.

3   Considering an aerofoil in a stalled condition, which of the following is correct:

    (a)   An aerofoil stalls at a certain speed.

    (b)   In a stalled condition, the lift has dropped considerably but not to zero.

    (c)   When an aerofoil stalls, the pressure over the top surface decreases considerably.

    (d)   At the onset of a stall, both lift and drag decrease abruptly.

4   Considering the forces acting on a rotor blade, which of the following is correct:

    (a)   The angle between the relative airflow and the chord line is called the blade angle.

    (b)   The angle of attack plus the inflow angle equals the pitch angle

    (c)   The angle between the chord line and the plane of rotation is called the angle of attack.

    (d)   The angle between the relative airflow and the chord line is called the pitch angle.

5   Which of the following is correct regarding airflow about the rotor:

(a)   The angle of attack and induced airflow are inversely proportional for a given rotor section and RPM.
(b)   The induced airflow remaining constant, the inflow angle and the Nr are directly proportional.
(c)   The inflow angle and the induced airflow are inversely proportional for a given rotor RPM (Nr).
(d)   For a given blade section and rotor RPM; for a reduction in induced airflow, the angle of attack decreases.

6   The speeding up and slowing down of the rotor blade during a given revolution accompanied by blade flapping is termed:

(a)   Hookes joint effect.
(b)   Control orbit.
(c)   Coriolis effect.
(d)   Phase lag.

7   Cyclic stick movement:

(a)   Alters the disc attitude.
(b)   Changes the coning angle.
(c)   Changes the "advance angle".
(d)   Alters the phase angle.

8   Translational lift at low forward air speeds, or in the hover for a given engine power, will:

(a)   Maintain a constant total rotor thrust.
(b)   Increase parasitic drag.
(c)   Maintain constant airspeed.
(d)   Cause the helicopter to climb.

9   Phase lag is the:

(a)   Time between the collective pitch increase and the restoration of the original rotor RPM.
(b)   Angle, in the plane of rotation, through which a blade moves between a pitch selection and the corresponding flapped position.
(c)   Angle, in the plane of rotation, though which a blade moves between a collective selection and the corresponding disc attitude.
(d)   That point where the blade receives the maximum alteration in cyclic pitch change 90° out of phase with the highest and lowest points of the control orbit.

10   Dynamic roll-over may be caused by:

(a)   Landing on a steep slope.
(b)   Lifting off near buildings.
(c)   An excessive rolling movement developing about a skid or wheel in contact with a slope or uneven ground.
(e)   An excessive movement of the cyclic control in the pitch axis causing a rocking motion in the helicopter.

11   In the event that on touch down, ground resonance exists, the more appropriate action to take is to:

(a)   Increase rotor RPM to change the resonant frequency.
(b)   Turn the tail into wind to reduce resonance effects.
(c)   Take off immediately if rotor RPM is high enough.
(d)   Operate the cyclic control to change the ground/rotor recirculating flow

12   Airflow reversal is associated with:

(a)   Retreating blade stall, starting at the root and progressing towards the blade tip.
(b)   Autorotation, and originates at the tip of a retreating blade.
(c)   Vortex ring state, and originates at the root of the retreating blade.
(d)   Flight at high speed and originates at the root of the retreating blade.

13   Should a helicopter suffer from retreating blade stall in flight, to reduce the effects:

(a)   Power should be reduced and the collective pitch increased to reduce speed.
(b)   Decrease the collective pitch to reduce the angle of attack below stalling angle.
(c)   Increase the backward pressure on the cyclic until the speed begins to decay, then apply more power.
(d)   Reduce collective pitch and increase the forward speed.

14   One secondary effect which the tail rotor tends to produce in the hover if not corrected, is sideways drift:

(a)   In the direction of any cross-wind present.
(b)   Can be either direction depending on the amount of tail rotor thrust being applied.
(c)   In the opposite direction to the main torque reaction from the main rotor.
(d)   In the direction of the tail rotor thrust.

15   Which of the following is correct regarding the vortex ring state of the main rotor blades:

(a)   Causes an even higher rate of descent when descending with power on.
(b)   It describes the developing vortex around the root ends of the blades.
(c)   The angle of attack increases at the blade tip.
(d)   The rate of descent will decrease by raising the collective pitch, but the pilot must act quickly.

16   The centre of pressure of a symmetrical aerofoil when increasing the angle of attack:

(a)   Moves very little.
(b)   Moves forward.
(c)   Moves rearwards.
(d)   Does not move at all.

17   Washout describes rotor blades that have:

(a)   Reduced blade angle at the tips.
(b)   Increased blade angle at the tips.
(c)   A neutral angle of attack at the roots.
(d)   A maximum blade angle at the ⅔ point.

18   Disc loading is defined as the:

(a)   Loading required to maintain the coning angle within safe limits.
(b)   Ratio of the total weight of the helicopter supported, per unit of the disc area.
(c)   Maximum centrifugal loading of the rotor hub assembly.
(d)   The disc area divided by the lift force in the hover.

19   Overpitching in a helicopter is where:

(a)   Too much forward (or rearward) cyclic control is used and insufficient power is available, and the helicopter descends.
(b)   Increasing the Rotor pitch angle beyond the RPM limitation.
(c)   A pilot attempts to climb at altitudes higher than the optimum height for blade efficiency and the helicopter either maintains height or descends.
(d)   Rotor pitch angle already being high at maximum power to maintain rotor speed is further increased and the helicopter blades cone upwards.

20   Overtorquing in a helicopter is where:

(a)   The pilot attempts to increase the rotor RPM without a corresponding increase in power.
(b)   The engine power is insufficient to maintain RPM with an increase in pitch.
(c)   If the rotor RPM reduces and the power to maintain total rotor thrust remains the same, the torque may increase over limits.
(d)   If the rotor RPM increases and the power to maintain total rotor thrust remains the same, the torque may increase over limits.

21   Flapback in a helicopter is where:

(a)   During transition, because of phase lag, the disc tilts forwards causing the helicopter to accelerate.
(b)   The disc tilts back in a horizontal airflow.
(c)   During acceleration, the disk tilts, but because of phase lag it tilts sideways towards the advancing side which has to be corrected by cyclic control.
(d)   Cyclic pitch takes place in horizontal flight where it increases in the forward blade, and decreases in the retreating blade causing the disk to tilt forwards.

22   A helicopter which may be susceptible to "mast bumping" should not be flown in such a manner as to induce negative 'G'. However, if negative 'G' is accidentally applied the pilot should:

(a)   Move the cyclic stick forward until the bumping stops, then level out.
(b)   Keep the cyclic stick central and move the collective up.
(c)   Immediately correct any roll by use of cyclic control.
(d)   Apply rearward cyclic to increase the angle of attack, then level the helicopter using the cyclic.

23   The angle between the relative airflow (RAF) and the chord line of a rotor blade is called the:

(a)   Angle of attack.
(b)   Coning angle.
(c)   Inflow angle.
(d)   Pitch angle.

24   The difference between a semi-rigid rotor and a fully articulated rotor is that a semi rigid rotor is free to:

(a)   Flap, feather, lead and lag, whereas the fully articulated rotor is free to feather.
(b)   Lead, lag and feather, whereas the fully articulated rotor is free to flap, lead and lag.
(c)   Flap and feather, whereas the fully articulated rotor can flap, feather, lead and lag.
(d)   Lead and lag, whereas the fully articulated rotor is free to flap and feather.

25   When in normal level flight, the advancing blade will:

(a)   Lag about its drag hinge.
(b)   Increase its angle of attack.
(c)   Lead about its drag hinge.
(d)   Flap up.

26   The effect of horizontal airflow over the rotor disc when hovering facing into wind is to:

(a)   Reduce induced flow considerably.
(b)   Initially to reduce induced flow but at the same time adding a component to the induced flow passing through the disc at right angles.
(c)   Induced flow remains constant, but a component of the horizontal airflow now acts at 90° to the rotor.
(d)   Induced flow will increase, allowing a smaller angle of attack, and therefore less collective pitch.

27   Movement of the tail rotor pitch of most types of helicopters is assisted by:

(a)   Tabs fitted to the trailing edge of each blade.
(b)   Delta Three hinges.
(c)   Drag hinges.
(d)   Counterbalance weights.

28   Some helicopter fins have a camber on one side to:

(a)   Counteract tail rotor thrust at high speeds.
(b)   Help in reducing tail rotor drift.
(c)   Improve low-speed stability.
(d)   Produce a side force to assist the tail rotor.

29   For a main rotor blade that turns anti-clockwise when viewed from above, movement of the cyclic control to the right produces the maximum rotor blade pitch when the blade is:

(a)   At the rearmost position.
(b)   On the advancing side.
(c)   On the retreating side.
(d)   At the foremost position.

30   The tail rotor compensates for the torque effect of the main rotor in the:

(a)   Horizontal axis.
(b)   Normal axis.
(c)   Lateral axis.
(d)   Fore and aft axis.

31   For a helicopter in forward flight, maintaining a constant height, heading and speed, the deployment of forces are:

(a)   Lift, equal and opposite to mass. Horizontal thrust component opposite but greater than drag, stabiliser producing positive lift.
(b)   TRT acting opposite to mass. Horizontal component of thrust acting forward, equal to drag. Stabiliser producing negative lift.
(c)   Lift, equal and opposite to mass. Horizontal thrust component opposite and equal to drag. Stabiliser producing negative lift.
(d)   Lift, opposite but greater than mass. Horizontal thrust component equal and opposite to drag, stabiliser producing positive lift.

32   With the main rotor blade, the drag force is compensated for by:

(a)   Engine power.
(b)   Blade dragging.
(c)   The effect of blades flapping.
(d)   The effect of cyclic pitch changes.

33   When the collective lever is moved upwards, the swash plate also moves upwards, this causes the rotor blades to:

(a)   Increase lift which is dependent on their position relative to the swash plate.
(b)   Increase blade angle which will change the orientation of total rotor thrust.
(c)   Increase the pitch angle on the retreating blade and decrease the pitch angle on the forward blade.
(d)   Increase blade angle equally and increases the total rotor thrust.

34   Airflow reversal is possible when:

(a)   In high speed flight, it originates at the root of a retreating blade.
(b)   In a vortex-ring state, it originates at the tip of an advancing blade.
(c)   In autorotation, it originates at the root of a retreating blade.
(d)   In high speed flight, it originates at the tip of a retreating blade.
(e)

35   To correct the effects of retreating blade stall in flight, the pilot would:

(a)   Increase the collective pitch to increase the angle of attack.
(b)   Push the cyclic stick forward to increase speed.
(c)   Reduce the collective pitch and reduce forward speed.
(d)   Immediately reduce power and increase the collective pitch to reduce speed.

36   In a turn and slip indicator, the ball:

(a)   Requires aircraft power off the bus bar and indicates correctly balanced turns.
(b)   Requires no power to operate and indicates slip, skid or balanced turns.
(c)   Requires battery power and will indicate slip or skid.
(d)   Requires no aircraft power and will indicate correctly balanced turns.

37   The pressure entering the forward facing orifice of a pitot tube of an aeroplane in flight is:

(a)   Dynamic pressure.
(b)   Static pressure.
(c)   Dynamic and static pressure.
(d)   Stagnation pressure.

38   Water in the pipelines of a static system:

(a)   Will not freeze if the pitot heater is on.
(b)   Will cause the Airspeed Indicator to over read.
(c)   Is automatically separated from the air by a water separator.
(d)   May produce inaccurate readings on pressure instruments.

39   A Directional Gyroscope operating under normal flight conditions can experience DRIFT. What degree of drift is considered acceptable:

(a)   15° per hour.
(b)   3° every 15 minutes.
(c)   0.3° every 15 minutes.
(d)   1.5° per hour.

40   Should an engine failure occur in flight:

(a)   The rotor RPM is quickly restored by the autorotative forces.
(b)   The rotor RPM is restored in the flare.
(c)   The freewheeling unit disengages the engine from the rotor.
(d)   The helicopter will tend to turn slowly in the opposite direction from the main rotor.

41   Should the disc loading increase, under certain circumstances, ie., during a flare, the total reaction can move closer to the axis of rotation, this result can be:

(a)   A decrease in rotor torque.
(b)   A decrease in the coning angle.
(c)   An increase in rotor torque.
(d)   An increase in rotor drag.

42   Considering a helicopter in autorotative flight, which of the following is correct:

(a)   If a helicopter is autorotating with forward speed, the angle of attack increases, and the inflow angle is reduced.
(b)   If a helicopter is autorotating vertically, following autorotation with forward speed, the inflow angle decreases and the pitch angle increases.
(c)   If a helicopter is autorotating with forward speed, the inflow angle will reduce as does the pitch angle.
(d)   If a helicopter is autorotating vertically, the inflow angle increases as does the mean pitch angle.

43   Assuming an engine failure occurs in a HOVER, which of the following is correct:

(a)   The rate of descent is directly related to the angle of attack.
(b)   The helicopter will accelerate downwards, until the autorotative force equals the helicopter mass, then the acceleration will decrease.
(c)   If for any reason, the angle of attack should increase, then there will be a rapid increase in the rate of descent.
(d)   The autorotative force will produce an RPM and rotor thrust equal to the helicopter mass, then the helicopter will descend at a constant rate.

44   In consideration of Tail Rotor Drift, with a helicopter that has a clockwise rotation of its main rotor, which of the following is correct:

(a)   The helicopter tends to rotate in the same direction as the main rotor torque reaction ie., anti-clockwise.
(b)   The helicopter tends to drift starboard when in ground effect.
(c)   The corrective anti-torque force set up by the tail rotor causes the helicopter to hover with the starboard skid low.
(d)   The helicopter tends to drift in the direction of the tail rotor thrust.

45   Hovering in ground effect (IGE), the high pressure area underneath the helicopter is considered to extend up to:

(a)   ½ of the main rotor disc diameter.
(b)   ¾ of the main rotor disc diameter.
(c)   A height equivalent to the distance from the main rotor head to the tail rotor.
(d)   ¼ of the main rotor disc diameter.

46   The fitting of a Tail Stabiliser on certain helicopters has the effect of:

(a)   Improving the directional control, particularly in slow speed flight.
(b)   Limiting the amount of yaw in gusty conditions.
(c)   Limits the amount of pitch-up of a fuselage and rearwards tilt of the disc in gusts.
(d)   Provides the pilot with improved pitch control particularly if the fuselage pitches downwards.

47   During the four stroke cycle, the sparking plug ignites the mixture just prior to:

(a)   The 'intake stroke'.
(b)   The 'exhaust stroke'.
(c)   The end of the 'compression stroke'.
(d)   The start of the 'compression stroke'.

48   The term "valve overlap" is given to the method of opening and shutting the inlet and exhaust valves. The use of this method is to:

(a)   Ensure that all the exhaust gases are removed from the cylinder after the intake stroke.
(b)   Improve the volumetric efficiency of the engine.
(c)   Increase the period of the compression stroke.
(d)   Increase the period of the exhaust stroke.

49   Carburettor icing takes place in the following conditions:

(a)   Only in cloud, above the freezing level and in the descent with a low power setting.
(b)   Only when the outside temperature is below freezing.
(c)   Is enhanced when flying at full throttle in humid air clear of cloud precipitation and fog.
(d)   In humid air where the temperature drop in the carburettor is due to adiabatic expansion.

50   Dual ignition is fitted to aero engines for the following reason:

(a)   To provide a back-up ignition system.
(b)   Only for safety reasons.
(c)   Provides better combustion.
(d)   In case of spark plug failure.

51   If a fuse protecting a particular circuit blows, the pilot should:

(a)   Immediately reset the appropriate circuit breaker.
(b)   Immediately isolate (switch off) all the electrics served by the particular fuse. Do not replace fuses in flight.
(c)   Only reset the circuit breaker if the electrics served by it are vital for flight safety.
(d)   Wait at least 2 minutes before re-setting the appropriate circuit breaker or inserting a fresh cartridge fuse.

52   In the event of an alternator or generator failure during flight:

(a)   Electrical loads should be reduced to a minimum and a landing made as soon as possible.
(b)   Master switch should be turned off and flight continued normally without electrical power, except at night.
(c)   If the aeroplane is being flown under IFR conditions, perform radio out routine, if being flown VFR, it will be quite safe to continue.
(d)   Master switch should be turned off particularly if the failure is a discharge or over-charge being indicated. Flight may be continued but there is limited electrical power available from the battery.

53   If a magneto becomes disconnected from its ignition switch:

(a)   A dead cut will result when the ignition check is carried out at high RPM and the other magneto is selected to "OFF".
(b)   Selecting the other magneto to "OFF" will fail to stop the engine.
(c)   The ammeter will show a continual discharge.
(d)   The pilot would notice the engine torque will reduce accompanied by slight rough running.

54   High tension supply for the spark plugs in a piston engine is derived from the:

(a)   Battery, and stepped-up by the magneto.
(b)   Battery during starting and the magneto once the engine is running.
(c)   Magneto's self contained generation and distribution system.
(d)   Alternator or generator stepped up through a capacitor on starting, then by the magnetos.

55   In the event of a cockpit fire, it is permissible to use a hand-held BCF extinguisher provided that:

(a)   The cockpit is ventilated after use.
(b)   A window is opened before the extinguisher is used.
(c)   Great care is used to avoid skin contamination.
(d)   All electrics are switched off.

Answers to Part 1 will be found on page: 285

PART 2 Aircraft (GENERAL) and Principles of Flight
Flight Performance & Planning

32 POWER REQUIREMENTS

32.1 **Introduction.** The power required to maintain level flight throughout the helicopter's speed range can be considered under three main headings:

1. **Rotor Profile Power**. Power required to drive the rotor and operate ancillary equipment and the tail rotor.

2. **Induced Power**. Power required to induce a flow and produce rotor thrust.

3. **Parasite Power**. Power required to overcome fuselage parasite drag.

32.2 The power required to meet the above requirements will vary from the hover to maximum forward speed of the helicopter. The reasons for such variations are now discussed in more detail.

32.3 **Work.** If an object is moved from one position to another then a force must be applied to overcome the resistance set up by the object being moved. When the object is moved work is said to have been done and it is calculated by multiplying the force used to overcome the resistance by the distance that the object has been moved. The resistance set up by the rotor blades when being rotated, or the resistance caused by moving the fuselage through the air is termed drag, and since in any equilibrium state force equals drag then work must therefore be equal to drag × distance.

32.4 **Power.** Power is defined as the RATE of doing WORK.

$$\text{Therefore POWER} = \frac{\text{WORK}}{\text{TIME}}$$

$$= \frac{\text{DRAG} \times \text{DISTANCE}}{\text{TIME}}$$

$$\text{But} \quad \frac{\text{DISTANCE}}{\text{TIME}} = \text{VELOCITY (Speed in a given direction)}$$

$$\text{Therefore} \quad \text{POWER} = \text{DRAG} \times \text{VELOCITY}$$

The equation for calculating DRAG is:

$$\text{Drag} = C_D \tfrac{1}{2} \rho V^2 S$$

Where,

C_D = Coefficient of drag
ρ = Air density
V = Velocity
S = Plan area of aerofoil (rotor)

$$\text{Power} = KV^2 \times V$$
$$= KV^3$$

32.5   The resistance or drag of a body moving through the air will vary as the square of the speed, but the power required to balance the drag will vary as the cube of the speed. Power is normally expressed in terms of horsepower, one horsepower being equal to 550 feet lbs/second or 33,000 feet/lbs/minute or 745.7 Watts.

32.6   **Parasite Power.** Parasite (or Parasitic) power is the power required to overcome the drag of the fuselage when the helicopter is moving in straight and level flight. If the drag is calculated for a given speed and the speed is doubled the drag will increase four times but the power required to overcome this rise in drag will increase eight times.

32.7   The curve to show parasite power against forward speed will have a Zero value when the helicopter is in the hover but will rise more and more steeply as speed increases. See fig. 32.1.

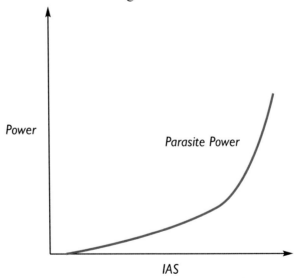

Fig. 32.1   *Parasitic power increases as the helicopter's speed increases.*

32.8   **Rotor Power.** In considering a helicopter hovering in still air, the total rotor thrust being produced by the rotor will be equal to the weight. Within limits, depending upon the type of helicopter, this total rotor thrust can be produced from a wide variation of collective pitch settings and rotor RPM but the drag and therefore the power will vary with each combination, and only one combination will give minimum rotor drag.

32.9   The power to drive the rotor can therefore be considered from two aspects:

1.   The power related to a variation in the blade's rotational velocity (RPM) for a minimum value of pitch or drag coefficient (C_D): *This is Rotor Profile Power.*

2.   The power related to a change in pitch or C_D for a constant otational velocity: *This is Induced Power.*

32.10   **Rotor Profile Power.** The power component related to the blade's rotational velocity for a fixed value of C_D is known as Rotor Profile Power. The C_D value of the blade will vary with collective pitch setting but it will be constant and have its least value when the collective pitch lever is FULLY DOWN.

32.11   The power will therefore vary only with changes in rotor RPM and with air density changes for a given RPM. However, whenever the main rotor is turning, ancillary equipment, associated drive shafts and the tail rotor will also be absorbing power, the power absorption varying in the main with the velocity of the main rotor. All these power requirements are included in calculating Rotor Profile Power.

32.12   Rotor Profile Power can therefore be defined as being:- *the power required to maintain a given rotor RPM when the collective pitch lever is fully down (minimum) and to overcome the drag of ancillary equipment, associated drive shafts and the tail rotor.*

32.13   Rotor Profile Power will have a starting point at some position on the vertical axis of the graph, see fig 32.2, the position depending upon the rotor RPM selected and the air density.

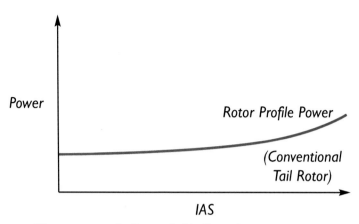

Fig. 32.2   Rotor profile power vs Indicated Air Speed.

32.14   Assuming a value of C_D, as forward speed increases, the power required to maintain this rotor RPM will increase. The reason for this rise in power is because in forward flight the increase in drag of the advancing blade will be greater than the decrease in drag of the retreating blade.

32.15   Consider a two-bladed helicopter running upon the ground in still air conditions with the collective pitch lever held fully down. Therefore to maintain a constant rotor RPM the power (DRAG × VELOCITY) required by the advancing blade will increase and for the retreating blade, decrease.

32.16   As the increase in power for the advancing blade is greater than the reduction in power for the retreating blade, considering the sections together, the total power required to maintain constant rotor RPM will INCREASE.

32.17   The effect in forward flight will be the same but there will be a saving in power because the tail rotor increases tail rotor thrust through translational lift, therefore less pitch and less power will be required by the tail rotor to keep the fuselage straight.

32.18   The tail rotor also flaps back and in so doing obtains flare effect and therefore a further saving in power. As forward speed increases, the curve to show Rotor Profile Power will rise only slowly at first but will rise more rapidly in the higher speed range, because the tail rotor drag and power is affected in exactly the same way as in paragraph 32.16 above. Rotor profile power accounts for approximately 40% of the power required to hover.

32.19   **Induced Power.** When the collective pitch lever is fully lowered there is virtually no rotor thrust being produced. In order to increase the rotor thrust it is necessary to raise the lever. This will give rise to:

1   An increase in rotor drag because the C_D value of the blade is increasing.
2   An increase in the mass of air flowing down through the disc. In order to maintain the rotor RPM constant more power must be applied to offset the rising drag which results from increasing the C_D value of the blade.

32.20   This increase in power is known as the INDUCED POWER because it is the extra power required to overcome the rise in drag when the blades are inducing air to flow down through the rotor. As explained in Helicopter General and Principles of Flight, paragraph 6.2. With translational lift, induced flow diminishes with forward speed and less collective pitch is needed to produce the required angle of attack.

32.21   The curve to show INDUCED POWER will have a starting point at some position on the vertical axis of the graph see figure 32.3, and will fall rapidly at first due to the onset of translational lift, and then fall more slowly as forward speed increases. The ground cushion effect will also reduce the induced power required to hover.

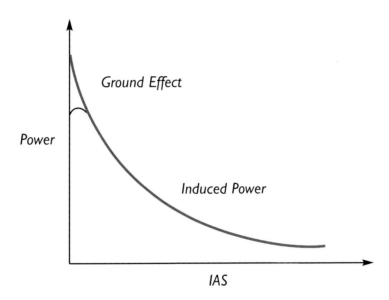

Fig. 32.3   Induced power vs Indicated Air Speed.

32.22   **Summary.**

1   *Rotor Profile Power*. Rotor Profile Power is the power require to drive all ancillary equipment and the tail rotor and to overcome the drag from the blades when the collective pitch lever is fully down. It accounts for approximately 40% of the power required to hover.

2   *Induced Power*. Induced power is the power required to maintain the rotor RPM when the drag from the blades increases as a result of the collective pitch lever being in any position other than fully down. It accounts for approximately 60% of the power required to hover.

32.23   **Power Required Curve.** The power required to maintain the helicopter in straight and level flight at any given forward speed will be the combination of Rotor Profile Power, Induced Power and Parasite Power for that speed. The curve to show power required will be as shown in figure. 32.4.

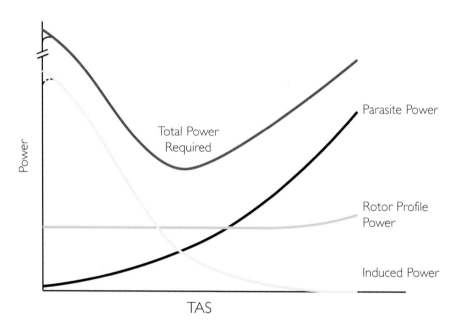

Fig. 32.4   Power required graph

32.24   **Power Available.** With propeller driven fixed wing aircraft, the power available curve takes into account the varying efficiency of the propeller with forward speed. With the helicopter the efficiency of the rotor system is taken into account in assessing the *Power Required* so the Power Available is therefore purely the power which is available TO the rotor and not FROM the rotor.

32.25   For any given altitude this power will remain more or less constant and it therefore appears on the power graph as a straight line. See figure 32.5.

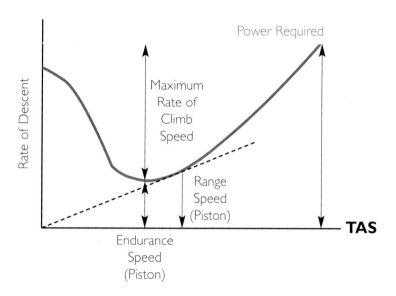

Fig. 32.5   Power required/Power available graph

32.26   Referring throughout to figure 32.5, the power required/power available graph can be used to obtain performance data in addition to that required for straight and level flight. Power in hand can be used for climbing.

32.27   If 60 HP is available beyond that required to maintain straight and level flight for a given speed, and the Mass of the helicopter is 6000 lbs, then the rate of climb expressed in feet per minute would be:

$$\frac{60\ HP \times 33\ 000}{6000} = 330\ \text{feet/min.}$$

Note: 1 HP = 33 000 ft lb per min.

32.28   The greater the power available the faster the rate of climb. The speed to give maximum rate of climb will therefore be where the two curves are furthest apart. The maximum forward speed will be where the two curves cross. Range speed will be that speed where a line drawn from the point of origin of the graph touches the power required curve at a tangent, although this will be true only for piston engine helicopters, the range speed for helicopters with gas turbines being appreciably higher. Endurance speed will be the speed for minimum power, the lowest point on the power required curve. **Range and Endurance is now treated in greater detail.**

32.29   **Range.** In figure 32.6, are shown the range performance of a light piston engine helicopter for a range of true airspeeds at weights from 1800 lb to 2150 lb. By interpolation between sea level and 5000 feet. Note that this graph is drawn for zero wind and ISA conditions. In this example, the maximum range is 228 nm at 5000 feet at a weight of 1800 lb. If the weight is greater, or the height reduced, then the maximum range is also reduced. Remember too that range is also reduced if flying at greater or less than optimum range speed.

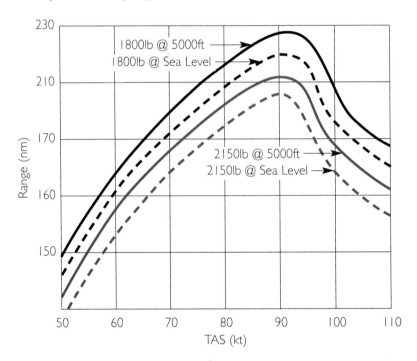

Fig. 32.6   Range – light single piston engine helicopter, standard temperature Zero wind.

32.30   For a given gross weight, the maximum range, and the required TAS from fig 32.5 can be established. Since the altitude to fly is often determined by meteorological conditions, the graph provides for different altitudes. These examples ignore temperature deviation. The range will also reduce in warmer than ISA conditions.

217

32.31   **Summary of Range Parameters.**

Condition	TAS	Effect on Range
Increase altitude	Higher	Increase
High Density Altitude	Higher	Decrease
Increase in Mass	Higher	Decrease
Headwind	Higher	Decrease
Tailwind	Lower	Increase

It must be noted that at higher altitude, the greater the range, however this must also consider the longer climb using a higher fuel consumption. The wind velocity is often the deciding factor as to which altitude to use.

32.32   **Endurance.** In figure 32.7 is shown an endurance graph similar to the range graph for a range of true airspeeds and Mass from 1800 lb to 2150 lb. By interpolation between sea level and 5000 feet. This graph, like the range graph, is drawn for zero wind ISA and conditions. In this example, the best endurance is 3h 40 minutes at low gross weight at 5000 feet and a TAS of 62 kt. The endurance will reduce rapidly if the speed increases towards V_{ne} values. (V_{ne} = Never exceed speed).

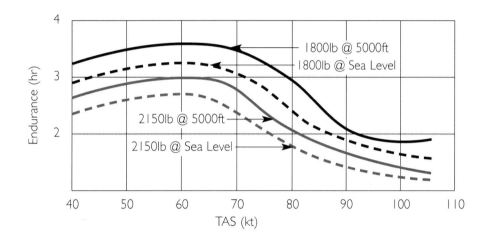

Fig. 32.7   Endurance – Light, single piston engine helicopter, standard temperature.

32.33   Endurance may be improved if there were altitude "in hand". The graph is constructed for ISA conditions, and if the temperature were greater than ISA then endurance will reduce.

32.34   **Summary of Endurance Parameters.**

Condition	**TAS**	**Effect on Endurance**
Increase altitude	Higher	Decrease
High Density Altitude	Higher	Decrease
Increase in Mass	Higher	Decrease
Headwind	~	No effect
Tailwind	~	No effect

32.35   **Factors Affecting Power Available/Power Required.**

1   *Power Available.* The power available from a piston engine is affected by density and altitude changes but the power output can be increased by supercharging. It can be generally stated that the power available curve will move up until the maximum efficiency of the supercharger is reached, then begin to move down as altitude is further increased.

2   *Power Required.*

(a)   *Density/Altitude* The power required by the rotor is affected by both helicopter all-up mass and air density and it has already been explained that the total rotor thrust can be obtained with varying combinations of pitch and rotor RPM.

Consider now a helicopter of a given weight hovering outside ground effect. If rotor RPM are kept constant as height is gained, Rotor Profile Power will decrease because of the reduction in air density, but if total rotor thrust is to be maintained the collective pitch must be increased to compensate for this density change and Induced Power must increase. If in raising the collective pitch lever the blade is moving towards its optimum combination of rotor RPM and pitch, then the reduction in Rotor Profile Power will be greater than the increase in Induced Power. Less power will be required to drive the rotor and the total power required curve will move down the graph. (Figure 32.5).

Once this optimum setting has been reached any further reduction in air density will result in the Induced Power required increasing faster than Rotor Profile Power is being decreased, consequently the power to drive the rotor will increase and the total power required curve will move up the graph.

(b) *Mass.* Any increase in mass will require a greater total rotor thrust and for a given rotor RPM this can only be achieved with increased collective pitch. The helicopter will therefore reach the height at which it will produce its optimum blade setting sooner than if the helicopter is lightly loaded.

32.36 **Summary.**

1 *Power Available.* Power available for the piston engine helicopter will increase up to the height where the supercharger is most efficient. Beyond this height power available will fall. With the gas turbine power available will remain constant within the permissible operating height of the helicopter.

2 *Power Required.* Compared with sea level performance less power may be required at altitude because of increased rotor efficiency but there will always be a given altitude beyond which the power required will increase, and for a given set of conditions the higher the all-up mass the lower this altitude will be. At some overseas stations the rotor may be operating beyond the conditions at which it is most efficient even when flying at sea level.

32.37 **Operation With Limited Power.** From the foregoing it will be seen that with changes in air density, weight and altitude, the power available and power required curves will move closer together and that power available may eventually be sufficient to hover but only with the assistance of ground effect. In extreme conditions there may be insufficient power to hover at all. Under these conditions there will now be a minimum speed below which, even with ground effect, the helicopter cannot maintain height. See figure 32.8.

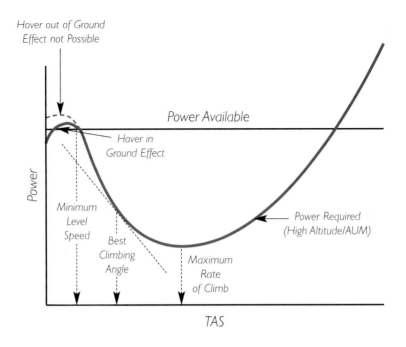

Fig. 32.8   The effect of reduced power available on helicopter performance.

32.38   **Power Checks.** Conditions at the take-off and landing areas may differ and in order that the pilot may make an assessment of the power available when airborne before committing himself to a landing, a simple power check can be carried out.

32.39   When flying straight and level at some pre-determined speed, and with landing rotor RPM selected, a note is made of the fuel flow or boost required to maintain that speed. Maintaining landing rotor RPM full power is then applied temporarily and the change in boost or fuel flow is noted. Depending upon the difference between the two values (i.e., the Power Margin) the pilot is able to determine from a prepared graph or set of tables the slow speed capabilities of the helicopter.

32.40   These calculations do not allow for wind effect, this being considered a bonus. A similar type of check can be carried out while hovering and before moving into forward flight in order to assess the take-off capabilities. The airspeed at which the landing check is carried out and the necessary boost or fuel flow required will obviously vary with different types of helicopter.

32.41   In making this power available check, some allowance must be made if the helicopter is operating above the altitude where the rotor is most efficient. Power required increases in the same proportion as TAS to IAS, therefore, to maintain a given indicated airspeed at a height where the TAS is twice the IAS, twice the power would be required.

221

32.42   If a graph is produced to show these power required curves against indicated airspeed, and it is assumed that sea level is the height at which the rotor is most efficient, it will be seen that the curve for altitude changes shape and moves upwards. Refer again to figure 32.8.

32.43   Therefore, if limited power checks at the same IAS are being carried out by two helicopters, one at sea level and one at altitude, the helicopter at altitude would require a larger power reserve to carry out the same low speed manoeuvres as the helicopter at sea level.

32.44   **Best Climbing Angle.**   When operating with limited power the helicopter must be moving forward in order to climb. In order to assess the steepest climbing angle it is necessary to find the best *rate of climb/forward speed ratio*. This can be determined by drawing a line from the point where the power available curve cuts the vertical axis of the graph (figure 32.8). Tangential to the power required curve, the speed relating to the position where the two lines touch is the speed for the *best or maximum climbing angle.*

32.45   It will always be less than the speed for maximum rate of climb. This point gives the best ratio of POWER MARGIN for climbing against *minimum forward speed.* Therefore the steepest angle. Note: the maximum rate of climb is where the power margin is greatest, this is at a higher forward speed. (Figure 32.8).

32.46   **Turning.**   In addition to providing a component to balance the mass and a thrust force to maintain speed, the total rotor thrust must supply a further component to change the direction of the helicopter in a balanced turn. The greater the angle of bank the greater this force must be. Its effect is similar to an increase in mass. With 30° of bank the apparent mass will increase by 15%. With 60° of bank the apparent mass will increase by 100%.

32.47   To maintain height in the turn more collective pitch and therefore more power will be required when turning and the effect on the power required curve is to cause it to move up the graph. The maximum angle of bank that can be achieved by a helicopter in a level turn is that angle of bank where the airspeed is the speed for maximum rate of climb. If bank is increased beyond this stage height will be lost and rotor RPM will decay.

32.48   **Limits of Nr (Rotor RPM).**   Because the area of the Rotor Disc reduces as the Coning Angle increases, the Coning Angle must never be allowed to become too big.

32.49   As centrifugal forces through Nr gives a measure of control of the Coning Angle, providing the Nr is kept ABOVE a laid down minimum, the Coning Angle will always be within safe operating limits.

32.50   There will also be upper Nr limits due to transmission (main rotor gear-box) considerations and blade root loading stresses. Compressibility, due to high blade tip speeds is also a limiting factor. Nr limits will be found in the relevant operating manual.

32.51   See also Over-torquing (sect: 5.7) and Over-pitching (sect: 5.8).

32.52   **Service Ceiling.** Definition: that height at which the Rate of Climb (R of C) becomes less than 100 fpm (0.5 m/s).

33 HELICOPTER PERFORMANCE

33.1 **Introduction.** Assuming that a helicopter engine and all components are operating satisfactorily, the performance of the helicopter is dependent on three major factors:

1   Density altitude (air density).
2   Gross Mass.
3   Wind velocity during takeoff, hovering, and landing.

33.2 In this section, item number 1 (density altitude) is discussed in some detail because of the importance in helicopter operations. Items 2 and 3 are covered elsewhere in these notes.

33.3 The factors which affect density altitude are altitude, atmospheric pressure, temperature and moisture content of the air.

33.4 **Altitude** has a direct relationship with air density, as the higher the altitude the lower the density, or the higher the density altitude. It is necessary to know for examination purposes what a particular density is at specific heights in a real atmosphere or the ISA atmosphere. It can easily be obtained on a CRP1 navigation computer, or from a graph as seen in figure 33.1, or by calculation.

33.5 **Atmospheric Pressure** at an airport or landing area at a given elevation can change from day to day, sometimes by a very noticeable amount which, when combined with other factors, could be significant. The lower the pressure at a given elevation, the less dense the air, and higher the density altitude and, as a result, the less performance the helicopter will have.

33.6 The daily and seasonal variations in atmospheric pressure at a given place will not have as significant effect on the density altitude as the daily and seasonal variations of temperature and moisture. The density altitude chart (figure 33.1) is based on pressure altitude, not indicated altitude. To determine the pressure altitude at any given place, if an altimeter is available, adjust the altimeter setting to 1013.2 mb and read the pressure altitude directly from the altimeter. (It is calibrated in the ISA atmosphere). However, do not forget to reset the altimeter to the current altimeter setting (QNH) if available, or to field elevation (QFE) if an altimeter setting is not available.

33.7 **Temperature.** Even when elevation and pressure remain constant, great changes in air density will be caused by temperature changes. The same amount of air that occupies 1 cubic cm at a low temperature will expand and occupy 2, 3, or 4 cubic cm as the temperature rises. Therefore, as temperature increases, air becomes less dense, density altitude is increased, and the helicopter performance decreases.

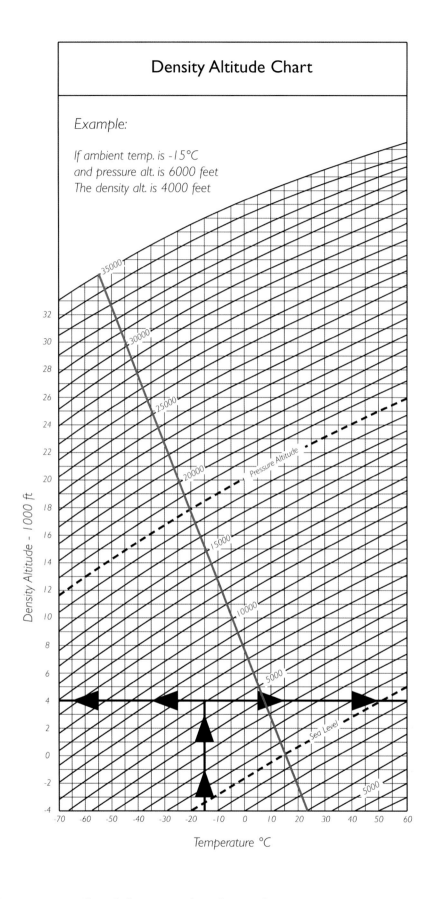

Fig. 33.1   Pressure Altitude/Density Altitude graph.

33.8   To use the density altitude graph - what would be the density altitude if the pressure altitude is 5000 feet and the temperature is 35°C ? Locate the 35°C vertical line at the bottom of the chart, follow this line up to its intersection with the 5000 foot pressure altitude (diagonal) line, then move horizontally to the left side of the chart where a density altitude of 8400 feet is read off. A helicopter operating at this elevation under these conditions would be flying in air with a density equivalent to that at the 8400 foot level. Therefore, the performance of the helicopter would be as though it were flying at the 8400 foot elevation.

33.9   **Moisture.** When temperature and pressure are constant, changes in the moisture content of the air will change air density. Water vapour weighs less than dry air. Therefore, as the moisture content of the air increases, air becomes less dense; density altitude is increased with a resultant decrease in helicopter performance.

33.10   The higher the temperature the greater the amount of moisture the air can hold. Relative humidity, which is expressed as a percentage, is the ratio of the amount of moisture in the air to the amount it is capable of absorbing at a given temperature. The moisture content of the air at a relative humidity of 80% and a temperature of 38°C will be much greater than with a relative humidity of 80% and a temperature of 10°C. *The greatest decrease in air density (increase in density altitude) due to moisture content will be at a high temperature.*

33.11   The density altitude chart (figure 33.1) does not take the moisture content of the air into consideration. It should be remembered that the actual density altitude can be much higher than that computed from this chart if the air contains a high moisture content (High Humidity).

33.12   The terms high density altitude and low density altitude should be thoroughly understood. In general, high density altitude refers to thin air; low density altitude refers to dense air. Therefore, those conditions that result in thin air, high elevations, high temperatures, high moisture content, or some combination thereof, would be referred to as high density altitude conditions. Those conditions that result in dense air, low elevations, low temperatures, low moisture content, or some combination thereof, would be referred to as low density altitude conditions. It is important to note that high-density altitudes may be present at low elevations on hot days with high moisture content in the air.

33.13   Students will be expected to establish Density Altitude (DA) from the parameters of temperature and altitude in the JAR examination, however, a conversion graph such as figure 33.1 may not be provided. The DA may be established by two methods, one by formula, and the second with the CRP1 Navigation computer.

33.14 Using a formula, first of all find the ISA temperature at the height given. Assume an aerodrome is 4000 feet AMSL. The ISA temperature at 4000 feet is 15° – 8°C. (Remember that ISA temperature is + 15°C at MSL, and decreases 1.98°C (2°C is close enough) for each 1000 ft of elevation.). Therefore, at 4000 feet the ISA temperature is +7°C.

Now assume that the actual temperature measured is + 12°C. This is 5°C above ISA, or more correctly, ISA + 5°C.

Density Altitude (DA) is greater than the Pressure Altitude (PA) by approximately 118.8 feet for each degree Centigrade by which the prevailing temperature exceeds that of the Standard Atmosphere at the same height.

Therefore, at this aerodrome, the temperature is ISA + 5°C
DA = PA + (5 × 118.8)
= 4000 ft + 594
= 4594 ft.

Conversely, if the actual measured temperature were to be less than the ISA temperature, ie., ISA – 5°C, then the DA would be the PA – 594 ft = 3406 ft.

If it is warmer than the ISA, then the DA will be higher (warmer air is less dense therefore the same as a higher altitude).

If it is colder than the ISA, then the DA will be lower (colder air is more dense therefore the same as a lower altitude).

33.15 **Using the Pooleys CRP-1 Navigation Computer.**

Inputting temperature use actual corrected (measured) temperature, as the scales will automatically allow for ISA temperature deviation.

Look for the AIR SPEED WINDOW. Set the measured temperature against the PA. The DA can be read off in the DA window. Unfortunately, the scales on the CRP-1 are rather small, so be as accurate as possible when inputting the aerodrome height and temperature.

Using the CRP-1 try the following example:

Assume the PA to be 10000 ft
Assume the corrected air temperature is +5°C
What is the DA ?

Set the temperature of +5°C against the PA of 1000 feet in the AIR SPEED WINDOW. Now look across to the DA window and read off 11200 ft DA.

Cross-check by formula: ISA temperature at 10000 ft = +15°C – (10 × 2) = - 5°C. Actual (measured) temperature is + 5°C. Therefore, the temperature deviation is ISA + 10 (It is 10°C warmer than ISA)

DA = PA + (118.8 × 10)
= 1000 + 1188
= 11188 ft

34 MASS & BALANCE

34.1 **Limitations on Aircraft Mass.** When the aircraft is operated in atmospheric conditions where the air is less dense than the International Standard Atmosphere, the aircraft performance will be reduced. The effect of this performance reduction is particularly important during the take-off and initial climb. Therefore, before flight, the pilot must ascertain that the all-up mass of the aircraft is within the correct limits applicable to the conditions in which it is to be operated. **He must also appreciate the probable adverse effects on aircraft performance if the permitted all-up mass or Centre of Gravity limits are exceeded.**

34.2 Pre-flight planning should include a check of the aircraft performance charts to determine if the aircraft mass could contribute to a hazardous flight condition. Payload, passengers, baggage, cargo and fuel load must be adjusted to provide an adequate margin of safety.

34.3 In this respect, it should be understood that in some light single engine, single rotor helicopters, it is not possible to fill all seats, baggage space and fuel tanks and still remain within the approved mass or balance limits. In many aircraft, the fuel tanks may not be permitted to be filled to capacity when a full complement of passengers and baggage is to be carried.

34.4 Aircraft are generally designed so that a full complement of passengers can be carried on short flights but not on extended flights when a full fuel load will be needed. The amount of fuel which can be off-loaded to allow for a greater payload is limited by the forward C of G location with empty fuel. The effects upon the performance characteristics of an over-weight helicopter is:

1   Reduced rate and angle of climb, lower ceiling altitude.
2   Shorter range.
3   Reduced cruising speed.
4   Reduced manoeuvrability.

34.5 **Limitations in Relation to Aircraft Balance.** Balance refers to the location of the Centre of Gravity (C of G.) of the aircraft. It is of primary importance to the safety of flight. Whilst it is necessary to ensure that the maximum all-up mass of an aircraft is not exceeded, the distribution of permissible mass, i.e. the balance of the aircraft, is vitally important.

34.6 **Method of Computing Balance.** The method of calculating mass and balance is shown in the manual for the aircraft. Unfortunately the manufacturers have yet to standardise these procedures so the following text is of necessity written in general terms. It is essential that pilots should refer to the manual and be in no doubt as to whether or not the aircraft is in balance before take-off.

34.7 The principle of all mass and balance calculations is the simple one illustrated in figure 34.1. Expressed in words it is that the force exerted by a mass on a beam is dependent upon its distance from the pivot point. In aircraft terms the pivot point should be regarded as the required position of the Centre of Gravity. Thus 100 lb (or kg) mass situated 50 in. (or mm) from the pivot point (C of G) will balance 50 lb (or kg) positioned 100 in. (or mm) on the other side of the pivot. By multiplying mass × distance, the answer, known as the Moment, may be expressed as pound:inches or, when metric units are used, kg:mm.

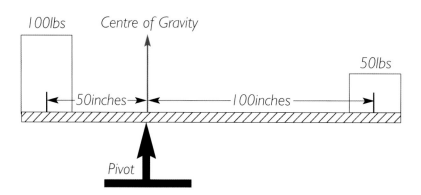

Fig. 34.1 Simple beam: Mass × Distance = Moment

34.8 Starting with the empty aircraft and its known moment (found previously by weighing, after all equipment has been installed) it is then necessary to compute the moments for all variable load i.e. passengers, baggage, fuel, etc. This is not the daunting task it might at first appear and to make it easier several methods are used.

34.9   The manual may include a plan of the cabin/baggage area with each seating, baggage or fuel location (Station) marked. To save calculating the moment for each station, which would entail multiplying the distance from datum to station by the load in that position, tables are often provided listing weights as a scale against which are shown the moments for that station. For small helicopters it is sometimes the practice to employ simple graphs. For the purpose of this exercise, an example of the working will be shown.

34.10   It is not possible to design an aircraft in which the lift, mass, thrust and drag forces are always in a natural state of equilibrium during straight and level flight.

34.11   The helicopter is also able to counteract any of the unbalance or unstable tendencies caused by movements of the Centre of Gravity, *provided that these movements are confined within certain limits.*

34.12   Information relating to examples of working out mass and balance problems is normally contained in the Flight/Owner's Manual/Pilot's Operating Handbook. The mass figures are given in pounds or kilograms.

34.13   If after the aircraft is loaded, the Centre of Gravity (C of G) does not fall within the allowable limits, it will be necessary to shift loads before flight is attempted. The actual location of the Centre of Gravity can be determined by a number of factors under the control of the pilot. Positioning of baggage and cargo items, assignment of seats to passengers according to mass, and arranging for the fuel load to be carried, are all items under his control. In light helicopters, these options are somewhat limited.

34.14   The all-up mass of an aircraft will vary during flight due to the consumption of fuel and oil. The alteration of all-up weight due to this fuel and oil consumption will usually change the position of the Centre of Gravity, unless the Centre of Gravity of the fuel and oil is coincident with the aircraft's Centre of Gravity.

34.15   Fuel tanks are normally aligned close to the midpoint of the basic Centre of Gravity in order to keep the Centre of Gravity changes from this source to a minimum. It must nevertheless be appreciated that in light helicopters the Centre of Gravity of the fuel carried is generally behind the rotor mast, and therefore **as fuel is used the aircraft's Centre of Gravity will move forward.**

34.16 **C of G ahead of allowable limits.** There could be a problem in a light helicopter when taking off with the C of G in the extreme forward position, or worse, taking off with the C of G ahead of the forward limit. The pilot would know this as soon as he took off because the helicopter would have a nose low attitude and an excessive rearward displacement of the cyclic stick will be required to maintain a hover in a no-wind condition, if hovering flight can be maintained at all.

34.17 Flight under this condition should not be continued since the possibility of running out of rearward cyclic control will increase rapidly as fuel is consumed, and the pilot may find it impossible to increase the pitch attitude sufficiently to bring the helicopter to a stop. Also, in case of an engine failure and a resulting autorotation, sufficient cyclic control may not be available to flare properly for landing.

34.18 Hovering in a strong wind will make this condition less easily recognised since less rearward displacement of the cyclic control will be required than when hovering in a zero wind condition. Therefore, in determining if a critical balance condition exists, the pilot should consider the wind velocity in which he is hovering and its relation to the rearward displacement of the cyclic stick.

34.19 **C of G aft of allowable limits.** Without proper ballast in the cockpit, this condition may arise when (as an example) a lightweight pilot takes off solo with a full load of fuel located aft of the rotor mast, or baggage in a rear compartment and substantial fuel. The pilot would recognise this condition after coming to the hover following a vertical take-off. The helicopter will have a tail low attitude and an excessive forward displacement of the cyclic stick will be required to maintain a hover in a no-wind condition, if a hover can be maintained at all. If there is a wind, an even greater forward displacement will be required.

34.20 If flight is continued in this condition, the pilot may find it impossible to fly the upper allowable airspeed range due to insufficient forward cyclic displacement to maintain a nose-low attitude. This particular condition may become quite dangerous if gusty or rough air accelerates the helicopter to a higher airspeed than forward cyclic control would allow. The nose would start to rise and full cyclic stick may not be sufficient to hold it down or to lower it once it rises.

34.21 The Air Navigation Order/JARs require that before takeoff, the commander of an aircraft shall satisfy himself that the load carried by the aircraft is of such mass, and is so distributed, that it may be safely carried on the intended flight. Therefore, before every flight, it is the captain's responsibility to ensure that his aircraft is loaded in such a manner that the all-up mass is not exceeded, and that the position of the Centre of Gravity remains within the limits for the particular aircraft.

34.22   In order to understand the principles of mass and balance calculations, a pilot will need to be familiar with the following terms:

Centre of Gravity (C of G).   The point about which an aircraft would balance if it were possible to suspend it at that point. It is the mass centre of the aircraft or the theoretical point at which the entire mass of the aircraft is assumed to be concentrated.

Centre of Gravity Limits.   The specified forward and aft points beyond which the Centre of Gravity must not be located during flight.

Centre of Gravity Range.   The distance between the forward and aft limits.

Arm (moment arm).   The horizontal distance, from the reference datum line to the Centre of Gravity of the item. The sign is (+) if measured aft of the datum and (-) if measured forward of the datum.

Datum (reference datum).   An imaginary vertical plane or line from which all measurements of the arm are taken. The datum is established by the manufacturer. After the datum has been established, all moment arms and the location of the permissible range must be taken with reference to that point.

Station.   A location in the aircraft which is identified by a number designating its distance from the datum. The datum is therefore identified as zero. The station and arm are usually identical i.e. an item located at station +50 would have an arm of 50 inches.

Moment.   The product of the mass of an item multiplied by its arm. Moments are expressed in pound inches or metric equivalent kg.m. or kg.mm.

Moment Index (or index).   The moment divided by a constant such as 100, 1000, or 10,000. The purpose of using a moment index is to simplify weight and balance computations where heavy items and long arms result in large unmanageable numbers. (Not usual on small helicopters)

Reduction Factor.   The constant which, when divided into a moment, results in an index.

Note: *The aircraft mass and balance schedule will contain information relating to the following terms:*

Basic Mass.   The basic mass is the mass of the aircraft and all its basic equipment and that of the declared quantity of unusable fuel and unusable oil. In the case of aircraft of 5700kg (12,500Ib) maximum authorised mass or less it may also include the mass of usable oil.

Basic Equipment. This consists of the unconsumable fluids, and equipment, which are necessary for the operation of the aircraft in any role for which it is certified.

Variable Load. Variable load is the mass of the crew and of items such as the crew's baggage, removable units, and other equipment the carriage of which depends upon the purpose for which the operator intends to use the aircraft, on that particular flight.

Disposable Load. This is the mass of all persons and items of load, including fuel and other consumable fluids carried in the aircraft, but excluding the basic equipment and variable load.

34.23 **Mass and Centre of Gravity Calculations.** To obtain the total loaded mass, it is necessary to add to the basic mass the masses of the variable and disposable load items to be carried, for the particular role for which the aircraft is to be used.

34.24 Flight/Owners Manuals vary in their methods of presenting mass and balance information but most of them show a mass and balance envelope (Centre of Gravity Moment Envelope) (See fig 34.4), so that a pilot can quickly check if the weight and balance is within limits after making his calculations.

34.25 These calculations must commence by referring to the Mass and Balance Schedule for the particular aircraft. The following information outlines the steps to be taken to determine the actual mass and balance of the aircraft. Referring to the Mass and Balance Schedule and the aircraft Flight/Owners Manual:

1 List the aircraft Basic Mass, Variable Load and Disposable Load.
2 Multiply the masses by their arms to obtain the moment of each item.
3 Add the respective masses to obtain the total loaded mass of the aircraft.
4 Add the moments to obtain the total moment.
5 Divide the total moment by the total weight to obtain the arm of the Centre of Gravity of the aircraft.
6 Compare the total mass obtained in step 3 to the maximum authorised all up mass (AUM).
7 Compare the calculated Centre of Gravity arm obtained in step 5 to the approved Centre of Gravity range of the aircraft.

34.26   If both the mass and position of the Centre of Gravity are within the permitted limits, the aircraft is safe to fly. If, however, the actual mass is greater than the maximum authorised mass or the calculated Centre of Gravity position is outside the permitted limits, the disposable load must be adjusted accordingly.

Fig. 34.2   Datum line near rotor mast, "arms" ahead of the datum are negative, and behind are positive.

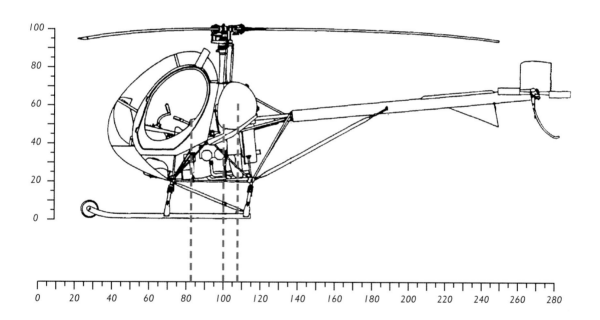

Fig. 34.3   Datum-line ahead of the helicopter, all "arms" are therefore positive.

34.27   Although it will be sensible to enter the masses of the various items first and then check that the total mass is within limits before carrying out the moment arm calculations, it must not be assumed that because the actual total mass is below the maximum all-up mass allowed that the Centre of Gravity will also be within the permitted limits.

Remember the calculations must determine two items:

1   The total all-up mass.
2   The actual position of the Centre of Gravity.

34.28   Some manufacturers chose the datum line at some point in the middle of the helicopter, sometimes in line with the rotor shaft. In this case, moments produced by masses ahead of the datum line are negative, and moments produced by masses aft of the datum line are positive. See fig 34.2.

34.29   Other manufacturers choose the datum line at or ahead of the most forward structural point on the helicopter, in which case all moments are positive. See figure 34.3. Notice that the fuel tank has an arm of +107 inches, and the pilot at +84 inches.

34.30   The mass and balance schedule will list the main aircraft details, manufacturer, serial number, maximum authorised mass, C of G limitations etc. Also, the aircraft basic mass, and whether there is any difference in the C of G limits with the undercarriage up or down (if applicable). Also, the position of the C of G datum and masses and lever arms for pilot/s passengers, baggage and fuel.

34.31   In this first example, the datum line is ahead of the aircraft so that all moments will be positive. It is assumed that the maximum allowable takeoff mass will be 1600 lbs, and the C of G limits are between 95 and 100 inches aft of the datum. (Note the very small C of G range – 5 inches, typical of a light single engine helicopter).

34.32   The following mass and balance calculations are worked out with the aircraft load in this case consisting of the pilot, one passenger, full fuel tanks and no baggage.

Item lb.in.	lb.	×	Arm in.	=	Moment
Basic Weight	Aircraft 1004		+101.0		101404.0
Variable Load	Pilot 165		+ 83.9		13843.5
Disposable Load	Fuel 150		+107.0		16050.0
	Oil *(included in the basic mass)*				
	Passenger				
	(one) 165		+ 83.9		13843.5
Baggage	nil				
TOTAL	1484		~		145140.5

34.33   At this stage, check that the total mass is within limits for the take-off conditions. Dividing the total mass into the total moment gives the position of the Centre of Gravity, in this case:

$$\text{C of G} \quad = \quad \frac{\text{Total moment}}{\text{Total mass}} = \frac{145140.5}{1484} = 97.8$$

34.34   As all the "arms" are positive, the C of G is therefore 97.8 inches aft of the datum. Reference is then made to the Centre of Gravity Moment Envelope contained in the Flight/Owners Manual to ensure that the C of G is within the limits. See figure 34.4 and 34.5 for two examples.

34.35   In the JAR examinations, students may be examined on one of several types of C of G envelope charts, and three types are included in these notes. A cautionary note concerns the stowing of baggage. It is not sufficient just to ensure that the baggage mass and stowage position does not cause the weight and balance limit to be exceeded. If it is not secured properly, a shift in the position of loose baggage during flight can negate the purpose of the balance calculations and possibly jam or interfere with the aircraft controls or lead to injury of the pilot or the passengers in the case of an accident.

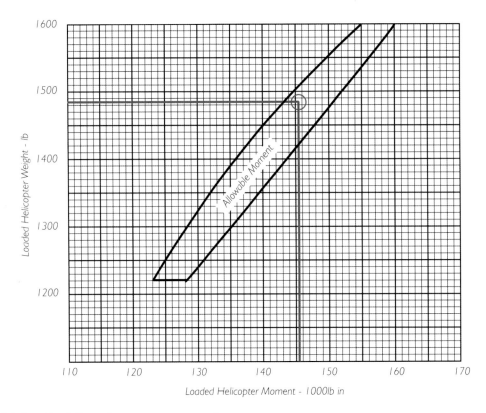

Fig. 34.4   C of G and gross mass envelope.

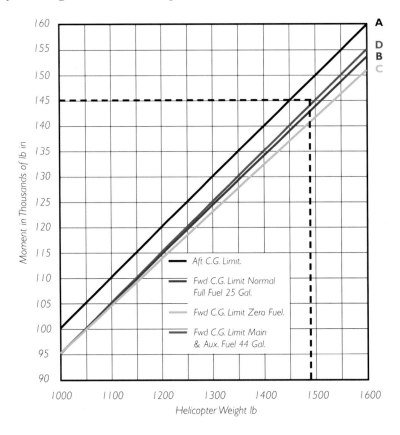

Fig. 34.5   Centre of Gravity Chart. The terms "Weight" in the above graphs are used as the graphs are from a manufacturer not working to the JAR definition.

237

34.36   The following mass and balance calculation (using metric units) assumes a helicopter has a maximum take off weight of 1800 kg, and the masses and moments are given:

ITEM (Kgmm)	Mass (kg)	×	Arm(mm)	= moment
Basic helicopter	1040		3110	3335808
Pilot	90		1440	129600
Co-pilot	90		1440	129600
Passenger	100		2290	229000
Baggage	25		1704	42600
Fuel	320		3069	982080
	1665	~		4848688

$$C \text{ of } G = \frac{\text{Total moments}}{\text{Total mass}} = \frac{4848688}{1665} = 2912 \text{ mm aft}$$

34.37   Having calculated the C of G position for a particular load, reference should be made to the limitations section of the pilots operations manual and see that the C of G is within the limits.

34.38   Referring to figures 34.4 and 34.5. These indicate quite well the very narrow C of G range available. It is normal (and safe) practice to compute the position of the C of G for take off and landing, particularly after a long flight, where most of the fuel would have been consumed.

34.39   An example is now presented and it is suggested that students rework all these loading calculations as test questions follow.

Given: Helicopter maximum take-off weight 2860 lbs.
Helicopter empty mass 1930 lbs
C of G limits 3 inches forward of station 0 to 4 inches aft of station 0.
Fuel load 45 US gallons (270 lbs)
2 pilots at 165 lbs
Baggage 26 lbs in rear compartment
Baggage 11 lbs in forward compartment
One passenger at 165 lbs

Note: *Arms are both positive and negative in this example.*

Arms:

Empty mass		+ 6 inches
Fuel tank		+ 2 inches
Pilots seats		-32 inches
Baggage comp (rear)		+ 7 inches
Baggage comp (fwd)		-31 inches
Passenger seat		+ 8 inches

Helicopter take off mass is:

Empty mass	1930 lbs
2 pilots at 165 lbs	330 lbs
1 passenger	165 lbs
Baggage (rear)	26 lbs
Baggage (fwd)	11 lbs
Fuel	70 lbs
TOTAL	2732 lbs

The actual take off mass is below the maximum for the conditions in this example.

Tabulation of masses and moments:

ITEM	Mass × (lbs)	Arm = (inches)	Moment(+)	Moment(-)
Basic mass	1930	+6	+11580	
Fuel	270	+2	+ 540	
Baggage (Rear)	26	+7	+ 182	
Passenger	165	+8	+ 1320	
Pilots (2)	330	-32		-10560
Baggage (Fwd)	11	-31		- 341
TOTALS	2732	~	+13622	-10901

Total moment   = +13622 -10901 = +2721 lbs ins.

C of G = $\dfrac{\text{Total moment}}{\text{Total mass}}$ = $\dfrac{+2721}{2732}$ = 0.995 inches aft

Assuming that the flight fuel consumption was 37 US gallons (222 lbs), what would be the position of the C of G when landing ?

The fuel load on landing would be 270 lbs less the burn-off = 270-222 lbs = 48 lbs

239

The revised tabulation is now:

ITEM	Mass (lbs)	×	Arm (inches)	=	Moment(+)	Moment(-)
Basic mass	1930		+6		+11580	
Fuel	48		+2		96	
Baggage (Rear)	26		+7		+ 182	
Passenger	165		+8		+ 1320	
Pilots (2)	330		-32			- 10560
Baggage (Fwd)	11		-31			- 341
TOTALS	2510		~		+13178	- 10901

Therefore the landing C of G would be:

$$\frac{\text{Total moment}}{\text{Total mass}} = \frac{+2277}{2510} = 0.907 \text{ inches aft}$$

It can be seen that in this flight, the C of G moved less than one inch forward.

34.40 **Lateral C of G position**. It is usually not necessary to determine the lateral C of G position as most optional equipment is located near the helicopter centreline. However, if an unusual installation or loading occurs which could affect the lateral C of G, (ie., single pilot operation) its position should be checked against the lateral C of G envelope.

34.41 The lateral C of G position can be calculated by multiplying the massws of all items that are not symmetrical about the centreline, times their arm from the centreline. Then considering all items on the right as positive and those on the left as negative, sum the moments and divide the total by the mass of the loaded helicopter. This will give the lateral position, which together with C of G in the calculated longitudinal position, can be compared with the allowable C of G envelope.

34.42 An example is now included as this too forms a question area in the JAR examinations.

34.43   To calculate the lateral C of G it is normal to calculate the longitudinal C of G in the first phase, as already described. The lateral ARMs of the empty aircraft, pilots, passengers, baggage and fuel will be given. Positive and Negative arms will be used. These will be multiplied by the respective masses to produce the moments. The calculation is then the same as for longitudinal C of Gs, in that

$$\frac{\text{Total Moment}}{\text{Total Mass}} = \text{C of G}$$

Inches or mm Left or Right of the datum. Reference is then made to the Lateral C of G envelope to establish that the C of G is within the safe area.

34.44   As an example, a complete calculation is now included to show the steps required.

GIVEN:

ITEM	Mass(lb)	Longitudinal Arm	Lateral Arm
Basic mass	1000	+93.0	+ 0.3
Pilot	160	+71.0	+12.0
Passenger	160	+71.0	- 12.0
Fuel	130	+96.0	- 9.1

First step, calculate the longitudinal C of G:

ITEM	Mass(lb)	× Longitudinal Arm	= Moment
Basic mass	1000	+93.0	93000
Pilot	160	+71.0	11360
Passenger	160	+71.0	11360
Fuel	130	+96.0	12480
TOTALS	1450	~	128200

$$\frac{\text{Total Moment}}{\text{Total Mass}} = \frac{+128200}{1450} = 88.41 \text{ inches Aft of Datum}$$

ASSUME the flight uses 110 lb of fuel. Therefore, on landing, the fuel left is the fuel uplifted less the fuel burn-off = 130 – 110 lb = 20 lb. The landing mass is now the take-off mass less the fuel burn-off = 1500 – 110 lb = 1390 lb. Substituting these two new values in the tabulation above, we have:

ITEM	Mass(lb) ×	Longitudinal Arm	=	Moment
Basic mass	1000	+93.0		93000
Pilot	160	+71.0		11360
Passenger	160	+71.0		11360
Fuel	20	+96.0		1920
TOTALS	1340	~		117640

$$\frac{\text{Total Moment}}{\text{Total Mass}} = \frac{+117640}{1340} = 87.79 \text{ inches Aft of Datum}$$

During this flight, the Longitudinal C of G moved forwards 0.62 of an inch. Look at figure 34.6 (Longitudinal C of G) and plotting the aircraft mass against the C of G see that the take-off and the landing C of G are within the safe envelope – Point "A" for take-off and point "B" for landing. The graph shows quite well the excursion of C of G when fuel is used.

Lateral C of G

ITEM	Mass(lb) ×	Lateral Arm	=	Moment
Basic mass	1000	+ 0.3	+ 300	
Pilot	160	+13.1	+1920	
Passenger	160	-13.1		-1920
Fuel	130	- 9.8		-1183
TOTALS	1450	+2220 = - 883		-3103

$$\frac{\text{Total moment}}{\text{Total mass}} = \frac{- 883}{1450} = - 0.608 \text{ Left}$$

As the moment is negative, the Lateral C of G is left.
This is point "C" on the lateral C of G (Figure 34.6) and within the safe envelope.

A further example of a Longitudinal and Lateral C of G problem:

Assume now that a single pilot operation is to take place, but the pilot sits in the Left Hand seat. First of all, the longitudinal C of G is:

ITEM	Mass(lb) ×	Longitudinal Arm =	Moment
Basic mass	1000	+ 93.0	93000
Pilot	160	+ 71.0	11360
Fuel	130	+ 96.0	12480
TOTALS	1290	~	116840

$$\frac{\text{Total moment}}{\text{Total mass}} = \frac{+116840}{1290} = 90.57 \text{ inches aft of datum}$$

Point "D" on the Longitudinal C of G (Figure 34.6)

Lateral C of G

ITEM	Mass(lb) ×	Lateral Arm	=	Moment
Basic mass	1000	+ 0.3		+ 300
Pilot	160	- 12.0		- 1920
Fuel	130	- 9.1		- 1183
TOTALS	1290			+ 300 - 3103
				= - 2803

$$\frac{\text{Total moment}}{\text{Total mass}} = \frac{-2803}{1290} = -2.172 \text{ Left}$$

This is point "E" on the Lateral C of G (Figure 34.6)

From the C of G envelopes, it can be seen that the Longitudinal C of G is within the safe limit, but the lateral C of G is outside the envelope, and therefore the helicopter is unsafe to fly.

243

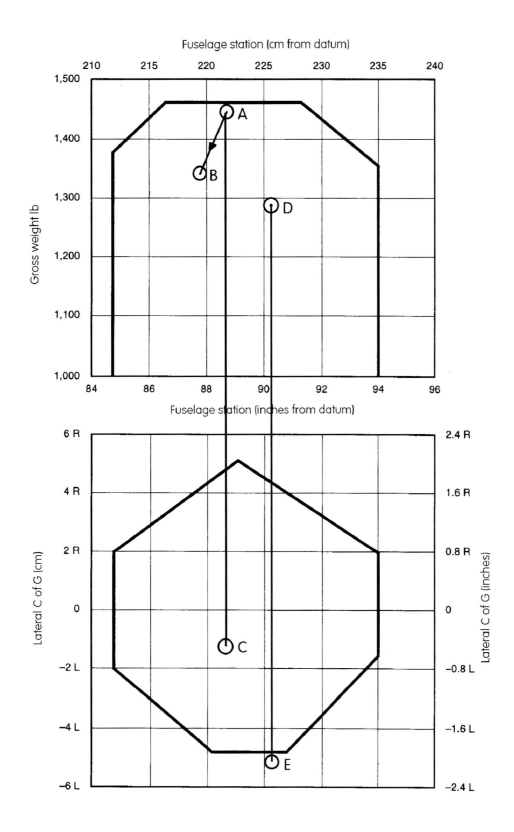

Fig. 34.6   C of G limits - Top Longitudinal, Lower lateral.

34.45   If a pilot loads up a helicopter, and finds after calculating the C of G that it is outside the safe operating envelope, then it is necessary to move the load in order to move the C of G within the safe limits. There is not a lot that a pilot can do in this respect except to move any freight or baggage. Fuel and pilots' seats remain fixed.

34.46   In the JAR examination on Helicopter Flight Performance, students are expected to know how to "re-calculate" C of G problems when the first calculation shows the C of G being out of limits. That is to say, how much should baggage or freight be moved, and what direction to meet the C of G limits. In order to illustrate this application, an example will be shown.

34.47   GIVEN:

Item	Mass lb	Arm inches	Moment
Empty mass	1460	80 Aft	116800
Pilot	160	63 Aft	10080
Baggage	150	72 Aft	10800
Fuel	210	84 Aft	17640
TOTALS	1980	~	155320

The maximum take-off mass is 1990 lb

The take-off mass is within limits.

$$C \text{ of } G = \frac{\text{Total Moment}}{\text{Total Mass}} = \frac{155320}{1980} = 78.44 \text{ inches Aft.}$$

Assuming the MAXIMUM AFT C of G is 77.1 inches Aft of datum, how far would the baggage be moved and in what direction to meet the new maximum limit ?

∴ as the mass remains the same at 1980 lb, the total moment must be reduced.

The limit C of G is 77.1 inches Aft

$$\therefore C \text{ of } G = \frac{\text{Total Moment}}{\text{Total Mass}}$$

$$\therefore 77.1 = \frac{\text{Total Moment}}{1980}$$

∴ Total Moment = 77.1 × 1980 = 152658 (The new total moment)

The difference between the OLD and NEW Total Moments

$$= 155320 - 152658$$
$$= 2662 \text{ lb inches}$$

The baggage original moment was 10800
The new moment must now be $10800 - 2662 = 8138$ lb inches

Baggage Mass × Arm = Moment
=   150 × Arm = 8138

New Arm   = $\dfrac{8138}{150}$ = 54.25 inches Aft of Datum

Therefore: the baggage must be moved from its original arm of 72 inches aft to 54.25 inches aft, which is **17.75 inches forward.**

To check the new C of G position using the new baggage Arm of 54.25 inches Aft

Item	Mass lb	Arm inches		Moment
Empty mass	1460	80	Aft	116800
Pilot	160	63	Aft	10080
Baggage	150	54.25	Aft	8138
Fuel	210	84	Aft	17640
TOTALS	1980	~		152658

C of G = $\dfrac{\text{Total Moment}}{\text{Total Mass}}$ = $\dfrac{152658}{1980}$ = 77.1 inches Aft.

The re-positioning of the baggage 17.75 inches forward brings the C of G to the **EXACT** Aft limit.

35   HELICOPTER ICING

35.1   The JAR PPL(H) examination also has questions about Helicopter Icing in Flight Performance & Planning, as well as in the Meteorological examination paper. Therefore additional icing information is now included and certain aspects that are unique to helicopters.

35.2   Icing on helicopters can present a very serious situation, more serious than fixed wing aircraft. Few helicopters are equipped to cater for icing, even light icing.

35.3   Some flight manuals state "flight into known icing conditions is prohibited". The helicopter is restricted for a number of reasons, and even in light icing (in some cases) to a maximum of 30 minutes duration due to the probability of damage from shedding ice.

35.4   Ice can readily form on an aircraft when flying in conditions of high humidity in precipitation, cloud or fog and low temperatures, particularly at 0°C or just below. However, even flying at positive temperatures, but near to the 0°C level, icing can still take place on those regions of an airframe experiencing a pressure drop. In the case of a helicopter, the region above a rotating rotor blade.

35.5   **Ice Accretion.**   The rate at which ice can build up on an airframe in dependent on:

1   Water content of the air (absolute humidity)
2   Temperature
3   Size of water drops
4   Kinetic heating
5   Shape of aerofoils

35.6   **Influence of Temperature and Drop Size.**   Icing encountered under normal conditions is produced by freezing of supercooled water droplets into solid ice in one form or another depending on the degree of supercooling. The water droplets are at temperatures below freezing, but still in the liquid phase, which can exist in the free atmosphere. Any disturbance to the droplets, such as a wing or rotating blade striking them, solidifies part of the drops instantaneously while the remainder flows back over the blade, freezing as it moves. 1/80 th of the volume of the drop freezes virtually instantaneously for each degree of super cooling. In general, the larger the drop size and the closer its temperature to the freezing point, the smaller the portion that turns to ice on impact and the larger the amount that flows back, releasing latent heat and freezing to a solid as it goes.

35.7   The type of ice is known as *clear ice* (also known as *translucent ice)*. It is hard, clear and dense, and therefore heavy. It is also very difficult to dislodge. If it does fly off, and because it is heavy and dense, produces dangerous flying debris. Flexing of blades can cause large lumps to fly off, and this in turn will unbalance rotor blades resulting in vibration. Most likely severe.

35.8   For small water droplets at temperatures well below freezing, a greater percentage of the water droplet will freeze on impact with the airframe. 1/80 of the volume for each degree of supercooling. Therefore, much less of the droplet volume will flow back. This type of icing is called *rime ice*. It is white in appearance, as it is contains a lot of air. It is not so dense as clear ice, but the danger here is the change of the aerodynamic contours of rotor blades, and reduction of efficiency.

35.9   The lower temperature limit for icing is deemed to be -40°C. At these temperatures, it is rare that there are no water drops in a supercooled state. Generally, suspended water is in the ice crystal state. They pose no danger to airframes as impact will not see any adhesion.

35.10   In the temperature range of -20°C to -40°C droplet sizes are generally small, and the percentage of the droplet freezing on impact is large. (See para: 35.8). This means a reduced icing hazard. If the helicopter is fitted with an anti-icing system, it can generally avoid a build-up of this type of icing. It must be remembered though that clear ice is far more dangerous than rime ice.

35.11   **Water Contents of Air.** Ice build up on an airframe is dependent on the amount of water contained in the air. Icing in Nimbo Stratus cloud can be severe because of the very high concentration of water drops, even though they are described as being small to medium in size. A further point to consider is flying in the neighbourhood of mountains. Droplet sizes can be enhanced due to orographic displacement aloft of the air. Icing is therefore also enhanced.

35.12   As updrafts enhance airframe icing as explained in para: 35.11, then thunderstorms which have considerable up-drafts can also lift large water drops upwards. The icing can therefore be very severe in a thunderstorm. Rain ice can be encountered flying ahead of an approaching warm front in the cold air ahead. The aircraft must be above the freezing level in the cold air, but below the freezing level of the warm sector. Precipitation from the warm sector penetrating the warm front interface is now falling through sub zero temperatures, and produces supercooled water drops. Flying in this segment produces clear ice (see para: 35.6). This type of icing is very rapid, and no anti-icing system will prevent it. The pilot will need to take evasive action VERY QUICKLY.

35.13   In polar regions, with very low temperatures, airframe icing is much less of a hazard than at lower latitudes or tropical regions because of the low water content. At higher temperatures there is a greater capability of holding more water vapour. In tropical latitudes, the freezing level is about 15000 to 17000 feet, so should a helicopter fly at this height, then icing in large cumulus would be severe.

35.14   Kinetic heating of airframes (when moving) and propellers and rotors takes place as a function of the speed/friction through the ambient air. With helicopters, the high rotational speed of rotors are heated this way. This has a bearing on the characteristic ice formation on the blades. Near the tips, ice may not form because of the higher local speed through the air. Some small diameter multi rotor helicopters experience icing though despite higher rotational rotor speeds.

35.15   **Shape of Aerofoils.** When flying though supercooled water drops, it has been observed that the drops can break through the thin boundary layer that is found on sharp objects facing the oncoming airstream. i.e., VHF and UHF aerials, leading edges of rotor blades, allowing ice to build up. Whereas, a more blunt object like a low speed lifting surface is not so susceptible as the airflow is directed (more slowly) around it retaining its boundary layer.

35.16   Windshields can also ice up. This takes place again in flying through supercooled water drops, or in sleet where there is a mix of supercooled water drops and snow or snow grains. Supercooled water drops will allow the dry snow or grains to stick to the windshield (or any part of the airframe). Snow will not stick in its 'dry' state. The windshield can also ice up inside. This is because it has become cold flying in cold air, and condensation on the inside can freeze.

35.17   **Mechanical Vibration.** Ice can be shaken off an airframe by vibration, and flexing of rotor blades. It has been observed that with a rotor blade, the maximum flexion forces exist about one third of its length from the root. High performance 'stiffer' blades do not shed ice so readily as more flexible blades.

35.18   As shedding of ice may seem to afford a degree of de-icing, the danger here is the unevenness of the ice coming off. This with a helicopter can be very dangerous as vibration being a consequence of rotor imbalance can have structural failure possibilities. A pilot experiencing this should land as soon as practicable. Note too, that this phenomenon can take place whilst running on the ground, should all the requirements be in place.

35.19 **Ice Formation at Different Temperatures.** It has been mentioned in earlier paragraphs, that icing is dependent on temperature and droplet size, however they are formed. In the temperature range of 0°C to about 6°C, ice will readily form on leading edges of rotor blades out to about 70% of its length. The tip is a section most likely remaining clear because of kinetic heating. At about 20% of the chord distance from the leading edge, the maximum ice deposit is seen in the affected area. At the blade root however, there is local turbulence which deforms the icing in this area. See fig. 35.1.

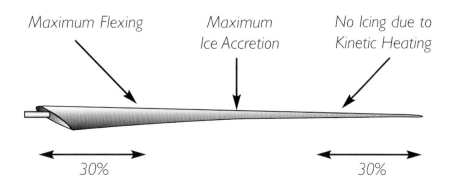

Fig. 35.1   Ice accumulation at approximately –3°C.

35.20 At lower temperatures, say from -6°C to about -18°C, what icing takes place will see the complete leading edge of the blade covered. Kinetic heating having less influence at these lower temperatures. Temperatures lower than this range means that the air is less moist, and hence airframe icing is reduced.

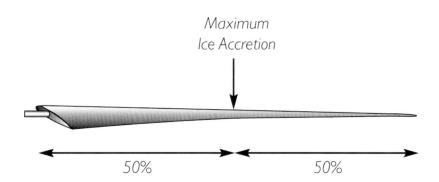

Fig. 35.2   Ice accumulation at approximately –10°C and colder.

35.21   The ice deposits that build-up depend to a large extent on the droplet size and the temperature. Large drops at just below freezing temperature are likely to produce clear ice, where the initial small portions of the drops turn instantaneously to solid ice. The remaining rearward flow, which is losing latent heat, solidifies as it flows back. This results in clear smooth dense ice. At temperatures of about -10°C and lower, smaller drops will see a higher volume of the drop freezing solid instantaneously, and a much smaller amount flowing back. Then the ice deposit has the characteristic of a rough lumpy surface. Also, it is white in appearance because of trapped air. See fig. 35.3.

Clear Ice - Smooth   Rime Ice - Rough

Fig. 35.3   Ice accretion on rotor blades, characteristic appearance of Clear and Rime ice.

35.22   Icing conditions present the following hazards :

1.   *Rotor Icing.* The build-up of ice on the main and tail rotor blades can have serious effects while building up and possible catastrophic effects when it breaks loose. Since the blades are going faster than any other part of the helicopter, they encounter more droplets per second, and because of their collection efficiency, accrete ice at a faster rate. Furthermore, compression of the air at the stagnation points on the leading edge of the blade raises the temperature (as much as 22°C) at the very tip. For this reason, tips are often free of ice while it builds up on inboard sections. Ice degrades the aerodynamic characteristics of the blade aerofoil by forming irregular shapes that increase drag and decrease maximum lift capabilities. The power increase due to the higher drag may give an alert pilot the first indication of ice.

2   *Autorotation.* The degraded aerodynamic characteristics will also jeopardize the ability to autorotate in case of engine failure. Autorotation with ice on the blades presents the following problems:

a.   Because the power required is higher, the autorotative rate of descent must be higher to produce that power from loss of potential energy. This gives the pilot less time to get the engine restarted.

b.   Because the rate of descent is higher, the collective pitch required to maintain normal rotor speed is lower. It is possible that the collective downstop may be too high to get the rotor speed up to a desired level.

c.   Because the maximum lift capability is lower, the safe minimum rotor speed will be higher. With lots of ice, the minimum safe RPM may actually be higher than the RPM on the downstop.

d.   Because the drag is higher, the ability to build up excess rotor speed in a cyclic flare will be lower.

e.   Because the maximum lift is lower, the load factor that can be generated in the final collective pull will be lower.

35.23   Blade ice will eventually be shed because of rotational forces, air loads, blade flexing, or flying into warmer air. When it does, it often goes from one blade at a time, or "asymmetrically" so that the rotor goes out of balance and out of track. This can produce severe vibration in the cockpit and damaging cyclic loads in the main and/or tail rotor support structures. At the same time, damage to the tail rotor may result from ice thrown off the main rotor or the other way round.

Self Test Questions for Part 2
Aircraft General & Principles of Flight

1   Who is responsible before a flight that the load is safely distributed and secured ?

    (a)   The Company licensed engineer.
    (b)   The Company Load master.
    (c)   The Commander of the intended flight.
    (d)   Any company engineer acting for the chief engineer.

2   What is the weight of 33 US Gallons of Av Gas at a specific gravity of 0.715?

    (a)   197 lb.
    (b)   201 kg.
    (c)   155 lb.
    (d)   179 kg.

3   A helicopter is flying at FL 80. The corrected outside air temperature is -1°C, what is the Density Altitude ?

    (a)   7174 feet.
    (b)   8826 feet.
    (c)   8194 feet.
    (d)   7380 feet.

4   An aerodrome which is 1800 feet above mean sea level, has an observed QNH of 998 mb. What is the approximate pressure altitude ?

    (a)   2107 feet.
    (b)   1580 feet.
    (c)   1956 feet.
    (d)   2250 feet.

5   If a helicopter is hovering over a fixed position, and there is a wind blowing, which is the most critical position of the Centre of Gravity ?

    (a)   Close to the aft limit.
    (b)   Close to the forward limit.
    (c)   Is of no consequence when hovering in ground effect.
    (d)   Aft limit in a headwind, forward limit in a tailwind.

6   Air density is reduced by:

   (a)   Decrease in temperature, decrease in humidity and decrease in pressure.
   (b)   Increase in temperature, decrease in humidity and increase in pressure.
   (c)   Increase in temperature, increased humidity and decrease in pressure.
   (d)   Increase in altitude, decrease in humidity and decrease in temperature.

Refer to the helicopter power graph below and answer the following two questions:

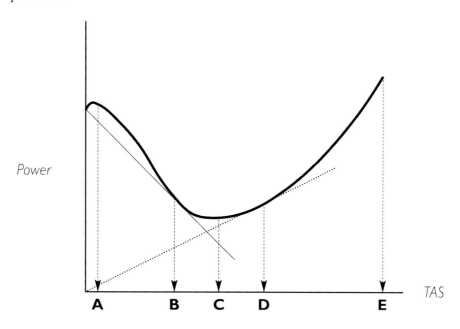

7   To fly for range, the best speed would be:

   (a)   B
   (b)   C
   (c)   A
   (d)   D

8   To fly for maximum rate of climb, the best speed would be:

   (a)   C
   (b)   E
   (c)   B
   (d)   D

9   The V_{ne} of a helicopter is determined by:

(a)   Compressibility effects at the rotor tips.
(b)   The tail rotor limitation to control the effects of main rotor torque at high speed.
(c)   The power of the engine.
(d)   Retreating blade stall.

10   Assume a helicopter is autorotating following an engine failure. The pilot may decide to operate at the shallowest angle of descent (range speed), or the maximum time in the air (endurance speed). Which of the following is correct?

(a)   The best still air range speed and best endurance speed under autorotation is the same as the lowest rate of descent speed.
(b)   The best still air range speed is slightly higher than the best endurance Speed.
(c)   The best still air range speed and best endurance speed are virtually the same but a little lower than the lowest rate of descent speed.
(d)   The best endurance is achieved at the tangential point on the 'rate of descent graph'.

11   A helicopter is loaded longitudinally and laterally as below: Calculate the Longitudinal and Lateral C of G's and answer the following two questions:

ITEM	Mass(lb)	Longitudinal Arm	Longitudinal Moment	Lateral Arm	Lateral Moment
Basic mass	1200	+91.4	!	+ 0.28	!
Pilot	150	+70.0	!	+11.8	!
Passenger	150	+70.0	!	-11.8	!
Freight	100	+82.0	!	- 8.1	!
Fuel	180	+92.6	!	-9.8	!
TOTAL's	!	~	!	~	!

The Longitudinal C of G is:

(a)   86.88 inches Aft of datum.
(b)   79.12 inches Aft of datum.
(c)   87.38 inches Aft of datum.
(d)   89.35 inches Aft of datum.

12   The Lateral C of G is:

(a)   0.812 inches Right of datum.
(b)   1.257 inches Left of datum.
(c)   0.964 inches Left of datum.
(d)   1.655 inches Right of datum.

13   Using the data from question 11, assume that the maximum Aft C of G is 86.5 inches, how far would the freight have to be moved in order to bring the Longitudinal C of G within limits:

(a)   14.98 inches rearward.
(b)   16.71 inches rearward.
(c)   14.68 inches forward.
(d)   15.78 inches forward.

14   GIVEN the following tabulation of Helicopter masses and arms, what is the position of the C of G.

Item	Mass lb	Arm inches	Moment
Empty mass	1196	80 Aft	!
Pilot	160	63 Aft	!
Freight	50	72 Aft	!
Fuel	185	84 Aft	!
TOTALS	!	~	!

(a)   78.50 inches aft of datum.
(b)   80.42 inches aft of datum.
(c)   83.97 inches aft of datum.
(d)   79.28 inches aft of datum.

15   Using the data from question 14, if the Aft C of G limit was 79.10 inches Aft of the datum, how far should the freight be moved in order to bring the C of G onto the maximum Aft limit.

(a)   6.83 inches forwards.
(b)   17.96 inches aft.
(c)   3.14 inches aft.
(d)   15.78 inches forwards.

16   Refer to **ANNEX "A"**, Longitudinal and Lateral C of G envelopes for a typical light helicopter. If the helicopter had a take-off mass of 1430 lb, and the Longitudinal C of G is 87 inches Aft of the datum, and the Lateral C of G is 1.4 inches right of the datum, which of the following statements is correct ?

(a)   Longitudinal and lateral limits are safe for take-off.
(b)   Longitudinal limits are unsafe, but the lateral limits are safe.
(c)   Longitudinal limits are safe, but the lateral limits are not.
(d)   Longitudinal and lateral limits are unsafe for take-off.

17   If 20 HP is available beyond that required for level flight at a given speed, and assuming the mass of the helicopter is 4000 lbs, what would be the rate of climb possible?

(a)   240 fpm.
(b)   317 fpm.
(c)   165 fpm.
(d)   126 fpm.

18   A helicopter is flying at a constant speed and altitude and in a correctly balanced turn, which of the following is correct ?

(a)   The horizontal thrust component is greater than the total drag.
(b)   The total rotor thrust is greater than the mass of the helicopter.
(c)   The total rotor thrust is equal to the mass of the helicopter.
(d)   In a 30° banked turn, the apparent increase in all up mass is 25%.

19   The service ceiling of a helicopter is defined as:

(a)   The highest altitude where the engine operating at maximum continuous power maintains a constant altitude.
(b)   The altitude where at climbing power the rate of climb is zero.
(c)   The altitude where a set engine boost is maintained at a given engine speed.
(d)   The altitude where the rate of climb can no longer be maintained at a minimum of 100 feet per minute.

20   Under conditions where the maximum power available for a vertical climb is insufficient, then the horizontal distance covered to clear an obstacle is dependent upon:

(a)   Helicopter gross mass, the temperature and pressure altitude.
(b)   The aerodrome elevation, the helicopter equipped mass and temperature.
(c)   The density altitude, the relative humidity and temperature.
(d)   Translational lift, temperature and density altitude.

21   If the QFE at the departure point is 1000 mb and at the destination is 1013 mb, and assuming the temperature at both points is the same, which of the following is correct?

(a)   The helicopter performance at the destination point is the same as at the departure point.
(b)   The helicopter performance at the destination point would be the same as the departure point because the temperatures are the same.
(c)   The helicopter performance at the destination point would be worse than at
        the departure point.
(d)   The helicopter performance at the destination point would be better than at the departure point.

22   A helicopter moves forward from a hover condition to forward flight. Which of the following is correct ?

(a)   The power required decreases, and the total rotor thrust remains constant.
(b)   Both the power required and the total rotor thrust will effectively increase.
(c)   Both the power required and the total rotor thrust will effectively decrease
(d)   The total rotor thrust decreases initially, but the power required remains constant.

23   Detailed performance information of a specific helicopter variant is listed in which of the following documents to meet legal requirements ?

(a)   Certificate of Maintenance Release.
(b)   The Helicopter Flight Manual.
(c)   The Certificate of Airworthiness.
(d)   Manufacturers engineering and performance manual.

24   A helicopter is operating off cross-sloping ground. As the pilot raises the collective, the helicopter rotates about the higher skid, and the cyclic does not arrest the rolling. The pilot should:

(a)   Apply yaw pedal towards the slope, then raising the collective, take off as soon as possible.
(b)   Apply yaw pedals away from the slope, reduce power immediately.
(c)   Lift off as soon as possible.
(d)   Lower the collective swiftly.

Examine the graph below, and answer question 25

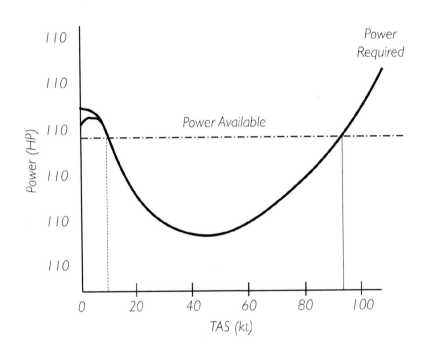

25   After examining the above graph, which of the following is correct ?

(a)   There is only sufficient power to hover in ground effect.
(b)   Only at speeds below about 10 kt is it possible to initiate a climb.
(c)   Level flight is only possible between about 10 kt and 93 kt.
(d)   The best climbing angle would be about 70 kt.

26   The best rate of climb speed results with:

(a)   The best obstacle clearance flight path.
(b)   The greatest increase in height with the shortest distance from take-off.
(c)   The greatest increase in height in a given time period.
(d)   The steepest climbing angle possible under given conditions.

27   A heli-pad is 850 feet AMSL, the QFE is 976 mb, what is the approximate pressure altitude:

(a)   1110 feet.
(b)   860 feet.
(c)   920 feet.
(d)   765 feet.

28   Flying in rain with an outside air temperature of -2°C causes:

(a)   The water droplet to freeze immediately and form rime ice.
(b)   Part of the water to freeze immediately, and the rest to flow back over the airframe becoming hoar frost.
(c)   4% of the droplet changes to rime ice.
(d)   97.5% of the droplet becomes clear ice.

29   Flying in rain with an outside air temperature of –25°C causes:

(a)   Relatively little icing as the temperature is too low to support high saturation.
(b) $^{25}/_{80}$ ths of the droplet freezes immediately, and the remainder flows back over the airframe to form jagged rime ice.
(c)   No icing on the rotor blade because kinetic heating will keep the blades clear.
(d)   The maximum rime icing will form only from the blade root out to about 30% of the blade span.

30   Assume a piston-engine helicopter is fitted with a carburetor.
      Icing can form in:

(a)   Clear air or in cloud when the temperature is –5°C to –25°C.
(b)   Cloud during a prolonged climb.
(c)   Clear air during summer in temperatures up to +25°C.
(d)   Moist Humid air during the cruise.

Answers to Part 2 will be found on page: 286

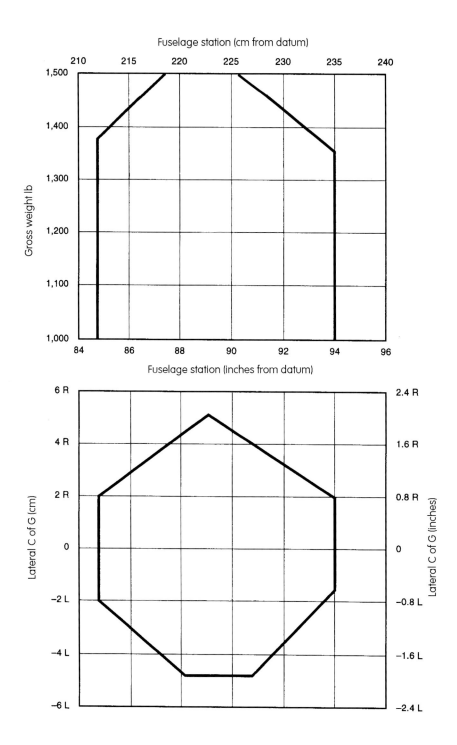

PART 3   Turbine Section

1   INTRODUCTION

1.1.1   Frank Whittle was granted a patent in 1930 for a gas turbine engine producing a propulsive jet. However, it took 11 years before his engine was used in an aeroplane and performed its first flight. A number of engines were produced from this basic design such as twin spool, by-pass, propfan, ducted fan, unducted fan, all developments from Whittle's original concept.

1.1.2   The adaptation of gas turbine power for helicopter use was a later innovation. This offers engines of light weight and greater power.

1.2   Basics

1.2.1   Before looking at the means in which gas turbine engines power helicopters, the basic gas turbine aero engine is described. The first engines, including Whittle's engine, were developed to propel an aeroplane by means of exhaust jet reaction. This is a practical application of Sir Isaac Newton's third law of motion. This states that for every action, there is an equal and opposite reaction. The jet engine produces a force to the rear of the aircraft, and the reaction of this jet propels the jet engine forward. As the engine is firmly attached to the aircraft, the aircraft too is propelled forward.

1.2.2   The thrust produced is similar to a propeller, in that a propeller displaces a large weight of air to the rear of the aircraft, causing a reaction force propelling the aircraft forward. With propellers however, the airstream is large but at relatively low speed. With jet engines, the displaced stream emitted from the engine is mainly gas at very high speed.

1.2.3   The simple jet engine consists of an air intake where air is drawn into the engine by the action of the compressor. In forward flight of a jet-powered aircraft, the forward movement augments the air going into the engine. The air is compressed by flowing through various stages of the compressor, which may have many stages of compressor blades. The air is then directed though a combustion stage, which consists of one or more combustion chambers. Fuel is introduced and ignited and the pressure rapidly increases. It is this pressure directed to the rear, which provides the propulsive reactive force.

1.2.4   The compressor must be driven, and the usual method is to connect a turbine wheel in the hot gas flowing to the rear. The turbine is connected by a drive shaft to the compressor. Turbines may be one or several stages. This basic configuration is called the gas generator. See figure 1.1 for a section through a basic turbo jet engine.

1.2.4   For gas turbines which drive helicopters, a further turbine is positioned aft of the gas generator turbine, and a shaft connects it to a drive shaft. The driveshaft passes concentrically through the gas generator shaft, and suitable gearing is used to bring the RPM down to required operating RPM. In this configuration, **as the turbine developing the power is not connected to the compressor, it is known as a free turbine.** See figure 1.3.

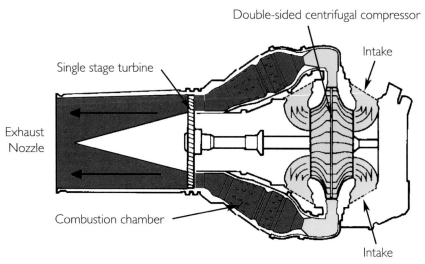

Fig. 1.1   Basic layout of a turbojet engine.

1.2.6   In figure 1.1, the air intake allows air to flow through the centrifugal compressor. It is compressed and enters the combustion chambers arranged around the engine casing. Fuel is introduced in these chambers and ignited. The resulting high-pressure gas is expelled outwards, and passes through a single stage turbine, which provides the power to drive the compressor.

1.2.7   Figure 1.1 is an example of an early variant of a turbo jet engine as the technology of centrifugal compressors was already available. A more efficient and more powerful compressor is the axial flow. See figure 1.2.

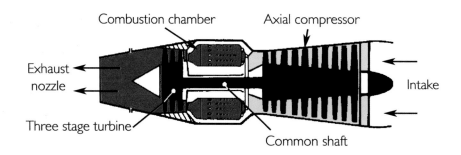

Fig. 1.2   A turbo jet with an axial flow compressor with 10 rows of axial rotors and a three stage turbine.

263

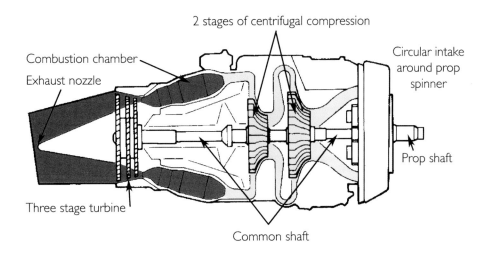

Fig: 1.3 A turbo-prop gas turbine engine.

1.2.8   Figure 1.3 shows a turbo-prop gas turbine engine. In this example, centrifugal compressors are used. There are two stages of compression. The compressors are arranged on a common shaft to the turbine, and in this example, the turbine has three stages. The air intake is directed around the propeller spinner and into the ducts leading to the first compressor. At the front of the common shaft, is the propeller reduction gear. Notice in this engine that a common shaft connects the compression stage with the turbine stage.

1.2.9   Figure 1.4 shows a turbo-shaft gas turbine engine. There are two compressors, the first stage being a four stage axial compressor, and the second stage being a centrifugal stage.

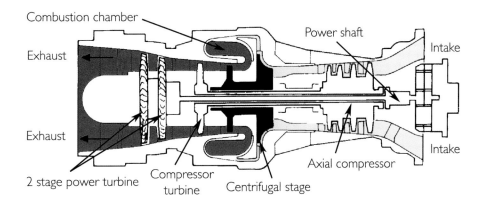

Fig. 1.4   Turbo-shaft gas turbine engine.

1.2.10 From figure 1.4 it can be seen that the first stage of compression is through an axial compressor. The compressed air is directed to the centrifugal stage where little additional compression takes place, but this stage is mainly to change the direction of the airflow quite abruptly into the combustion chambers. The air is directed through divergent stator blades where velocity is changed to pressure. The centrifugal compressor has its own turbine. The next turbine downstream in the hot gas is the axial compressor turbine, and further downstream the power turbine. Note that the power turbine shaft is not connected to any of the compressors, but its shaft passes concentrically through the gas generator compressors and turbine. This shaft is then connected to a gear box to reduce the RPM. This configuration is termed a free power turbine.

1.3 Gas Turbines General

1.3.1 **Introduction.** The gas turbine engine is a heat engine. Air entering the engine is accelerated, this increases its kinetic energy, the pressure energy is increased at the compressor stage, and this is followed by an increase in heat energy at the combustion stage, and then final conversion back to kinetic energy at the exhaust stage.

1.3.2 The working cycle of a gas turbine engine can be compared to the working cycle of a four-stroke piston engine. There is an induction stage, compression, combustion and exhaust stages. **However, the gas turbine engine works at constant pressure and the four stroke piston engine works at constant volume,** although a piston engine works intermittently, and the gas turbine engine works continuously. Because of this, a gas turbine engine is more powerful as it does not have 'wasted cycles or strokes'. This means more fuel is burnt per unit time and greater power is produced for a given size of engine.

1.3.3 As the gas turbine engine has a continuous burning action, and also that the combustion chamber/s are not enclosed spaces, the air pressure does not rise but its volume increases. This is heating at constant pressure, and not fluctuating pressure as in a piston engine.

1.3.4 The change of the variations in which the gas is subjected can be shown in a *pressure-volume diagram.* The area bounded by the four curves show the effect of the heat added. This heat can be used for work, either to produce propulsive jet reaction, or mechanical shaft power. See figure 1.5.

1.3.5 As the gas turbine engine is a heat engine, the higher the temperature in combustion, the higher will be the expansion of gas and the greater will be the power. However, limits are imposed by the metals used in the turbines.

1.3.6   To convert heat into mechanical work requires a differential in temperature of a gas. Looking at figure 1.5, it can be seen that at point 'A' is the local ambient condition of the atmosphere as it enters the engine. Along the line A-B, the air is progressively compressed. At point 'B' the air enters the combustion stage. When the air is progressively compressed, it progressively decreases in volume (and increases in temperature – Boyles Law). There are however, frictional losses, so in fact, actual volume/pressure is not quite as ideal as the diagram illustrates. More work is actually required than if the flow were ideal.

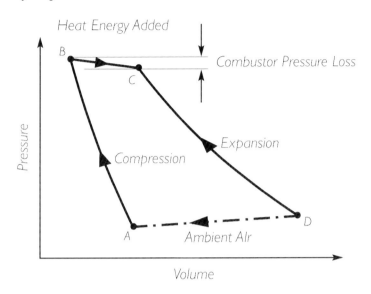

Fig. 1.5   The pressure volume working cycle.

1.3.7   Combustion (heat added) from point 'B' to point 'C'. To obtain maximum efficiency in the combustion process, the pressure should remain constant, however, due to turbulence and fluid dynamic frictional forces there is always a pressure loss: point 'C' is lower than point 'B'. From point 'C' to point 'D' is the expansion of the gas through the turbine and exhaust nozzle. Note at point 'D' the expansion of the gas rarely reaches atmospheric pressure (point 'A'). Not all the gas energy has been used.

1.3.8   The engine designer is faced with a number of thermodynamic and fluid losses along the path the gas has to follow at different engine stages.

1.4   Helicopter Turbo Shaft Engine

1.4.1   A typical Turbo Shaft engine as used in the single engine single rotor helicopter is the Detroit Diesel Allison 250-C20J. Some of the salient features of this engine are now described, *with acknowledgements to Detroit Diesel Allison.*

1.4.2   The dynamic components consist of – The engine and drive train, which consists of the transmission, the tail rotor drive shaft and the tail rotor gear box.

1.4.3   The engine weighs about 72 kg and is rated at 313 kW   (420 SHP), although the engine is flat rated to 236 kW (317 SHP).

1.4.4   The engine consists of a multi stage axial/centrifugal flow compressor, a single combustion chamber, a two stage gas generator (or producer) turbine, and a two stage power turbine which supplies the power output of the engine. See figure 1.6.

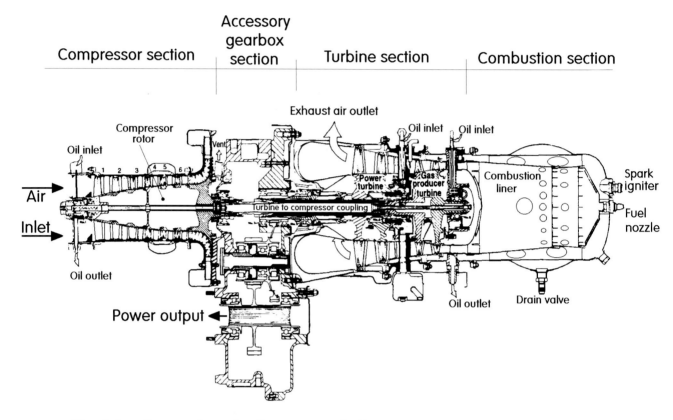

Fig. 1.6   *Section through a Detroit Diesel Allison model 250-C20J Turbo Shaft Gas turbine engine.*

1.4.5   At first sight, it looks like the engine is 'back to front'. Air is directed into the air inlet (Bellmouth intake), and passes through the 6 stage axial compressor, from there it is directed radially (90° to the central shaft) by a centrifugal stage. Two ducts to the rear of the engine duct the compressed air where it passes into the combustion section. (See fig: 1.7). Here, it is mixed with fuel and ignited. The high-pressure gas is directed **forward** through the first two stage turbine, which in turn is coupled to the compressor. The turbine to compressor coupling is a shaft mounted co-axially (inside) the power turbine shaft.   This is the **'Gas Generator' or 'Gas Producer'** assembly. The next stage (still going forward) the high-pressure gas passes through is a two stage **Power Turbine.** The power turbine shaft is connected to the accessory gearbox section where the main power take-off (output) is connected. The gas, at this stage has given up most of its power through the turbines, and is then exhausted through two outlets mounted on top of the engine. The engine is a free turbine, where the gas generator stage is not connected to the compressor.

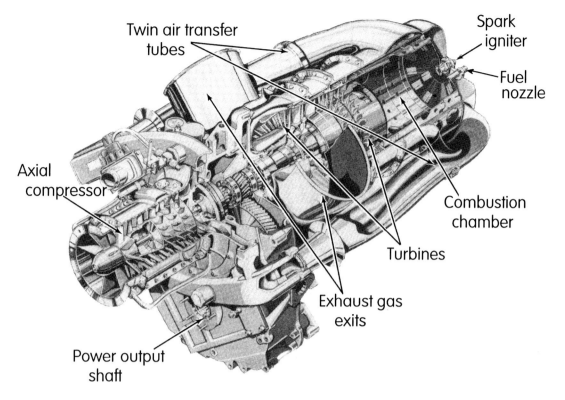

Fig. 1.7   General layout of the Detroit Diesel Allison 250-C20J Turbo-shaft Gas turbine engine.

1.4.6   For this particular engine, the following parameters apply:

Note: *These figures are for student guidance only, and should not be used for any particular helicopter. Refer to specific engine and helicopter flight manuals that are in current use and are up-dated.*

Weight	71.67 kg
Power/Weight Ratio	2.66:1
Airflow	1.56 kg/sec
Pressure ratio	7.2:1
N_1 Gas producer speed	53000 RPM
Power turbine	33290 RPM
Output drive shaft speed	6016 RPM (at 100%)
Rotor Drive shaft	394 RPM
Take-off power (5 min)	420 SHP (313 kW)
Maximum continuous	370 SHP (276 kW)
Cruise at 90%	333 SHP (248 kW)
Cruise at 75%	278 SHP (207 kW)
Ground idle (Gas producer)	33000 RPM
Ground idle (Power turbine)	24968 RPM at 75%
In autorotation (Gas producer)	33000 RPM
In autorotation (Power turbine)	32725 RPM at 98%
In autorotation (Output shaft)	5900 RPM at 98%

1.4.7   The following sections apply in general to a Bell 206B Jet Ranger Helicopter being an example of a modern single rotor, single gas turbine powered light utility helicopter. The arrangement of the main drive shaft to the Rotor transmission gear box, and the free wheeling units can be seen in figure 1.8

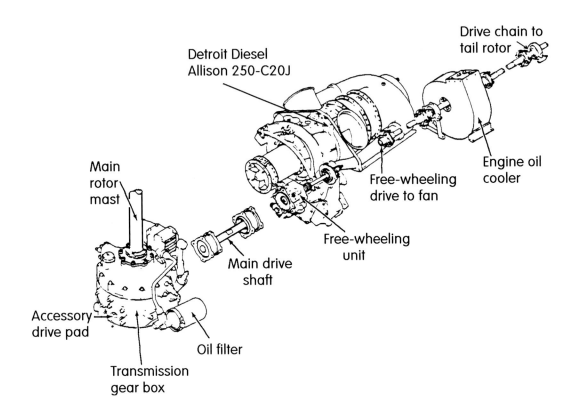

Fig. 1.8   Arrangement of the drive to the main rotor, fan drive and start of the drive chain to the tail rotor.

1.4.8   The engine is coupled to the transmission through the freewheeling unit and the main drive shaft. See section 13 "Helicopter transmission systems" Part 1. The sprag type free-wheeling unit is mounted on the engine gearbox. During autorotation, it provides a disconnect from the engine and allows autorotational forces of the main rotor to drive the transmission, tail rotor and all transmission accessories.

1.4.9   The power turbine and gas generator **tachometer generators** are mounted on the front of the engine on the left and right side respectively. The **starter/generator** is located on the right side. A turbine outlet temperature harness relays temperature measurements to an indicator on the instrument panel. An ENG OUT warning light on the caution panel is illuminated when the gas generator RPM falls below a pre-set value.

1.4.10   There is an anti icing system, which directs hot compressor discharge air over the compressor inlet guide vanes and front bearing hub. A switch on the radio pedestal controls the system.

1.4.11   An **hour meter**, mounted in the battery compartment operates in conjunction with the engine RPM sensor. It gives an accumulative total of the engine running time.

1.4.12   A start counter, mounted on the engine, records the total starts, counting one each time the ignition system is energised.

1.4.13   The twist grip. On the end of the collective lever is a twist grip, which controls the engine governor. **It is not an engine throttle,** as is fitted to most piston engined helicopters, and in normal flight is always in the fully open position. If, with the lever fully down the twist grip is fully closed, the governor will reduce engine rpm to ground idle.

1.4.14   Anti Icing Valve. Whenever the outside air temperature (OAT) is below 4°C the anti icing selector on the right side of the roof console should be put to the 'ON' position immediately after starting the engine. Operation of the valve bleeds hot air to the engine air intake and you will see that the only indication of its operation is a slight rise in Turbine Outlet Temperature. (TOT)

1.5   The Engine Oil System

1.5.1   The engine oil system is a circulation dry sump type with an external reservoir and oil cooler. Pressure and scavenge pumps are mounted within the engine and are driven by the accessory gearbox. All engine oil system lines and connections are internal with the exception of the pressure and scavenge lines to the front and rear bearings. See fig. 1.9 for a schematic.

1.5.2   A blower driven by the tail rotor drive shaft provides cooling air to the oil cooler. An oil temperature bulb installed in the supply tank is connected to an indicator on the instrument panel. A chip detector illuminates a light on the caution panel when metal particles are detected in the system.

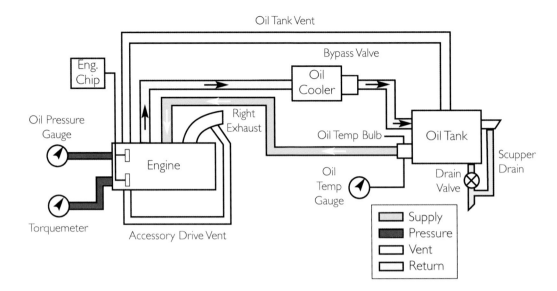

Fig. 1.9   Engine oil system schematic.

1.6   Fuel System

1.6.1   A single fuel cell located in the aft passenger seat bench with a fuel capacity of 344 litres (91 US gallons). It's reinforced to stand a 50 foot drop test. See fig. 1.10 for a schematic.

1.6.2   An engine-driven fuel pump and a fuel filter are both mounted on the engine. Two electric submerged boost pumps are located in the fuel cell, connected in parallel to the engine fuel supply line. A fuel pump caution light informs the pilot if either of the boost pumps malfunctions. Two fuel-level transmitters are connected to one indicator on the instrument panel. A filler cap is located on the right side of the helicopter, aft of the passenger door. A grounding plug is located nearby. An electric fuel-sump drain valve, operated by a push-button is located just below the filler cap. A fuel shut-off valve is electrically operated by a switch on the instrument panel. A transducer activates the fuel pressure gauge.

1.6.3   Engine starting. This is essentially automatic. However, the pilot must monitor the Turbine Outlet Temperature (TOT) to see that the start-up transient temperature is not exceeded. (In the order of 793 – 927°C, 10 second maximum limit). Also, the pilot must monitor the oil pressure immediately after starting, as is the case with all aero engines. Should the TOT reach, or pass the limit, or there is low oil pressure, **ABORT THE START.**

1.6.4   Should the fuel pressure rise too rapidly, there is a possibility that fuel is introduced into the combustion stage before the RPM is high enough for a satisfactory light-up. This is due to the mixture being too rich. This could result in a "Hung Start". This is where the engine lights up but the pilot would see the engine RPM rising to a figure below the "idle" RPM, and not go any higher. Fuel flow would be low and the TOT would be high. Should this happen, the fuel switch must be selected off.

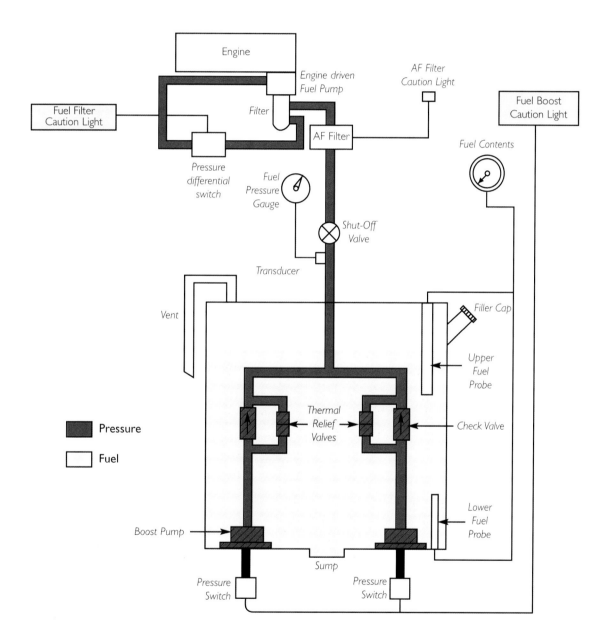

Fig. 1.10   Fuel system schematic.

1.6.5   For normal starting, the starter motor will accelerate the gas generator section of the engine, and the fuel pressure will rise as the engine driven pump also accelerates. The fuel introduced into the combustion section will ignite, and the resulting gas pressure will accelerate the engine to "Self Sustaining Speed". This is the speed (RPM) where the engine will run without assistance from the starter motor.

1.6.6   If an engine fails to start, ie., a Hung Start, it may be necessary to perform a "Vent Run". This is to turn the engine with the starter motor in order to dry out excessive unburned fuel in the engine. Igniters OFF. It must be remembered however, that the unsuccessful start may have resulted from low battery power. Also, time must be observed for engine starter cooling, particularly on a hot day.

1.7   The Transmission

1.7.1   The transmission is coupled to the engine by means of a short drive shaft. Basically, the transmission is a reduction gearbox which transmits engine power to the main rotor at reduced RPM by means of a **spiral bevel gear** and a **planetary gear**. The transmission, with a total of eight precision gears, reduces the engine output RPM to the rotor from 6016 to 394 RPM.

1.7.2   A self contained lubrication system for the transmission and the free-wheeling unit is incorporated. An accessory-drive bevel gear on the forward left side drives the transmission oil pump. It, in turn, is equipped with a pad on which the hydraulic pump is installed, and the hydraulic pump is equipped with one on which the tachometer generator is installed.

1.7.3   The transmission oil pump is a constant-volume submersed type that forces oil out of the sump to a filter on the left side and on to an oil filter and oil cooler on the aft side. Both the filter and the cooler are mounted on the transmission.

1.7.4   From the cooler, the oil is circulated to oil jets in the transmission and free-wheeling unit. The oil filter assembly contains a bypass valve, a high-temperature warning switch, a thermobulb, a magnetic chip detector and a drain valve. It has a replaceable filter element.

1.7.5   The oil cooler contains a thermal valve that allows oil to bypass until it warms up. The self-contained transmission lubrication system has a capacity of 4.1 litres (5 US Quarts).

1.7.6   Lights on the **caution panel** warn the pilot of loss of oil pressure and/or excessive oil temperature.

1.7.7 An electric **chip detector** is located in each oil sump (transmission and free-wheeling unit). These detectors have a permanent non conduction magnet surrounding an electric probe. When a sufficient number of metal particles accumulate to complete the circuit, the **TRANS CHIP** light on the caution panel illuminates. The detector has a self-closing valve, which serves as a drain plug.

1.7.8 A breather-type filler cap and an oil level **sight gauge** are located on the transmission top case and the right side of the lower case, respectively.

1.7.9 **The main rotor mast** is a tubular steel shaft that transmits rotational speed to the main rotor. Splines on the lower portion mate with those of the transmission planetary gear.

1.7.10 The main rotor of the Bell 206 is a semi-rigid, teetering type with two interchangeable blades. Certain advantages are available to the pilot, for instance, the onset of retreating blade stall does not induce pitching moments as in articulated rotors.

1.7.11 The root end of the blade, reinforced with doublers and grip plates, is secured to the blade grips by a retaining bolt. The grip plates extend inboard beyond the retaining bolt to a blade latch mechanism. This mechanism constrains the lead-lag motion of the blade. Trim tabs are located on the outboard trailing edge for tracking adjustment. The flap restraint prevents excessive flapping that may occur during startup and shutdown under gusty wind conditions. The flap restraint mechanism is installed on top of the trunnion and engages between 100 and 125 RPM. See fig. 1.11.

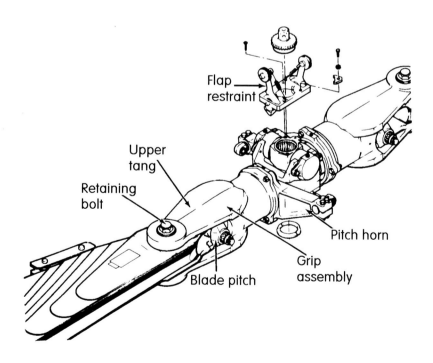

Fig. 1.11   Blade root assembly.

1.8   The Tail Rotor Drive Train

1.8.1   The Drive train extends from the free-wheeling unit to the tail rotor gearbox. (See fig. 1.12). The drive train is made up of eight individual drive shafts: three short ones extending from the free-wheeling unit to the tail boom, and one short shaft and four longer, interchangeable shafts extending along the top of the tail boom. The engine oil cooler blower is installed on and driven by the second shaft from the free-wheeling unit. The first two shafts are steel and the remainder are aluminum alloy. Steel laminated flexible couplings requiring no lubrication are used to connect the individual shafts to each other and to the tail rotor gearbox. Bearing hangers support and maintain the drive shaft alignment.

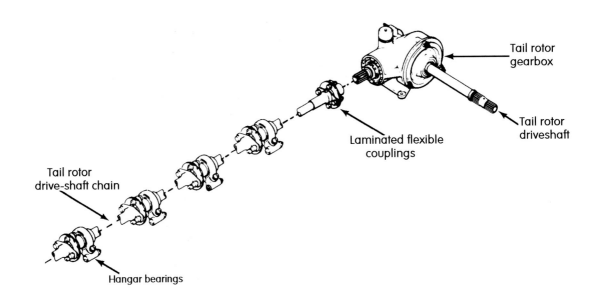

Fig 1.12   The tail rotor drive chain.

1.8.2   The tail rotor gearbox contains two spiral bevel gears which change the direction of drive 90° and provide a speed reduction of 2.35 to 1.0. It has its own, self-contained lubrication system with a capacity of 0.1 litre (0.375 U.S. pints). The gearbox assembly includes a breather-type filler cap, an oil level sight gauge, and a combination electrical chip detector and self-closing valve. The self-closing valve makes it possible to check the electric chip detector for metal particles without draining oil from the gearbox. Anti-torque control is provided by the two bladed, semi-rigid tail rotor mounted on the left side of the tail boom. The tail rotor is a **delta-hinge** type with two interchangeable blades and a changeable pitch controlled by directional pedals. See fig 1.13.

275

Each rotor blade is retained by two bolts. The pitch horn is a ring with a centre cross-piece that bolts onto the root end of the blade. A pitch link connects the horn to a crosshead assembly mounted on the tail rotor control tube outboard of the hub. The pitch links are non-adjustable and use non-lubricating bearings.

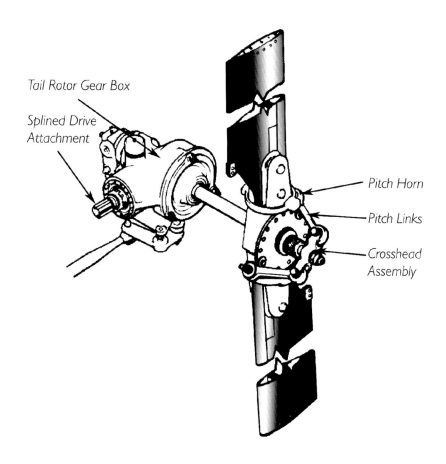

Fig. 1.13   Tail rotor and gearbox. (The gearbox incorporates a chip detector).

1.9   The Electrical System

1.9.1   The system is a 28-volt dc, single-conductor. All circuits are single wire with a common "negative" ground. Primary electrical power is supplied by a 30-volt, 150 ampere air cooled starter/generator (derated to 105 amperes). It serves the dual function of starter and main generator.   An electronic starter/generator control unit functions as a regulator. In the event of failure of the starter/generator, essential dc loads are supplied by the secondary system, a 24-volt, 13-ampere-hour, nickel-cadmium battery installed in the nose section. The capacity of the battery is 10 ampere-hours at the 5-hour discharge rate. At 65% power the battery will permit six starts at 32°C (90°F) and will perform a start down to -32°C (-25°F).

1.9.2   The engine may be started from battery power or by connecting an external 28-volt dc power source to the power receptacle in the nose. The ignition system consists of a single igniter plug and an ignition exciter box, provided by the engine manufacturer. The engine starter switch is located on the pilot's collective control stick. The igniter plug is only energised during the start sequence, or re-light action.

1.9.3   The battery temperature is monitored by thermal switches mounted under the battery case. A caution light indicating that the battery temperature is above normal and a light indicating the battery temperature is excessively high are provided in the caution panel. The pilot, warned of a battery malfunction, can disconnect the battery from the electrical system.

1.9.4   All instruments on the instrument panel have integral white lights supplied by 5-volt dc power. All other lighting is 28-volt dc white lighting. A rheostat in the roof panel controls the light intensity.

1.9.5   Three **Navigation lights** are installed: one on either side of the horizontal stabilizer and one on the end of the tail boom. A red anti-collision **strobe light** is located on top of the tail fin.

2   **EMERGENCIES**

2.1   The following listing is generally accepted as the safe procedure to adopt. **This list does not supercede procedures listed in the aircraft operations manual, which must be referred to for a specific aircraft.**

2.2   Illumination of transmission warning light indicates transmission temperature is at or above 110°C. Reduce power, check oil pressure, land as soon as possible.

2.3   Illumination of transmission pressure light indicates transmission pressure is below minimum. Land as soon as possible.

2.4   Fuel pump warning light illuminates when one or both booster pumps are inoperative. With single booster pump failure cavitation may occur causing engine to flame-out. Land as soon as practicable maintaining subsequent flight conditions optimised for carrying out a successful Engine Off Landing (EOL).With double booster pump failure the risk of cavitation and subsequent engine flame-out is increased. Land as soon as reasonably possible maintaining subsequent flight conditions optimised for carrying out a successful EOL. In either case make power changes gently.

2.5   Illumination of either filter indicates 'clogging' of that filter. Following illumination of both fuel filter lights the engine will be receiving unfiltered fuel. In either case land as soon as practicable.

2.6   Illumination of engine out light means engine failure. Audio warning occurs simultaneously. Reduce pitch immediately.

2.7   Illumination of engine tail rotor or main rotor chip lights indicates metal particles in the oil. Land as soon as practicable.

2.8   Illumination of rotor low RPM warning light indicates RPM is below normal. Reduce collective pitch - check for full throttle.

2.9   Engine failure. Power collective so as to maintain rotor RPM between 90 - 107%. Adjust forward speed 58-69 mph (50-60 kt). It is recommended to make touch down by 70% rotor rpm. Maximum autorotation speed 115 mph (100 kt).

2.10   Tail rotor drive failure. Enter autorotation, maintain 58 mph (50 kt) during approach. A run on landing is recommended with throttle at flight idle. Ventral fin may permit flight at low power levels. But flight idle landing must be made. Tail rotor pitch failure (control failure etc.) Power adjust as required to minimise excessive yaw. Adjust airspeed to determine best velocity to minimise excessive yawing.

2.11   Fuel control and/or governor failure giving change of power or RPM. Control power with throttle if engine overspeeds. Maintain RPM with collective if engine underspeeds. Establish autorotation if power is very low. Prepare for an EOL.

2.12   In the event of hydraulic system failure feed back forces will be evident. Control motions will be normal except for increased force required.

     a)   Reduce airspeed 70-80 mph (60-70 kt).
     b)   Check if hydraulic control circuit breaker - IN. **Hydraulic control switch - ON, OFF if power is not restored.** Land as soon as practicable and investigate (slow slide on landing recommended).

2.13   Electrical power failure is indicated by loadmeter. Necessary power will be provided by battery for short periods of time.

    a)   Cycle generator switch - if power not restored - OFF.
    b)   All electrical equipment OFF.
    c)   Required electrical equipment on as required.
    d)   Reduce height to below 5000 ft and land as soon as practical.

2.14.   Failure of engine fuel pump of duel element type will not result in engine failure. However, failure of a single element pump will require execution of engine failure procedure.

2.15.   Engine fire during start normally caused by overloading of fuel in combustion chamber,

    a)   Fully close throttle,
    b)   Continue to operate starter.
    c)   Main fuel switch - OFF.

2.16   Turbine engine surge on starting. This may occur when the pressure of the burning fuel is greater than the pressure of the air entering the combustion chamber. This causes unstable burning and a breakdown of flow through the engine and the high pressure in the combustion stage is expelled through the compressor. This may cause a loud bang. Other indications to the pilot is a rise in engine temperature and a banging or rumbling sound.

    a)   Fully close throttle.
    b)   Continue to operate the starter.
    c)   Main fuel switch - OFF.

Self Test Questions for Part 3
Turbine Engine Section

1   In a gas turbine engine, the Gas Generator is that section that consists of the:

    (a)   Combustion section and the power turbine.
    (b)   Compressor and the first turbine.
    (c)   Power turbine and the combustion section.
    (d)   Compressor and combustion section.

2   In a turbo-shaft gas turbine engine, a free turbine is a turbine:

    (a)   Used to drive ancillaries and the tail rotor drive shaft.
    (b)   Connected to the compressor of a gas generator stage.
    (c)   Not connected to the power output shaft.
    (d)   Not connected to the compressor of the gas generator stage.

3   The Gas Turbine Engine is a:

    (a)   Constant pressure engine.
    (b)   Constant volume engine.
    (c)   Constant cycle engine.
    (d)   Constant velocity engine.

4   A Free-Wheeling unit on a turbo-shaft gas turbine engine:

    (a)   Allows a disconnection between the drive shaft and all the ancillary drives in the event of engine failure.
    (b)   Automatically disengages the power drive in the event of engine failure.
    (c)   Allows the pilot to disengage the engine from the drive chain when shutting down the engine.
    (d)   Automatically disengages the power drive from the gear-box at a pre-set RPM.

5   Self Sustaining Speed for a gas turbine engine is where the engine speed is running:

(a)   At a constant RPM, such as in the cruise.
(b)   At a constant RPM set by an engine speed limited.
(c)   Without further input from a starter motor.
(d)   At minimum throttle setting.

6   A free turbine engine drives the main rotor and tail rotor from suitable gearing off:

(a)   The compressor shaft.
(b)   A dedicated turbine.
(c)   The first power turbine stage.
(d)   The Gas Generator section.

7   The Twist Grip on the end of the collective of a turbine helicopter is:

(a)   Used to set the cruise power.
(b)   Normally fully closed.
(c)   Used to keep engine torque within limits.
(d)   Normally fully open.

8   When starting a turbine engine, the pilot must monitor:

(a)   Oil pressure and Turbine Outlet Temperature.
(b)   Low torque and oil temperature.
(c)   Rotor speed and torque.
(d)   High torque, oil temperature and Rotor speed.

9   If the pressure in the combustion stage is greater than the air entering this stage, it can cause a Turbine Engine Surge. This produces the following indications:

(a)   A drop in TOT and increase in fuel flow.
(b)   A rise in TOT and decrease in fuel flow.
(c)   A rise in TOT and banging sounds.
(d)   A drop in TOT, intermittent fuel flow and rough running.

10   If the pilot selects the Anti-Icing Valve on, the only indication of satisfactory operation is a slight:

(a)   Rise in Turbine RPM.
(b)   Rise in Turbine Outlet Temperature.
(c)   Drop in Turbine RPM.
(d)   Drop in Turbine outlet Temperature.

11   A "Hung Start" is where the:

(a)   RPM fails to increase and the engine does not light up.
(b)   Mixture is too rich, the engine lights up but fails to increase the RPM to the idle speed.
(c)   Mixture is too lean and the engine fails to light up.
(d)   The engine lights up, but cuts out when the RPM increases to above ground idle.

12   A "Vent Run" is carried out:

(a)   Only by the licensed engineer after an engine wash.
(b)   Before starting on a very hot day.
(c)   Before starting on a very cold day.
(d)   After an over-rich start.

13   The thermal valve in the oil cooler system, is for allowing oil to bypass the cooler if:

(a)   It becomes clogged.
(b)   The pressure is too high.
(c)   The temperature is too low.
(d)   If the oil cooler leaks.

14   Chip detectors in engines and gearboxes are used to:

(a)   Indicate metal particles in the oil .
(b)   Prevent oil filters from becoming blocked.
(c)   Indicate oil bypass valve in operation.
(d)   Indicate that oil must changed on next daily inspection.

15   The Pilot operated ignition system in a helicopter gas turbine engine is:

(a)   On continuously during engine running.
(b)   Only available while the helicopter is on the ground.
(c)   Only available during re-lighting in flight.
(d)   Only on during engine starting and re-lighting.

16   In the event of a single fuel booster pump failure, the pilot should:

(a)   Land as soon as practicable, making power changes smoothly.
(b)   Be able to continue flying as fuel is supplied by a second (back-up) pump.
(c)   Expect an engine flame-out and prepare for an engine out landing.
(d)   Be able to descend, but be aware that full power may not be available.

17   Should the Chip Detector illuminate on the tail rotor gearbox, the pilot should:

(a)   Continue the planned flight but report the occurrence to the engineer after landing.
(b)   Immediately shut down the engine, declare an emergency and perform an engine out landing.
(c)   Declare an emergency, and land as soon as practicable.
(d)   Immediately perform an autorotation (as there is no torque reaction), land immediately.

18   When starting a turbine helicopter engine, should an engine fire occur, the pilot must:

(a)   Switch off the fuel and operate the engine fire extinguisher.
(b)   Switch off the fuel, open the throttle, continue to operate the starter.
(c)   Close the throttle, switch off the fuel, continue to operate the starter.
(d)   Switch off all electrics, isolate the starter, fuel switch off.

19   A fuel tanker holding AVTUR JET A-1 fuel, displays the following markings:

(a)   AVTUR in red on a yellow background.
(b)   AVTUR in yellow on a black background.
(c)   AVTUR in white on a black background.
(d)   AVTUR in black on yellow background.

20   The colour of AVTUR fuel is:

    (a)   Dark green.
    (b)   Dark blue.
    (c)   Light green.
    (d)   Light straw.

Answers to Part 3 will be found on page: 287

Answers to Self Test Questions

Part 1 – Aircraft General & Principles of Flight

1	c	29	a
2	d	30	b
3	b	31	c
4	b	32	a
5	a	33	d
6	c	34	a
7	a	35	c
8	d	36	b
9	b	37	c
10	c	38	d
11	c	39	b
12	d	40	c
13	b	41	a
14	d	42	c
15	a	43	d
16	a	44	d
17	b	45	b
18	b	46	c
19	d	47	c
20	c	48	a
21	b	49	d
22	d	50	c
23	a	51	d
24	c	52	a
25	a	53	b
26	b	54	c
27	d	55	a
28	d		

Answers to Self Test Questions

Part 2 – Flight Performance & Planning

1	c
2	a
3	b
4	d
5	a
6	c
7	d
8	a
9	d
10	b
11	c
12	b
13	d
14	a
15	b
16	a
17	c
18	b
19	d
20	a
21	d
22	a
23	b
24	d
25	c
26	c
27	a
28	d
29	a
30	c

Answers to Self Test Questions

Part 3 – Turbine Section

1	b
2	d
3	a
4	b
5	c
6	b
7	d
8	a
9	c
10	b
11	b
12	d
13	c
14	a
15	d
16	a
17	b
18	c
19	c
20	d